ASIAN HISTORICAL DICTIONARIES
Edited by Jon Woronoff

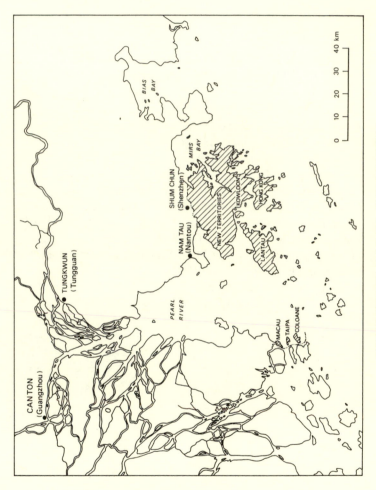

HONG KONG, MACAU, AND CANTON

Historical Dictionary

of

HONG KONG
& MACAU

by

ELFED VAUGHAN ROBERTS

SUM NGAI LING

PETER BRADSHAW

Asian Historical Dictionaries, No. 10

The Scarecrow Press, Inc.
Metuchen, N.J., & London
1992

British Library Cataloguing-in-Publication data available

Library of Congress Cataloging-in-Publication Data

Roberts, Elfed Vaughan, 1946–
    Historical dictionary of Hong Kong and Macau / Elfed
Vaughan Roberts, Sum Ngai Ling, Peter Bradshaw.
        p.   cm. — (Asian historical dictionaries ; no. 10)
    Includes bibliographical references.
    ISBN 0-8108-2574-0 (acid-free paper)
    1. Hong Kong—History—Dictionaries.   2. Macao—
History—Dictionaries.   I. Ling, Sum Ngai.   II. Brad-
shaw, Peter.   III. Title.   IV. Series.
DS796.H757R64   1992
951.25′003—dc20   92-20816

Manufactured in the United States of America

Printed on acid-free paper

To Dorothy, Elizabeth and Mo Kwan
and to the memory of
John William Roberts

CONTENTS

MACAU

EDITOR'S FOREWORD

Hong Kong is unique. There has never been a place quite like it nor will there ever be another one. Regarded with askance when first acquired by Great Britain, it survived long enough to become one of its last overseas possessions. Described as "a barren island with hardly a house upon it," it gradually became a teeming city and then a resplendent one with the most imposing skyline in the Orient. What had long been a financial drain became an economic powerhouse that grew at an extraordinary pace although it lacked every natural resource, including land and water, and could only develop thanks to human resources like hard work, courage, and vision.

When Hong Kong reverts to China in 1997, one of history's most unusual adventures will come to an end. But the fascination should linger and the interest remain keen. How could such a place, a haven for Chinese and other refugees, a colony run by expatriates, a political oddity, have been governed? How could it achieve an economic takeoff, almost an economic "miracle," when so many better endowed places failed? How, as it approached the 1997 deadline, could its people adjust their lifestyles and look hopefully into the future? Finally, what role can it play in China? Will it be absorbed and fade away? Or will it revitalize that vast country?

This book can answer many of the questions about Hong Kong and, as a special bonus, describes the situation in neighboring Macau. It provides considerable insight into their economies, societies, and governance. It documents the past and present and provides hints on the future. Through a comprehensive bibliography, it directs readers toward other works that deal with the past and present and try to fathom the future. But just what the future will bring only time can tell.

Books on Hong Kong (and Macau) should be written by people who not only know them but respect them. Both qualifications were met by an exceptional team of authors. Elfed Vaughan Roberts, who took the lead, has lived in Hong Kong for over a decade and lectures on political science at the University of Hong Kong. He recently coauthored a *Political Dictionary for Hong Kong*. Sum Ngai Ling, who was born there, has also written extensively on Hong Kong. Peter Bradshaw, seconded by the British Open University, is preparing distance learning materials on Hong Kong society for the Open Learning Institute of Hong Kong.

Jon Woronoff
Series Editor

PREFACE

When we were first asked to write this Historical Dictionary of Hong Kong and Macau it seemed to us a difficult but not impossible task. We set ourselves a time limit and then proceeded to extend it as the scope of the project began to dawn on us, to the reasonable annoyance of the publishers. Our first task was to attempt to select the number of entries and that in itself was not easy. We were constantly faced with decisions about what to include and, more significantly, what to exclude. Having come to that decision, the temptation was always to write long entries. As this would have made the Dictionary much too cumbersome we had to consider the appropriate length for the particular entry. The result, as it must always be in a Dictionary, is that the reader might find some entries unduly detailed, some which in the eyes of the reader need expanding, and some entries, looked for but not included. To those readers we present our apologies but derive a degree of comfort from the thought that an extensive bibliography accompanies this book and can be profitably employed for further reading.

One problem which faces an author using a language which does not employ the western alphabet is that there are a number of romanized vocabularies. In the case of Chinese the two systems most widely employed are the Wade-Giles system and the Pinyin. In addition some spellings, e.g., Canton province are not in either of these two systems (Kwantung in Wade-Giles and Guangdong in Pinyin) but are known almost universally in an English form.

Pinyin is based on the official language Putonghua, the standardized northern dialect of Chinese, and all mainland Chinese sources now use the Pinyin spelling. However, many historical texts written before the establishment of the People's Republic of China, and indeed many since, still use the older Wade-Giles. For instance, one of the standard history texts on Hong Kong, Endacott, G.B. *History of Hong Kong.* Hong Kong: Oxford University Press, 1973, employs the Wade-Giles system, while Cameron, N. in his more modern work *An illustrated history of Hong Kong.* Hong Kong: Oxford University Press, 1991, uses Pinyin. As a result place names differ, as in the case of Kwangtung and Guangdong and Peking and Beijing, in Wade-Giles and Pinyin respectively. (For those who want even greater complications Peking used to be termed Pekin in the nineteenth century!) Similarly, personal names also differ; for instance, Mao Tse-tung (Wade Giles) and Mao Zedong (Pinyin).

To compound the problem even further Hong Kong is almost a rule unto itself. In the colony the local dialect is not Putonghua (often referred to as Mandarin) but Cantonese. Consequently, many place names and personal names are translations based on an approximation of the pronunciation in that dialect. Even then there is often no standardization of translation. To illustrate the case there were two students registered in our class who were brothers and had deliberately chosen to spell, in English, their common surname Lee and Li. We have, therefore, in the case of Hong Kong places and surnames, used those terms commonly found in government texts.

To convert everything into Pinyin artificially imposes a set of names which nobody uses. To employ only Wade-Giles or English potentially confuses a reader who uses modern official Chinese government sources or refers to texts employing Pinyin. Our solution is to use Wade-Giles spelling most of the time, to use English occasionally, and to record the Pinyin in parentheses where appropriate. Sometimes we use only the Pinyin when the meaning is clear. We have also, when necessary, put entries in Pinyin and invited the reader to "see" the entry under Wade-Giles (e.g., Deng Xiaoping; see Teng Hsiao-p'ing). Finally, we have included at the end of the book a list which gives both versions so that the reader can check in the case of any confusion.

In Macau the official language is not English but Portuguese. Many of the place names, personal names, government, and other organizations are in that language. Fortunately the meaning, in nearly all cases, is fairly obvious. We have italicized the Portuguese terms.

We would like to take this opportunity of thanking all those who helped us in the writing of this book. It would be impossible to thank everybody but some deserve particular reference: members of the Department of Political Science at the University of Hong Kong and, in particular, Dr. Norman Miners, whose encyclopedic knowledge of Hong Kong we drew on unmercifully; Dr. David Clark and Professor Ian Scott who alerted us to sources of information on some of the more esoteric entries; Dr. Patrick Hase who helped with the precolonial introduction to the book and read many of the entries and corrected many of the inevitable errors; Joseph Ting of the Hong Kong Museum of History for his entry on archeology and Philip Bruce of the Hong Kong Branch of the Royal Asiatic Society for his entry on that organization; Doreen King who wrote the entry on architecture (to our great relief); and Mrs. D. Shroff for her entry on the Parsees. We would also like to thank Lara Mushkat, Carrie Sung, Dawn Roberts, Fred Yeung, and Ellen Jones for their invaluable help in finding dates and information and helping to type and correct parts of the book. Finally, our heartfelt gratitude goes to Mr. Patrick Lam who helped with the word processing; Mr. Y. C. Wan, the curator of the Hong Kong collection library who withstood our predatory attacks with good humor and patience, and Dr. Richard Irving and the Cartography unit of the Department of Geography and Geology who prepared the maps.

The authors
November 1991

ABBREVIATIONS

AMCHAM	American Chamber of Commerce
BDTC	British Dependent Territories Citizen
BL	Basic Law
BN(O)	British National (Overseas)
CBF	Commander British Forces
CCP	Chinese Communist Party
DB	District Boards
EC	European Community
EEC	European Economic Community
ERP	Electronic Road Pricing
FCO	Foreign and Commonwealth Office
FO	Foreign Office
GATT	General Agreement on Tariffs and Trade
GDP	Gross Domestic Product
GIS	Government Information Services
GNP	Gross National Product

HKSAR	Hong Kong Special Administrative Region
HMS	His (Her) Majesty's Ship
ICAC	Independent Commission Against Corruption
ICCPR	International Covenant on Civil and Political Rights
IEM	Instituto Emissar de Macau
ILO	International Labor Organization
JLG	Joint Liaison Group
KCR	Kowloon-Canton Railway
KMT	Kuomintang (Guomindang)
LEGCO	Legislative Council
MFA	Multi-Fibre Arrangement
NCNA	New China News Agency (Xinhua)
NIC	Newly Industrializing Country
NIE	Newly Industrializing Economy
NPC	National People's Congress
OMELCO	Office of the Members of the Executive and Legislative Council
PLA	People's Liberation Army
PRC	People's Republic of China
REGCO	Regional Council

RICO Act   Racketeering Influence and Corrupt Organizations Act

ROC   Republic of China

RTHK   Radio-Television Hong Kong

SAR   Special Administrative Region

SEZ   Special Economic Zones

UMELCO   Unofficial Members of the Executive and Legislative Council

UN   United Nations

UNHCR   United Nations High Commission for Refugees

URBCO   Urban Council

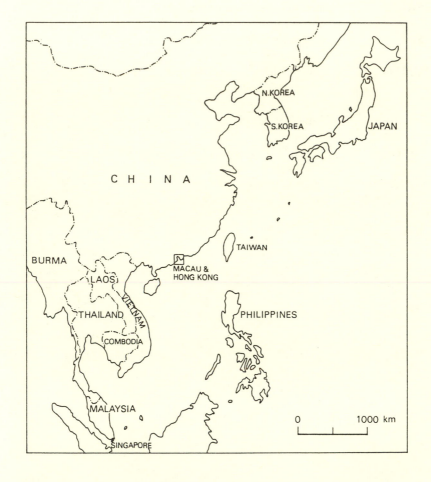

HONG KONG AND MACAU IN ASIA

xviii

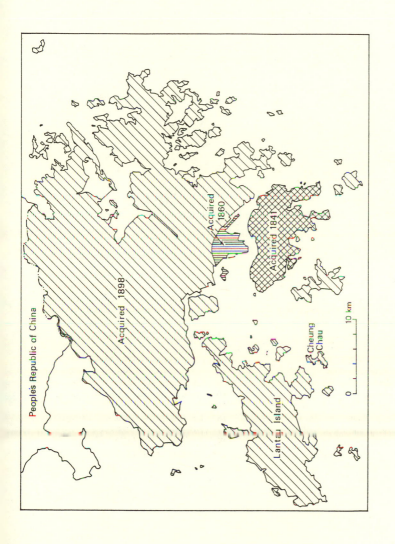

People's Republic of China

Acquired 1898

Acquired 1860

Acquired 1841

Lantau Island

Cheung Chau

0   10 km

HONG KONG—DATES OF ACQUISITION

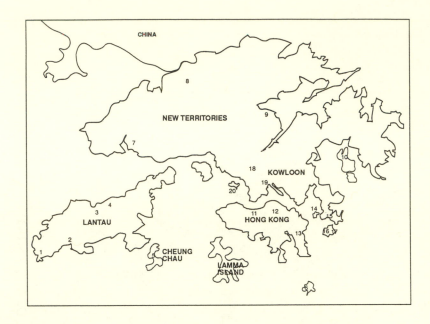

KEY

1. Fan Lau Fort
   Ch'ing (Qing) Dynasty
   (1644–1912)
2. Ancient Rock Carving
   Shek Pik
3. Tung Chung Fort
4. Tung Chung Battery (1817)
5. Ancient Rock Carving
6. Ancient Bronze Age
   Rock Carving. Po Toi
7. Tuen Mun. Important
   Naval and Military Base
   — Under various
      Chinese Dynasties
8. Man Lun Fung
   Ancestral Hall. Late 17th Century
9. Taipo - Major Pearl Fisheries
   by 10th Century
10. Ancient Rock Carvings at
    Kau Sai Chau

11. Flagstaff House
    (1846) Residence of British
    Commander in Chief
12. Tin Hau Temple. Uncertain date
13. Ancient Rock Carving. Big Wave Bay
14. Site of old Chinese Custom Station
15. Rock inscription Joss House Bay,
    Sai Kung. AD. 1274
16. Ancient Bronze Age Rock Carving
17. Tung Lung Fort
18. Lei Cheng Uk Tomb — Eastern Han
    (AD25–220)
19. Kowloon Walled City
20. Stonecutters Island

HONG KONG HISTORICAL SITES

INTRODUCTION

Hong Kong is situated at the mouth of the Pearl River in the southern part of China, 90 miles south of the great trading city of Canton (Guangzhou). In terms of its political origins, but not its physical geography, it can be divided into three parts: Hong Kong Island; Kowloon and Stonecutters Island; and what are called the New Territories. These three parts make up the Crown Colony of Hong Kong. The first two were ceded and the third leased to Britain by the Chinese government during the nineteenth century. The first, Hong Kong Island (35.5 square miles), was ceded in 1841 and formalized as a British colony in 1843. In 1860 Kowloon Peninsula (three square miles) and Stonecutters Island (half a square mile) came under British control. Finally, the New Territories were acquired under a ninety-nine year lease in 1898. These added a further 355 square miles, and are composed of territory on the mainland together with a large number of islands lying off the coast. The capital city of the colony is Victoria which is situated on Hong Kong Island. However, the title is rarely used and urbanization on the island has been so extensive as to make it impossible to recognize any distinct city in the area which used to be known as Victoria.

The most salient issue for all this territory is that at the stroke of midnight on June 30, 1997 sovereign control over it reverts to the People's Republic of China. The Colony then becomes a Special Administrative Region of the People's Republic of China (PRC). With that transfer of control 156 years of colonial administration (four years of it under Japanese occupation) will come to an end. Two years later the Portuguese possession of Macau will undergo a similar change.

There are some precedents similar in form to those which will take place in Hong Kong and Macau. But far more common in the case of the British and the Portuguese has been the granting of sovereign independence to their previous colonial possessions. Sometimes decolonization was smooth; sometimes the result of bitter struggle. Rarely have territories been handed over to the control of a third party in the face of considerable opposition from the local population.

In the case of both Hong Kong and Macau the Chinese Government has maintained that both possessions are, and always have been, an integral part of the sovereign state of China. They are seen as having been merely temporarily occupied by the foreign powers in question. The two territories have always been part of the motherland and, as such, they must be returned. Both the British and the Portuguese have eventually accepted that position.

There can be no question that the two territories were part of China for hundreds of years before the Portuguese and British arrived on the scene. They were administered in exactly the same way as all other parts of Kwangtung (Guangdong) Province. Moreover, even since the establishment of colonial status in the 1840s (1550s in the case of Macau), the influence of China has been massive. It would be impossible to understand the present or future of either Hong Kong or Macau without looking at the past, and in particular at the struggle between the western powers eager to "open up" China in the interests of trade, and the Chinese government equally eager to resist that attempt in the interests of preserving its independence.

Reaching even further back, Hong Kong has been inhabited for thousands of years, and was the site of flourishing Neolithic, and later, Bronze Age cultures. These settlers found an abundance of fresh water and plenty of fertile soil. There would have been little problem with migration along the coast. Close proximity to the sea provided a rich harvest of fish and shellfish, and the inland forests were full of game. In these circumstances, the occurrence of early settlement is not surprising. Excavations on the offshore islands of Lantau and Lamma (which are part of Hong Kong) have, in fact, uncovered two neolithic cultures with the oldest being dated in the region of 4000 B.C.

Bronze Age artifacts from between about 1200 B.C. and about 220 B.C. have also been found. Unfortunately, little is known about these Bronze Age people. It has been conjectured that they may have been the ancestors of the Yiu people, who were still inhabiting the more remote mountain areas near Hong Kong in the early nineteenth century. The Bronze Age inhabitants, however, were essentially a people of the seashore, whose remains have consistently been located on the coast, adjacent to suitable landing sites for small boats. The most spectacular remains of these people are the spiral form rock carvings which have been discovered on rocks overlooking the coast at nine sites in Hong Kong. Some of the ritual objects of these people, especially the decorated bronze knives, and the stone disks, as well as the stone carvings, are fine, and suggest a well-developed cultural identity. Nothing equivalent to these carvings has been discovered outside Hong Kong.

During the Ch'in (Qin) dynasty (221–207 B.C.) and the Han (Han) dynasty (206 B.C.–220 A.D.) the south of China was brought under Chinese control by military conquest. At first, only the area immediately around Canton (Guangzhou) was controlled. The aim of conquest was control of trade: the south was feared and hated by the northerners as the abode of evil spirits and fierce animals, of men who, in the northerners' eyes, were at best half-human. It was seen as a pit of foul diseases, a death-ridden hell-on-earth, but it was also the source of ivory and rhinoceros horn, pearls and medicinal drugs and dyestuffs, all of which were extremely valuable. Early evidence of direct Chinese contact with the inhabitants of the Hong Kong area tends to be mainly in the form of stray Chinese coins, probably evidence of trade. Trade was followed by the settling of the region by Chinese people, again initially in the area immediately around Canton (Guangzhou).

However, it is not yet completely clear when Chinese troops or settlers first came into the Hong Kong area.

The earliest evidence of Chinese settlement in the Hong Kong area, apart from stray coins, is the Han (Han) dynasty tomb found at Lei Cheng Uk in Kowloon, dated about 220 A.D. This tomb, as fine as tombs of the same period in the immediate Canton (Guangzhou) area, may well be evidence of Chinese settlement of some sort nearby. The tomb is entirely Chinese in design and detail. The existence of the tomb implies bricks available in the area, masons, ritual specialists, and makers of tomb furniture. These may all have been brought down to the site from Canton (Guangzhou), but this would have been a hugely expensive undertaking, as well as a pointless one. It is far more likely that the tomb is of someone of importance resident in the area.

The earliest known Chinese settlement is the naval base at Tuen Mun. For this we have no written evidence earlier than one of the poems of Han Yue of the early ninth century. It is very likely, however, that the naval base was much older than Han Yue, and it may well date back far enough to be connected with the Han tomb. The Buddhist monastery at Tuen Mun has a traditional foundation date of the mid-fifth century. This is not impossible, since Buddhist monasteries were being founded at about that date outside a number of other government centers in the area. Written evidence of the existence of the monastery, however, exists only from the mid-tenth century. Trade between China and Indochina was of great significance from the fourth and fifth centuries, and most of this trade was conducted at Canton (Guangzhou). Tuen Mun is extremely well situated as the forward naval and customs post for Canton (Guangzhou), where incoming ships could be stopped and searched before being permitted to pass up river, and this was almost certainly Tuen Mun's function in the time of Han Yue, and doubtless for a long period before. Military installations, such as Tuen Mun, were usually protected by an exclusion zone around them in which no civilians (other than convicts in forced labor camps providing food for the garrison) were permitted without military authority, and the existence of this naval base may well have left the previous inhabitants in the mountains more or less untouched.

Contacts between the area's original inhabitants and the Chinese are more evident at the other major early Chinese settlement, Tai Po. Tai Po was a major source of pearls, from at least the eighth century, and it became, in consequence, a strongly defended imperial monopoly estate from the ninth century at the latest. This estate, and its exclusion zone, survived without change right through to the mid-fourteenth century. The local aboriginal people were conscripted into the pearl fisheries, a hardship that resulted in protests at various dates throughout the period. It is likely that Kowloon was yet another early imperial estate, probably subordinate to Tuen Mun. If, as seems likely, the Tuen Mun exclusion zone covered all the islands in the Pearl River delta, then a second naval station east of the Kap Shui Mun channel would have been a practical necessity. Salt-farms were a secondary imperial interest at Kowloon, and at various other places on the coast throughout the region. In any event, when the last Sung (Song) emperor was in the area, it was thought appropriate for him to stay at Kowloon, strongly suggesting that this was an imperial estate in the mid-thirteenth century.

Given the existence of these two or three imperial estates and their exclusion zones—which must have covered most, if not all, of the Hong Kong area—it is, perhaps, not surprising that, despite the evidence of early Chinese military and imperial interest in the area, there is no evidence of civilian Chinese settlement until the very end of the eleventh century. At that date Tang Fu-hip, a retired official, set up home for himself and his family at Kam Tin, apparently with imperial permission. Shortly afterwards well-connected members of the Wong and Lee families secured imperial grants of Cheung Chau Island and Lantau Island respectively. All three areas would have been in the exclusion zone of Tuen Mun, and it seems likely that the Government was following a policy of allowing settlement within that old exclusion zone—

possibly a change of policy connected with the increasing shortage of cash plaguing the Sung (Song) Government around this time. From the thirteenth century on, settlement can be seen elsewhere in the region, and particularly in the area around Kowloon City. Here many of those involved seem to have been members of the Court of the last Sung (Song) Emperor, abandoned after his suicide in the face of the invading Mongols. Only the Tolo Harbor catchment, the exclusion zone of Tai Po, remained without any signs of settlement at this date.

Despite the increasing pace of settlement in the area through the twelfth and thirteenth centuries, the probable reduction in the imperial military presence (which the abandonment of the exclusion zones seems to imply) left the area open to problems. The area was, in fact, a "frontier" land, with all the social and political problems that suggests. Unfortunately, very little information survives about this period in the history of the area, but it seems very likely that the area fell more and more into the hands of the Ho family. The Ho family seem to have treated the whole area as a personal fief, and controlled it through an army of personal retainers.

The head of the Ho family, Ho Tsan, used his local power and his personal army to support the first Ming (Ming) Emperor in his bid for the throne in the mid-fourteenth century, and was rewarded with the title of Earl of Tungkuan (Dongguan). With the title went land, and Ho Tsan seems to have received among these lands the old exclusion zone of Tai Po (where the pearl beds had become exhausted). He was closely connected with the descendants of Tang Fu-hip. It also appears that a major reorganization of settlement, with groups of the Tangs being relocated to strategic locations in various parts of the area, occurred at this time. Ho Tsan's son, however, fell from imperial favor at the very end of the fourteenth century, and was executed with all his family. In the resulting confusion, the Tangs and other groups previously subordinate to the Ho's became the local landowners without any landlords above them, and, with this, the early modern period of Hong Kong's history begins.

In the fifteenth and sixteenth centuries, the area was deprived not only of imperial troops, but also of Ho Tsan's militia forces. As a result, the area was ravaged by bandit and pirate gangs (one of which was able to capture, and control for nine years, the city of Tapeng (Dapeng) just northeast of the Hong Kong area) throughout the period. Eventually the Imperial Government was forced to treat coastal defence in the area as a major priority and in 1571, after a particularly heavy battle with a pirate band, the area was set up as a separate county. This meant that a senior official was available to keep an eye on the defenses on a full-time basis. The county consisted of the Hong Kong area, plus the area just to the north in the Nant'ou (Nantou)-Shen Tsen (Shenzhen)-Tapeng (Dapeng) zone. A network of small forts was set up to guard the coasts, centered on major garrisons at major centers, and with a respectable fleet of war-junks to patrol the seas offshore.

Unfortunately, however, even these precautions were not entirely successful. In 1661, the coastal ravages of Koxinga, the pro-Ming figure who had set himself up as ruler of Taiwan with a powerful fleet, became so much a problem for the new Ch'ing dynasty that the Government decided on a "scorched earth" policy, driving away all residents living within 50 *li* (approximately 12 miles) of the coast, and pulling down their houses. Not until 1669 was this Coastal Evacuation Order rescinded. The displaced families had lost their land and the grain it could grow, but the Government had provided nothing in its place. Thousands died of starvation. Village tradition in the area states that at most a third returned from their eight-year exile.

Up until 1669, all the land residents of the Hong Kong area had been Cantonese speaking—in common with the rest of the lands bordering the Pearl River estuary. After 1669, however, the depleted Cantonese clans were unable to bring back into cultivation all the lands they had previously controlled. The Imperial Government, anxious not to lose the taxes from these lands, urged the old families to sell off their no longer needed lands to new settlers, mostly *Hakka* speakers from the northeast. Between 1669 and the mid-eighteenth century hundreds of *Hakka* groups moved into the area, taking up the more marginal lands in the mountains, particularly in the eastern part of the area. It was this mixed society, of old Cantonese clans in the fertile west, newer *Hakka* families in the less fertile east, plus a few groups of *Tanka* and *Hoklo* boat people, that characterized the area when the British first appeared on the scene early in the nineteenth century.

In 1841, when Hong Kong Island was ceded to Britain, the area (including Kowloon and the New Territories not acquired at this point) had some 700 villages, of which about 400 were *Hakka,* and a population of about 180,000, of which rather more than half were Cantonese speaking. Major market towns existed at Tai Po, Yuen Long, and Kowloon, with subordinate markets at Shamshuipo, Sheung Shui, Ha Tsuen, and Kam Tin. Fishing ports, which also served as markets for the immediately adjacent land people, existed at Cheung Chau, Tai O, Ping Chau, Sai Kung, Hang Hau, and what are now called Stanley and Aberdeen. The largest town was Cheung Chau, with 200 shops and workshops, and a total population of about 2,500. Yuen Long, Tai O, and Kowloon each had between 100 and 150 shops and populations of up to 2,000; Tai Po, and Aberdeen were a little smaller, and the other towns very much smaller. The area was entirely rural, subsisting on the rice and vegetables grown by the farmers themselves: the area had very little trade except for the essential local trade of the market towns. Only three items were traded beyond the local area: tableware, fish, and stone. The kilns at Wun Yiu, near Tai Po, supplied tableware to the whole county, and even further afield. The fishing ports were important in the South China coast trade in dried fish. Stone quarries, especially in the area around Kowloon and on the north shore of Hong Kong Island, cut stone for shipment to Canton (Guangzhou)—at about the time the British arrived the little town of Shaukeiwan was beginning to develop as the port for the biggest group of quarries. The area was, in fact, an entirely typical part of Kwangtung (Guangdong) province, long settled and peaceful, with its local schools, temples, respectable local elites, markets, ports, and small-scale industries.

The Macau area does not have quite the depth of history of the Hong Kong area. What is now Macau is found on the mud-flats of the West River Delta, and these were too marshy to attract settlement at an early date. The first interest in the area was shown by *Hoklo* boat-people. These people, originating from the area near the borders of Kwangtung (Guangdong) and Fukien (Fujien) Provinces, operated the big trading junks which moved up and down the coast. They found the harbor at Macau a useful center for their trade—in part at least because there was no earlier population there to interfere. Around the year 1400 these *Hoklo* boat people established the great temple of Tin Hau from which the town takes its name (A Ma Kau—"Anchorage of the Honorable Old Lady"). They also founded the major agricultural village of Mong Ha, with its temple to Kuan Yin, at about the same time. During the fifteenth century a few boatyards and other workshops developed near the Tin Hau Temple, but the place was by no means a major settlement before the Portuguese arrived in 1557.

To understand their interest it is helpful to comment first on the importance of Canton (Guangzhou) and the Pearl River. Canton (Guangzhou) has always been the major port for China's foreign seaborne trade. There is very little east of China except Japan and the vast emptiness of the Pacific Ocean. Moreover, for much of its history even Japan was unwilling to trade, even with China. Thus, almost all China's seaborne trade has always come up, from the south, from Indochina, with the Pearl River estuary often being the first landfall in China. Up this route came trade from Indochina in the fourth century, from India in the fifth century, and from Arabia in the sixth. Consequently Canton became, from the fourth century onwards, the most cosmopolitan and mercantile of all Chinese cities.

When Europeans first reached China by sea early in the sixteenth century, they, too, came up the coast from the south, and they, too, saw in Canton (Guangzhou) the obvious destination for their trade. In the sixteenth century the Portuguese traders needed two-and-a-half years to make the round trip from Lisbon to China, and this was impracticable without a base on the China coast for repairs and restocking. At first the Portuguese wanted Tuen Mun, in Hong Kong, and they made several determined attempts to take it by force early in the sixteenth century (forming a part of the "pirate and bandit gangs" which caused the local magistrate so much trouble). Some of these were successful for a short time, but all were defeated eventually by the local forces of the county magistrate. Tuen Mun is close to the deep sea channel to Canton (Guangzhou), and its strategic significance to the Pearl River has been recognized since the earliest times. Macau was very much a second best choice for the Portuguese, but one which they were eventually forced to accept as the best they could get. Even then it is said that the Imperial Government was only prepared to allow them to settle there after Portuguese help in destroying a major pirate fleet in the area which had proved too powerful for unaided local resources. The Portuguese eventually opened a trading station at the mouth of the Pearl River to conduct trade with the South of China in 1557.

The British did not establish their presence in Canton (Guangzhou) until 1685, but within two years the East India Company arrived in Macau. It was granted a monopoly over trade by the British government which was to last for the next 150 years. In the early years the East India Company, which also had a monopoly in India, oversaw a major increase in trade with China, mostly in tea and silk. This trade was organized by private companies with no foreign governments entering into formal diplomatic relations with the Imperial Government at any level. Foreign traders could only operate through the *Hoppo* (Chinese customs superintendents) and Chinese merchants, known as *Hongs,* who in turn, were granted monopolies by the Chinese Imperial Government. These *Hongs* were the only means by which foreign traders were able indirectly to petition the Chinese government either for improvements in conditions or for redress of grievance.

Although the British had a relatively late start, by the late eighteenth century they dominated trade with China. The number of ships leaving Britain for Canton in 1751 was only 19, but by 1792 it had risen to 57. The main exports to England were tea, raw silk, chinaware, and rhubarb. In return came wool products, lead, iron, copper and furs. The East India Company, by now effectively the government in India, imported from China quantities of nankeen cloth, alum, camphor, pepper, sugar, and chinaware and in return exported quantities of raw cotton, ivory, sandalwood, silver, and opium.

Demand for goods from China, particularly tea which was becoming a popular beverage, was expanding rapidly during this period. Unfortunately for the British the demand in China for British goods was not as buoyant with the result that a massive trade imbalance developed. This had to be paid for in silver bullion which led to a massive outflow of reserves by the East India Company. This problem for the Company was compounded by the trading restrictions imposed in Canton (Guangzhou). These regulations were first promulgated in 1759, but were gradually tightened until by the end of the eighteenth century resistance began to grow among foreign merchants. For their part, the Chinese authorities, while willing to trade with the West, were increasingly aware of the growing challenge to their position from the foreigners. They refused to allow the traders to expand their operations into other parts of China and closely supervised the conditions under which trade took place. The foreign merchants in

Canton were only allowed a limited period of residence in the city during the trading season from approximately October to January; for the remaining period they had to return to Macau. No foreign wives were allowed in the city, and the traders had to live within a designated area, set apart from the Chinese, in Canton. Further irritations to the Europeans were caused by corruption in some of the *Hongs,* the imposition of duties and taxes, and a distaste for certain aspects of Chinese law.

Accordingly, the British, chafing under the lack of freedom to trade, and under pressure from the merchants to seek an improvement in the situation, attempted to regularize relations with the Imperial Government. Missions were sent to Peking (Beijing) in 1793 and 1816, but both failed miserably. The requests by Lord Amherst in 1816 for the removal of grievances in Canton, free trade between China and Britain, the abolition of the Hong system, the opening of more ports in areas to the north of Canton, and the setting up of a diplomatic mission in Peking were all refused.

Meanwhile an even greater problem was developing with the growth of the opium trade in China. In the attempt to reduce the trade imbalance opium, which was grown mainly in India, was shipped into China to feed a growing demand. Between 1817 and 1834 nearly three-quarters of the value of British imports to China came from opium. This reversed the trade imbalance dramatically. Silver bullion now flowed out of China damaging the domestic economy at the same time as the drug it paid for created social tragedy. Much of the trade was conducted, not by the East India Company, but by a growing number of private merchants operating illegally but openly. In 1829–1830 one such trading company, Jardine Matheson and Company, exported over 5,000 chests of opium into China. This represented one-third of the total imports of the drug.

These private merchants, imbued with the philosophy of free trade, were opposed to the monopoly of the East India Company, were vociferous in their complaints against the restrictions imposed on them by the Chinese authorities, and were active in lobbying the British government to improve matters. However, and not surprisingly, the Chinese government responded, not by allowing greater privileges, but by actively attempting to suppress the opium trade.

Clearly matters were coming to a head, and two particular events led to the breakdown of relations. The first was the ending of the East India Company's monopoly in China by the British government in 1833. In response, the Chinese government, anxious to have someone with whom to deal, asked the British government to establish a *Taipan* (Head Merchant) in Canton to represent British trading interests. The response from Britain was to appoint Lord Napier as the Chief Superintendent of Trade. In a way this changed the ground rules of the British relationship with China as Lord Napier saw himself as a representative of government itself and not merely a spokesperson for the merchants. He was also given explicit instructions from London to negotiate for an extension of trade beyond Canton. This was going far beyond that which the Chinese had asked for, and constituted a clear demand for diplomatic relations which broke with the status quo.

The second incident was the Imperial Order of 1836 to suppress the opium trade. In 1839 attempts by Imperial Commissioner Lin to destroy completely any opium activities finally triggered a military confrontation. On 18 March 1839, Lin ordered British merchants to surrender all stocks of opium held in Canton, a demand which the British, led by Captain George Elliot, rejected. Lin then confined British merchants to their factories forcing the British to comply with his demands, and when the British retired to Macau Lin appeared to have won a major victory.

The British government was now faced with a number of options: they could accept the Chinese position and do business on their terms; they could close down operations in China; or they could fight. The first two were unacceptable, and the British believed that military force could bring about the changes they sought at limited cost. Accordingly, an expeditionary force was assembled under the control of Admiral Elliot, with his cousin Captain George Elliot as the second in command.

In June 1840 the British military force arrived and proceeded to conduct military operations in both the south of China and further north. The gap in military capability quickly led to the defeat of Chinese forces, and in turn led to the opening of negotiations. Under the Treaty of Chuanpi (Chuanbi) in January 1841, Hong Kong was ceded to Britain. Paradoxically, both governments eventually refused to accept the treaty: not only on the grounds that it was negotiated by subordinates and without the authority of the central governments, but also because, on reflection, the terms were unacceptable to both parties. Accordingly, hostilities broke out once more with the Chinese suffering further military defeats. Following a brief truce, the war entered a decisive phase when on 27 May 1841 Sir Henry Pottinger, who had by this time replaced Captain Elliot, went on to the offensive and imposed humiliating defeats on the Chinese by seizing important strategic points and cities on the Yangtze River. Eventually, on 29 August 1842, the Chinese Imperial Government signed the Treaty of Nanking (Nanjing). By this treaty Britain achieved its major objectives, which included the ceding of Hong Kong, the opening of new ports for trade, the abolition of many of the trade restrictions in Canton, and an indemnity to cover the cost of the British military expeditions.

In fact, the British had already anticipated the situation, and George Elliot had moved to Hong Kong as early as January 1841. The island was well situated for British purposes. Geographically it was close to the estuary of the Pearl River and hence Canton (Guangzhou); it had a deep harbor for shipping; and it was sparsely populated. British merchants quickly set up businesses on the island, an administrative framework was established, British laws were introduced, land sales began, and military barracks were built. However, although British authority was quickly established on the island, it was not until after the signing of the Treaty of Nanking (Nanjing) that the question of Hong Kong's status as a true colony was settled.

On April 5, 1843, Queen Victoria used her prerogative to declare Hong Kong a colony under the Order in Council. She then issued the Royal Charter, which established the office of Governor and the basic executive, legislative, and judicial institutions. These documents formed the core of the constitution of the newly established colony, but they were also supplemented by the Letters Patent and the Royal Instructions. These were given to the Governor and outlined in more detail the ways in which the various political institutions were to be established, the powers of these institutions, and the relationship of the colony to the metropolitan power in London.

The basic structure of the government was not complicated and followed that used elsewhere in many of Britain's other colonial possessions. The Governor was given considerable powers of decision making. He appointed the Executive and Legislative Councils to provide him with advice, but he could overrule any of this advice. The formal powers of the Governor were formidable, but he was answerable to the Government in Britain should he take undue advantage of those powers. Any legislation passed in the colony could be overruled by the British Parliament. No Bill of Rights was included in the basic constitution, although the freedom of religion was established. The judicial system was to be based on English Law, but laws based on Chinese customs were permitted providing they were not repugnant to English Law. Also, there was no mention of local government.

Effectively the political structure was designed to provide a simple set of procedures to oversee, but only become minimally involved in, the evolving commercial and social framework. There were, however, initial problems in the colony particularly with the high incidence of disease and with the difficulties experienced in encouraging further growth in trade. Significantly the expatriate merchants formed a powerful and increasingly influential group throughout the nineteenth century, and they were particularly resistant to any increases in government activity which they regarded as harmful to trade. The local population was initially excluded from participation in politics. Only grudgingly and slowly were they allowed a limited access to positions of potential influence.

The relatively stable political climate and the rapid growth of Hong Kong as a base for trade led to an increase in demand for labor. In the commercial field banks were established, the currency was organized on a more sound footing, the government raised sufficient revenues for its limited purposes, and trade eventually prospered. The colony was primarily seen as an entrepôt through which free trade could flow into and out of China. Indeed, the colony was to retain this status and not develop into a manufacturing center of any significance until the latter half of the twentieth century. There was, however, a demand for workers which was to attract a ready supply of cheap labor from the mainland where wages and conditions were less attractive than those in Hong Kong. The population itself, just over 7,000 in 1841, increased to approximately 24,000 in 1848. With the acquisition of Kowloon in 1860 and further growth on the island, the number went up to over 122,000. The acquisition of the New Territories in 1898 added another 100,000 to the estimated 254,000 already in the colony. The population was overwhelmingly Cantonese Chinese with all other minorities both from the mainland and other areas making up a very small percentage of the total.

Throughout the nineteenth century improvements in social conditions failed to keep up with the increase in population. The government did little despite its evident awareness of the need for regulation of housing, sanitation and water supplies and the increasing need for basic education, hospital, and other social services. Explanations for this inaction lie partly in the vociferous opposition to the raising of taxes by the expatriate community, partly in the unwillingness of the government to involve itself in matters it regarded as beyond its purview, and partly in the hostility among many of the local population, who regarded any action on housing and sanitation as an imposition upon traditional Chinese culture.

However, the British were more active in dealing with the potential disputes with China left unresolved by the Treaty of Nanking. The arguments about the freedom of the British to export goods (particularly opium) into China, and the reluctance of the Chinese to observe the details of the treaty led to the second Anglo-Chinese Wars. These ended with another Chinese military defeat and the ceding of Kowloon and Stonecutters Island to the British in 1860. The final addition to what is today known as Hong Kong came in 1898 when the Chinese ceded a large area known as the New Territories on a ninety-nine year lease.

The early twentieth century saw continuing growth of the population; from around 500,000 in 1916 to over 840,000 in the early 1930s. Virtually all the influx came from the surrounding province of Kwangtung (Guangdong) with the numbers swollen by the instabilities which followed the downfall of the monarchy and the setting up of rival groupings in the new republic. Hong Kong was by no means immune from these upheavals, with the nationalist sentiments in China often spilling over into the territory in the form of strikes and boycotts of British goods in the 1920s. Instability in China worsened further in the 1930s when the Japanese mounted their attacks on the mainland.

On 8 December 1941 the Japanese launched an invasion of Hong Kong itself, and quickly overran the British defenses. The surrender of the colony took place on 25 December 1941. The population of the colony which had risen to an estimated 1.6 million was rapidly depleted. During the period of occupation trade dwindled to a standstill, government operated without any recourse to the needs of the population, and the colony languished.

With the surrender of Japan in August 1945 the British quickly reestablished their authority over Hong Kong. Early attempts to introduce reforms in the institutional structures came to nothing. Certainly the authorities had to face major problems in restructuring the shattered economy and in dealing with the flood of refugees, flocking into the colony from the ever increasing instability on the mainland. Unemployment was high, housing conditions were very poor, investment was low, and by 1951 Hong Kong was seen by some as a dying city. The problems, already seemingly insurmountable, were compounded by the triumph of the communists in China in 1949. Hong Kong's importance as an entrepôt for trade to and from the mainland which had formed the bulk of its economic activities virtually disappeared.

However, the colony was soon to make major gains from the turmoil over the border. A huge reservoir of cheap labor entered the territory along with an influx of capital and expertise from entrepreneurs fleeing from the new regime in China. Immigrants from Shanghai in particular quickly set up textile factories to meet an increasing demand for textiles in Europe and North America. The economy of the colony began to be transformed into a manufacturing center with almost full employment, rising wages, and rising expectations.

Against this background, however, the terrible social conditions in the colony remained. The government, still wedded to *laissez faire,* was reluctant to intervene in the provision of social welfare. Squatter areas proliferated as new refugees continued to flood into the colony, and pressures on the inadequate education, social welfare, and health provision gradually increased. In 1954, following a huge fire in one of the major squatter areas, the government did introduce the first public housing schemes, but even there the provision was basic in quality and minimal in scope.

The government also saw no reason to change the political system in anything but the most minor and incremental fashion. Its concept was that of benign paternalism firmly rooted in nineteenth-century thinking. The Executive and the Legislative Councils were nonrepresentative and the civil service paid little attention to public opinion or the rising Chinese middle classes. These local elites, which had hitherto been only partly accommodated, became anxious to play a part in decision making on a more equal footing with the traditional expatriate elites.

The complacency of the government was heavily challenged by the riots of 1966 and 1967. The 1966 riots were ostensibly over a minor local issue but reflected a wider dissatisfaction, particularly among the young, over the conditions in the territory. The 1967 riots were much more violent and were an overspill from the turmoil on the mainland caused by the Cultural Revolution. Both prompted the government to rethink its traditional assumptions, and to introduce political reforms.

These reforms which were to remain in place, with only incremental improvements until the early 1980s, did not however envisage representative government in the form of an elected and accountable system. It was argued that there was no real demand for this in the territory. Rather they moved towards government by consultation and, it was hoped, consensus. Local elites were drafted on to advisory bodies and consulted over major policy proposals; localization of the civil service and the Legislative and Executive Councils was speeded up; and public opinion was more carefully monitored.

These reforms, minor though they were, succeeded in removing many of the most pressing political grievances in the colony. The government in London which had rarely intervened in the internal affairs of the colony was to grant, with very rare exceptions, virtual autonomy over the affairs of Hong Kong retaining only a say in the external matters which affected the territory.

Even more significant were three other major changes that were taking place. The first was the substantial rate of economic growth in the late 1960s and the 1970s. The colony's manufacturing base widened, from its reliance on textiles, into watches, plastics, and electronics. The service sector also grew considerably, with Hong Kong becoming a major financial center. The Gross Domestic Product, despite occasional lean years, averaged a growth rate of 10%.

The second major change was the arrival of a dynamic and reformist governor, Sir Murray MacLehose. MacLehose introduced a major public housing program that was eventually to provide shelter for nearly half the population; he increased educational provision; hospital and health services were improved; and the social and community services were expanded. He also tackled corruption which by the early 1970s had reached serious proportions in the public sector in general and the police force in particular. In many respects the period 1967–1979 was one of political stability combined with a prosperity undreamed of previously in Hong Kong.

The third set of changes in the 1970s occurred outside the territory in the People's Republic of China (PRC). The Cultural Revolution was largely a spent force by the early 1970s, and the government in Peking (Beijing), slowly at first, but more rapidly as the decade wore on, determined on a more liberal economic course. The new policies included the so-called "four modernizations" and the setting up of Special Economic Zones, including one immediately to the north of Hong Kong in Sham Chun (Shenzhen). Tensions and crises emanating from the mainland also now assumed less significance. Relations between Britain and the People's Republic of China showed greater reciprocity and the time seemed ripe for some opening of negotiations on the future of the colony. This future had to be discussed given the diminishing period before the point in 1997 when the New Territories, leased to Britain in 1898, were due to return to China.

So it was that in 1979 the then Governor Sir Murray MacLehose visited Beijing and raised the question of the settlement of the 1997 issue—an issue that had not been formally discussed at any level between the two governments previously. The scene was now set for substantive negotiations, the outcome of which was an agreement ending British administration totally in 1997 and the reversion of all of the colony to the People's Republic of China.

The actual negotiations took place from 1982 to 1984 between the governments of the People's Republic of China and the United Kingdom of Great Britain and Northern Ireland. The citizens of Hong Kong were excluded from the talks and were effectively faced with a fait accompli on their conclusion. Only the traditional elite in the colony were consulted or were aware of the progress of negotiations. After a most difficult period the question of sovereignty was settled in China's favor and Britain had to accept that administration of the colony would revert in 1997 to the People's Republic of China. The document which emerged was entitled "A Draft Agreement between the Government of the United Kingdom of Great Britain and Northern Ireland and the Government of the People's Republic of China on the future of Hong Kong" (26 September 1984). That document, more commonly referred to as the Joint Declaration was duly endorsed by the legislative bodies in London and Beijing in the same year.

Its provisions were to allow a high degree of political, economic, judicial, and social autonomy to the Special Administrative Region (SAR), which would be created in 1997 under the overall sovereignty of the People's Republic of China. In particular, the government was to be made more representative than hitherto, and socialism was not to be introduced for at least fifty years after the hand over of power.

Because the autonomous nature of the system had apparently been guaranteed there was, at first, little overt anxiety in Hong Kong, where many of the increasingly articulate middle classes were relatively optimistic about the establishment of a more representative government in which they could play a part. Certainly the rapidly emerging group of local Chinese liberals expressed a desire to guarantee and promote a system which was modelled broadly on capitalist economic principles and which promised minimal interference from the communist system on the mainland. On those two principles there was a high degree of consensus, although there were differences between those who advocated gradual political reforms and those who wanted a fully democratic system in place by 1997.

Whatever the outcome might be, the Joint Declaration had to be legitimized by the National People's Congress under a Basic Law. Because the Basic Law was seen by the PRC as an internal matter, it appeared appropriate that it should be drawn up by the Chinese authorities, without the participation of the British Government. A Basic Law Drafting Committee was set up in 1985 with 59 members of whom 23 were invited from Hong Kong. That drafting committee submitted its proposals in 1990, and these were duly adopted by the National People's Congress in the April of that year.

However, the provisions of the Basic Law fell short of what many in Hong Kong had hoped for. A fully and directly-elected Legislative Council was not included, and the maximum percentage of directly elected members allowed would eventually be only 50% of the total. The Chief Executive would not be directly-elected and the Executive Council would be appointed. Events in the years since the signing of the Joint Declaration only served to underline the unease with which the local population viewed the future of Hong Kong. Emigration from the territory increased dramatically as uncertainty over the degree of control which might be exercised over the future SAR intensified.

The Joint Declaration had stipulated that the British would continue to administer the territory until 1997. At the same time the political system in Hong Kong would continue to function under its colonial constitution. As a consequence, the government in the colony was to come under pressure from a host of sources both external and internal. Its tentative steps to widen the base of political representation were seen by some as too little and too late, and by others as too much and too soon. Criticized from within the territory, the Hong Kong government had also to deal with a British administration anxious not to alienate Peking (Beijing). In turn, the PRC government was equally determined not to allow full democratic representation, and issued warnings about attempts to bring this about. There was also considerable disquiet in Hong Kong concerning the unresolved problems left over from ambiguities in the Joint Declaration. These included such problems as the proposed size of the People's Liberation Army garrison in the territory, the influence the PRC should have over any major economic or political changes which spanned the period before and after 1997, the degree of human rights granted to the territory, and the location and composition of the final Court of Appeal.

Matters came to a head in the T'ien-an-man (Tiananman) Square incident in June 1989. There had been considerable support in Hong Kong for the democratic movement in China which had expressed itself in huge, but overwhelmingly peaceful demonstrations in the colony. The violent suppression of the democratic movement in Beijing and other cities led to a huge dip in confidence in the territory's future. This was followed by the PRC authorities labelling some of the Hong Kong supporters of the democracy movement in China as being subversive. Almost simultaneously, pressure for the granting of the right of abode in the United Kingdom, from all sectors of the local community, which had been building up in the late 1980s, was met with a response by the British Parliament granting right of abode for only 50,000 heads of households and their dependents—far short of the figures hoped for in Hong Kong. The result of these setbacks and of disappointment with the Basic Law was a major increase in applications for emigration to the United States, Canada, Australia, and New Zealand.

Internally the government in Hong Kong was under pressure, particularly from the liberal groups to quickly introduce full and direct elections for the Legislative Council; to introduce a full Bill of Rights at the earliest possible opportunity (and certainly before 1997); and to ensure an independent and robust judiciary as a bulwark against any incursions from the mainland after sovereignty was transferred. The government response was to introduce 18 directly-elected seats into the Legislative Council by 1991 and a further two in 1995. The People's Republic of China responded by stating unequivocally that the Basic Law would not allow for a full and directly-elected legislative body and was not negotiable. Direct elections to the Legislative Council which were held in September 1991 showed considerable support for the liberal group, which gained 12 of the 18 seats, thereby routing the more conservative business-orientated groups and eclipsing the few candidates with pro-Beijing leanings.

Other major advances for liberal positions were made with the government introducing legislation for a Human Rights Ordinance in March 1990, despite considerable opposition from the People's Republic of China, abolishing capital punishment (which was on the statute books although never in practice carried out), and decriminalizing homosexuality (1991).

Throughout the 1980s major changes were also taking place in the economy. The manufacturing base continued to decline while the service sector expanded. Full employment was maintained and wages went up with the shortage of labor which followed the abrupt halt to immigration from neighboring provinces in 1980. Hong Kong was also allowed to become a full and independent member of the General Agreement on Tariffs and Trade (GATT) organization and was active in setting up trade missions in many of the world major centers.

The greatest change, however, came from the huge expansion of the economic relationship with the People's Republic of China. Imports and exports to the mainland grew massively and re-exports showed impressive gains. A large amount of Hong Kong investment moved into the Special Economic Zone in Sham Chun (Shenzhen) where labor costs and factory space were lower than in the increasingly expensive colony, but this only seemed to increase the general prosperity of the region. Also, despite worrying signs of inflation, the currency, with a stable Hong Kong dollar, linked to the U.S. dollar since 1983, remained relatively stable.

The government made major efforts to improve education provision, particularly in the tertiary sector. Attempts were made to increase the training of professionals needed for the advanced sectors of an economy which remained buoyant but which was potentially threatened by a loss of skilled staff through emigration. Housing provision was improved in the public sector and the New Towns in the New Territories grew rapidly, helped by an increasingly efficient communication system. Life expectancy was among the highest in the world. Corruption in the public service had been brought under control and, with the T'ien-an-man (Tiananman) Square incident becoming less significant, prospects in all but the political sector were not unduly worrying. Business confidence, undermined by the events of 1989, returned to the colony and the British and Chinese negotiators, who had suspended discussions after 1989, returned to discuss the outstanding areas not yet resolved over the Joint Declaration.

The future of the territory between 1991 and 1997 and beyond is uncertain. Over 5-½ million people are being put under the final authority of an avowedly socialist system in direct contradiction to the capitalist way of life developed in Hong Kong. The optimists argue that the People's Republic of China will honor the agreements and allow the Special Administrative Region considerable autonomy, thus allowing the Hong Kong "way of life" to continue very much as it did under British administration. They further argue that the economy will continue to flourish and remain a paradigm for less developed systems to emulate. The fifty-year transition period before final absorption into the People's Republic of China, when the differences will supposedly have withered away, is for many people long enough into the future not to cause too much anxiety. Optimists would also suggest that the transition on the mainland with the modernization of the economy will lead to the relaxation of control by the Communist party and a greater reciprocity between the two systems.

Pessimists, on the other hand, argue that the People's Republic of China will not allow the system to continue in anything like its present form. They point to the refusal of the PRC to allow for real autonomy, or to allow full and direct elections to the central political institutions. Above all, they return to the continuing absence of western notions of democratic rule on the mainland. They further argue that even if the government in (Peking) Beijing does not destroy the system by direct intervention they might just do it by incompetence and a misunderstanding of what is needed to maintain economic growth in Hong Kong.

It is clearly still too early to predict accurately the set of outcomes upon which unfortunately so many people's futures rest. If the history of Hong Kong is anything to go by then a cautious optimism is not out of place. Carved out of a barren rock, with no natural resources beyond its magnificent harbor and its geographical location, it had to rely on the resilience and ingenuity of its people. The population, which grew so rapidly, transformed Hong Kong into one of the most successful economies in the world, able to respond rapidly and efficiently to changing demands. It remains today a society with a robust free press and media, where the rule of law largely pertains, a highly-educated population exists, and a standard of living, rapidly approaching that of the developed western systems, is emerging. Its crime rate remains one of the lowest in Asia; while its life expectancy is one of the highest. There is emerging a new generation of local politicians who seem determined to press for the retention and expansion of pluralistic democratic principles in the future.

On the negative side, the fragility of the economic framework, the nascent political reforms, and the societal nexus may find it difficult to absorb too many shocks emanating from the mainland. It is to be hoped that the authorities in Beijing will be able to reconcile Hong Kong's needs with those of the rest of the People's Republic of China. As they recognized the importance of Hong Kong in the past, so it is hoped that they can make full use of Hong Kong's potential contributions to the PRC as a whole while at the same time remaining sensitive to the needs of the Hong Kong people.

We wish Hong Kong well.

THE DICTIONARY

ABERDEEN (Shek Pai Wan). A settlement situated on the southeast coast of Hong Kong Island and named after Lord Aberdeen, the British Foreign Secretary at the time Britain acquired the colony. The community, now known as Aberdeen, was originally a fishing village, but was also known since the sixteenth century as a base for pirates. In October 1841 it was selected, along with Happy Valley and Stanley, as one of the first areas for development for town lots. It became one of the centers for the development of the Chinese deep sea fishing fleets and still retains many connections with the sea.

ABERDEEN, GEORGE HAMILTON–GORDON. Fourth earl of Aberdeen. (1784–1860). British Foreign Secretary in the Tory administration (1841–1846) at the time of the acquisition of Hong Kong and later Prime Minister (1852–1855). He was opposed to the permanent occupation of the territory stating, in Spring 1842, that the acquisitions made from China "were not to be regarded in the light of permanent conquest." He saw Hong Kong's worth as particularly dubious if held against Chinese wishes. His instructions were not followed by Sir Henry Pottinger, soon to be formally appointed as the island's first governor, and on 26 June, 1843 with the ratification of the Treaty of Nanking (Nanjing) Hong Kong was declared a British colony. (See Anglo-Chinese Wars; Nanking (Nanjing), Treaty of; Pottinger, Sir Henry.)

1

ACTING GOVERNOR. A position, outlined under Article XVII of the Letters Patent, to provide a temporary chief executive if the Governor was absent from the colony. The Chief Secretary assumes this office when necessary. (See Chief Secretary.)

ACTS OF PARLIAMENT. A Bill becomes an Act of Parliament after it has been passed by the House of Commons and the House of Lords and received the Queen's assent. Despite Hong Kong being a colony, acts only apply to the territory where this is specifically stated or implied. However, even if an act is not specifically operative in Hong Kong, it is likely to be applied if this is in line with opinion in Britain. The Murder Act of 1967 illustrates the point. Here the British Parliament virtually abolished the death penalty, but this did not specifically apply to Hong Kong. However, when in 1973 the then Governor of Hong Kong, Sir Murray MacLehose with the agreement of the Executive Council refused to quash a death sentence, he was overruled by the British Secretary of State.

In Hong Kong bills passed by the Legislative Council are referred to as ordinances rather than acts, but for all practical purposes the two are the same. (See Capital Punishment; House of Commons; Legislative Council; Parliament, British.)

ADMINISTRATION. Given the government's attachment to a *laissez faire* stance, for much of Hong Kong's history the extent of government activity and administration was minimal. Administrators were few in number, generalists in training, and overwhelmingly expatriate non-Chinese in background. However, with the growth of the population, the expansion of the economy and the demand for a better provision of government services after the Second World War, the administration expanded rapidly. It was also restructured following a major report by the international consultants, McKinsey and Co., in 1973.

Also significant in recent years has been the process of localization of the administration. Since 1985 only locals have been offered permanent terms at the Administrative Officer (the highest) level. This process will accelerate as 1997 approaches. No expatriate may hold the highest office of Secretary of a Branch in the Civil Service in the Special Administrative Region although provision has been made to allow certain expatriates to hold office at lower posts. (See Basic Law; Local Government; Localization; MacLehose, Sir Murray.)

ADVISORY BODIES. Attempts to develop a representative system of government have been slow to arrive and limited in aspiration. Membership of the Legislative and Executive Councils has been largely based on government appointments plus functional representation of key interest groups. More recently, the number of directly-elected members has increased but the legislature is far from being composed of directly-elected members based in geographical constituencies which is common in most Western democracies. An alternative form of representation has developed through the system of co-opting representatives of local interests onto the large member of advisory bodies used in the development and implementation of public policy.

There are now over 400 advisory bodies which advise on such diverse sets of policies as education, journalism, urban planning, banking, and a host of other matters. Their increasing importance is to some extent reflected in their growth in numbers. In 1950 there were 50; in 1960, 62; in 1970, 100; in 1980, 165: and in 1990, over 200. (See District Administration; Executive Council; Legislative Council; Political System.)

ADVISORY COMMITTEE ON CORRUPTION. A prototype of this important committee was first established in 1956. It was re-named the Advisory Committee on

Corruption in 1958. Its main function was to advise on ways of dealing with the rising incidence of corruption in the territory and it was instrumental in the setting up of the Independent Commission against Corruption in 1974. (See Independent Commission Against Corruption.)

AGRICULTURE. Hong Kong's dearth of easily cultivated land has led to a limited role for agriculture in the territory's economy. Upon their arrival the British found a small population, reliant mainly on fishing and subsistence farming of rice and vegetables. The growth in population exacerbated this situation and led to an increasing reliance upon external sources, particularly the mainland of China, for the importing of foodstuffs.

The New Territories, acquired in 1898, had a larger area of cultivable land particularly in the West, and were to retain their rural economy long after this had virtually disappeared in Kowloon and Hong Kong Island. However, in 1972 the government decided to encourage urban development in the New Territories to alleviate the overcrowding of other parts of Hong Kong with the result that agriculture there became even less significant.

By 1970 only 2% of the territory's Gross National Product was accounted for by agriculture, and that fell to 1% by 1985 and less than 0.3% by 1989. By the late 1980s only 2,230 hectares of land were under cultivation, with most of that being given over to vegetables and flowers. Some pigs and poultry are also reared. Despite the small area under cultivation, the territory still manages to provide 34% of its inhabitants' needs for fresh vegetables, 18% live pigs, and 37% live poultry. It was estimated in 1990 that only 6.7% (72 sq.km) of Hong Kong's land area is cultivable, down from 13% in 1954 and 7.8% in 1980 respectively. (See Economy; Trade.)

AKERS-JONES, SIR DAVID. Sir David Akers-Jones was Chief Secretary when the then Governor Sir Edward

Youde died in office. As a consequence, he became the Acting Governor from December 1986 until April 1987. With the appointment of the new Governor, Sir David Wilson, he remained for a short period as special advisor to the new incumbent. (See Chief Secretary; Governor.)

AMERICAN BAPTIST MISSION. The American Baptist Mission established a Chinese Church at Sheung Wan market as early as 1843. However, support for the Mission in the territory fluctuated, and, with the opening up of China in the 19th century the Mission moved out of the territory. In the 1950s following the establishment of the People's Republic of China, which actively discouraged Christian missions, the organization relocated in Hong Kong. Its specific function in the early 1950s was to help the mass of refugees who arrived in Hong Kong from the mainland generally, and Shantau (Swatow) in particular.

The Baptist Mission is not a church in the formal sense of the term. It also has no schools of its own, but it is affiliated with about 20 Baptist churches and supplies teachers to various educational establishments. It also provides financial aid and social work through the running of two community centers and other agencies. (See Religion.)

AMERICAN CHAMBER OF COMMERCE. The American Chamber of Commerce was established in the territory in 1969 as a consequence of the growing economic involvement of America in the increasingly important financial and industrial affairs of the territory. In 1970, for example, the United States accounted for 13% of the territory's imports and 42% of its exports. To safeguard the interests of American business a formal organization was established, the main aims of which were, and still are, as follows:

1. To foster the development of commerce.
2. To promote trade between the United States and Hong Kong and the Pacific Region.
3. To help maintain demand for United States products exported to the territory and to generally promote U.S. products.
4. To influence the structure of U.S. trade in the Colony.

Although the value of trade between Hong Kong and the United States has increased enormously in value its relative importance has declined. In 1989 8.2% of all imports came from the United States, putting it behind the People's Republic of China, Japan, and Taiwan. However, exports of Hong Kong goods (excluding re-exports mostly from the PRC) to the United States accounted for 32.2% of the total, making it still the territory's most important single market. (See Appendix; Economy; Trade.)

ANGLO-CHINESE PARLIAMENTARY GROUP. The Anglo-Chinese Parliamentary group is made up of British members of Parliament from all political parties. It is not a government body and has had little real power over Anglo-Chinese relations. During the negotiations over the future of Hong Kong prior to the 1984 agreements, its stance was generally supportive of the PRC government. It tended to underplay the significance of local sentiment when this clashed with the will of the PRC. (See House of Commons; Joint Declaration; Parliament, British.)

ANGLO-CHINESE WARS. A series of wars between the British and Chinese which are sometimes referred to as the Opium Wars (although the second war is also sometimes known as the Arrow War). Although hostilities first broke out in 1839, war was not formally declared until January 1840. The conflict was temporarily resolved by the Convention of Chuanpi (Chuanbi) in 1841, when the Chinese government ceded the Island of Hong Kong to the British, thus establishing a permanent base for the pursuance of foreign trade. However, hostilities reopened in February 1841 after the breakdown of further negotiations. As in the previous year, the strategic Bogue forts were occupied and Canton (Guangzhou) threatened. This led to the Chinese authorities accepting the need to come to terms with the military threat both in the south and further north. In the Spring of 1842 the British took Shanghai and moved the fleet up the Yangtze (Yangzi) River. With Nanking (Nanjing) threatened, the Chinese sued for peace. The Treaty of Nanking (Nanjing) was signed on 29 August 1842 on board the HMS *Cornwallis*.

The terms of the Treaty were harsh upon the Chinese and included even more than the British had aimed for at the outbreak of hostilities. Some of its more important provisions were:

1. The ports of Amoy (Xiamen), Canton (Guangzhou), Foochow (Fuzhow), Ningpo (Ningbo), and Shanghai to be opened for foreign trade. Residents and Consuls representing British interests to be appointed in those ports on preferential conditions.
2. Hong Kong Island to be ceded to the United Kingdom in perpetuity
3. China to pay $6 million in compensation for the opium that had been confiscated in Canton (Guangzhou) in exchange for "the lives of British subjects"—the ostensible though questionable cause of the outbreak of hostilities in the first place.
4. The Co-*Hong* monopoly (a guild of Chinese merchants with a virtual monopoly of the Canton trade) to be abolished and foreigners allowed to trade freely. Three million dollars to be paid to British

merchants by Chinese merchants to settle outstanding debts.

5. The Chinese government to pay $12 million to the British for the war (which, arguably, was largely forced upon them by Britain in the first place).

The Treaty of Nanking (Nanjing) was ratified by both governments on 26 June 1843. The colony of Hong Kong was thus formally established.

The second of the Anglo-Chinese wars broke out following an incident in 1856 on the British-registered ship the *Arrow* which was berthed in Canton (Guangzhou). Chinese authorities boarded the ship, imprisoned its crew, and charged them with piracy. This proved to be the spark to ignite the smoldering disagreements between the two nations which had existed since the signing of the Treaty of Nanking (Nanjing). Since the signing of this Treaty the British had tried to expand its provisions, but had been frustrated in this by the Chinese. After protracted and largely fruitless negotiations, hostilities recommenced, and Canton (Guangzhou) was taken by the British forces in 1858. Further north the military successes of a joint force of French and British pressurized the Chinese to sign the Treaty of Tientsin (Tianjin). Once again the Chinese authorities vacillated, and after further hostilities had broken out the Allied forces took Peking (Beijing) giving the Chinese little choice but to sign the Convention of Peking (Beijing) in 1860.

In terms of benefits to the British in Hong Kong the Treaty of Tientsin (Tianjin) ceded Stonecutters Island, Kowloon Point and Hong Kong Island in perpetuity. The clear benefits accruing to Britain were the virtual legalization of the opium trade; the expansion of territory onto the mainland (Kowloon), thus making the territory more defensible; and the profits that would be made by the trafficking of "coolie" labor through the colony. (See Bogue, Treaty of; Chuanpi (Chuanbi), Convention of;

Nanking (Nanjing), Treaty of; Peking (Beijing), Convention of; Tientsin (Tianjin), Treaty of.)

ANNUAL REPORTS. The Annual Reports are published by the Government Information Service and provide information on such matters as the economy, constitution, financial and political structure, crime statistics, health and weather patterns for the whole of the post-Second World War period. As government publications the information they contain is usually accurate and detailed, but is subject to government selection and interpretation.

AOMEN (MACAU). SEE MACAU. The Chinese Pinyin name for Macau, a Portuguese administered enclave some 40 miles from Hong Kong. Situated on the western side of the Pearl Estuary it is the oldest colony in the Far East. It is due to return to Chinese sovereign administration in 1999.

APPLICATION OF ENGLISH LAWS ORDINANCE. An ordinance (law) passed in Hong Kong in 1966 to clarify the relationship between laws passed in the United Kingdom and their applicability in the territory. This particular law will be modified in 1997 or before. (See Acts of Parliament.)

APPOINTED MEMBERS. The term "appointed members" was clearly spelled out in the Letters Patent (1917) which in turn were drawn from the Hong Kong Charter (1843) and the Royal Instructions (1917). The two documents were concerned *inter alia* with the constitutional powers of the Governor relative to the membership of the institutional bodies in the territory. These documents allow the Governor, upon the formal permission of the Crown, to appoint members to the Legislative Council and the Executive Council. In the case of the

Urban Council, District Boards, and Regional Council power to appoint is given by the respective ordinances. Until the 1980s this technically meant that all members who were not ex-officio were appointed members. However, despite the technical meaning, the term has often been used to describe non-civil servants who were appointed to the Legislative and Executive Council by the Governor.

The importance of these members was reduced slightly in the 1980s, when from 1982 an indirectly elected element was introduced into the District Boards and, from 1985, the Legislative Council. After 1997 there will be no appointed members in the Legislative Council, but appointments to the Executive Council will remain in the hands of the Chief Executive. (See Basic Law; District Administration; Executive Council; Legislative Council; Letters Patent; Regional Council; Urban Council.)

ARCHEOLOGY. Archeological evidence suggests that the first settlement of Hong Kong came 6,000 years ago in the Neolithic period. The earliest inhabitants of Hong Kong were related to the Bacsonial people of South East Asia, themselves successors to the Pleistocene gatherers known as Hoabinhian. There are, however, a growing number of scholars who believe that the prehistoric cultures within the South China region had evolved locally and independently of influences from outside the area.

Recent excavations have revealed two main neolithic cultures, the first showing both coarse cord-marked pottery and fine pottery sometimes painted and decorated with incised lines and perforations. In the second and more modern phase, beginning in the third millennium B.C., the artifacts are more sophisticated with polished stone tools, and ornaments such as rings, in a range of sizes made from quartz and other suitable stones.

The final phase in Hong Kong's prehistory was the Bronze age spanning the second millennium B.C. Although bronze artifacts were not in common use several good specimens of weapons, tools, and fish hooks have been excavated.

Although the linguistic and ethnic origins of the ancient peoples are not known, the earliest Chinese records speak of a maritime people inhabiting the South Eastern seaboard who were known as the *Yueh*. These people almost certainly made the rock carvings (unique to Hong Kong) at various sites in the territory such as Shek Pik, Kau Sai, Po Toi, Cheung Chau, Tung Lung, Big Wave Bay, and Wong Chuk Hang.

The military conquest of the area by the Ch'in (Qin) (221–207 B.C.) and the Han (Han) (206 B.C.–220 A.D.) had a major influence on the population of the territory. Coins have been discovered, but the most important discovery was the Han (Han) tomb at Lei Cheung Uk in 1955, thought to relate to the middle Eastern Han (Han) period.

To date remains from later periods are scarce. Recent work has given some clues about life under the T'ang (Tang) dynasty (618 A.D.–907 A.D.). Evidence has come largely from the study of the lime kilns which obviously were of some importance given their numbers. There are also links with the Mongol incursions and the last period of the Sung (Song) dynasty in the 13th century. Inscriptions, coins and celadon of Sung (Song) type have been found on various sites such as Tin Hau, Nim Shue Wan, Lantau, Shek Pik, and Mai Po.

The most recent digs are beginning to throw fresh light on events in Hong Kong during the Ming (Ming) dynasty (1368–1644) and the Ch'ing (Qing) (1644–1911). Two of the most interesting excavations were at Penny's Bay, where substantial quantities of Ming (Ming) export porcelain were found, and on Tung Lung Island, where a Ch'ing-(Qing) period fort gives fascinating details of the internal arrangements of the fortification and the everyday utensils of a remote garrison during the final stages of Imperial China.

One of the great problems facing archeology in the territory is the extent of construction work taking place. With the development of the New Territories in general and the smaller islands in particular there is much concern that many sites not yet discovered might be lost forever. (See Ch'in (Qin) Dynasty; Han (Han) Dynasty; Lei Cheng Uk Tomb; Ming (Ming) Dynasty; Sung (Song) Dynasty.)

ARCHITECTURE. Early "colonial" building, both public and private, followed European examples of 19th-century Neo-Classicism, Baroque or Victorian Gothic, with architectural adaptations such as colonnades and verandas to suit the climate. The oldest of the few remaining examples in Hong Kong is Flagstaff House, built in 1846 as the headquarters for the British Military Commander. Flagstaff House has since been converted into the Museum of Teaware.

Indigenous rural architecture dates mostly from the Ch'ing (Qing) dynasty (1644–1912) and was built with the vernacular characteristics of Southern China villages in design, materials, decoration, and *fung shui* (wind and water) principles. Some village buildings have been declared "historical buildings" but diminishment of the agrarian lifestyle and urban growth patterns have affected much change.

Temples to the Chinese deities and villas for the prosperous Chinese were built in the Chinese style, although the latter often adopted a mixture of East and West. Other religious architecture followed accepted practices of respective cultures.

At the turn of the century, major reclamation and consolidation of Hong Kong as an important port gave rise to a new business center of commercial and public buildings in neoclassical or baroque splendor, replacing much of the vernacular "shophouse" style.

Contemporary architecture in Hong Kong is notable for the large scale of concentrated developments in both commercial and residential sectors as redevelopment programs in the 1970s ushered in high-rise buildings, hotels, and indoor shopping malls, including the largest interconnected precinct in the world (Ocean Terminal/Ocean Center).

Huge housing projects were a common feature of the government's new towns program, introduced to meet the demands of a rapidly expanding post-World War II population. Clusters of high-rise apartment blocks, springing from previously rural settlements, now dominate the landscape of the New Territories. About 95% of the residential buildings in Hong Kong are apartments and over half the population live in government subsidized housing.

The attempt to maximize the development potential of urban sites has in the context of Hong Kong's competitive society provided an arena for the economic power of developers to flourish often at the expense of aesthetic values. More recently, however, a new set of aesthetics has penetrated the local architecture, not least of which are several buildings of international repute, such as the "High Tech" crafted Hong Kong and Shanghai Bank (1986) by Norman Foster and I.M.Pei's Bank of China, which was built shortly afterwards. The Bank of China is a symbolic megastructure which at the time of its construction was the fifth tallest building in the world.

ARMED FORCES. One reason Hong Kong was acquired as a colony was to allow elements of the British armed forces to be permanently stationed in the area in order to promote and defend British interests in China. A naval dockyard and army garrisons were quickly set up not only to defend Hong Kong, if necessary, from external attack, but also to provide a base from which expeditions could be sent to China. The further extensions to the colony in 1860 and 1898 were also partly based on strategic considerations. The harbor was protected for naval vessels, and extra territory allowed an in-depth defence against any possible attacks on Hong Kong from overland. In 1900, for instance, Hong Kong was used as a base for sending units to the mainland to deal with the Boxer Rebellion.

These deterrent measures were, however, of little use when in 1941, despite the presence of a defence force of 30,000 men, the colony rapidly fell to the Japanese invading forces. The battle began on December 8 and was concluded with the surrender of the British forces on December 25.

With the defeat of the Japanese in 1945 the British presence was reestablished. It was even briefly strengthened in 1949 in response to the victory of the communists in China. However, it was soon acknowledged that resistance to a determined attack by the People's Liberation Army was not feasible. Throughout the 1950s there was a rundown of British forces. In 1958 the naval dockyard was closed with the ships withdrawn to Singapore. In 1975 the British government further reduced the size of the army, and between 1976 and 1979 the strength of the armed forces was as follows: four Infantry Battalions (three Gurkha and one British), one Gurkha Engineering Squadron, five naval patrol craft and one Royal Air Force Helicopter squadron. A further agreement concluded in 1975 established that the Hong Kong government should shoulder a percentage of the cost of maintaining a garrison in the colony.

Under the 1984 agreements on the future of Hong Kong the British garrison was to remain in the territory until 1997. Its role until the complete withdrawal is as much a political as a military statement. It serves to underline the British administrative presence and commitment in the transition period leading up to 1997, but it is not intended as a military deterrent to the People's Republic of China. It also had an important, though declining, role in patrolling Hong Kong's land and sea borders to restrain illegal immigration into the territory. (This role is to be taken over by the Royal Hong Kong Police from 1992.) In the late 1980s the garrison was slowly depleted and under the terms of the 1984 agreements it will be completely withdrawn when the territory becomes a Special Administrative Region of the People's Republic of China.

After 1997 units of the People's Liberation Army (PLA) will be stationed in the territory but their size, composition, and precise location is not yet established. (See Basic Law; Gurkhas, Brigade of; People's Liberation Army; Second World War.)

ARROW WAR. The ostensible cause of this war between the British and Chinese—which led to the Treaty of Tientsin (Tianjin) in 1858 and the Convention of Peking (Beijing) in 1860—was an incident involving a ship called the *Arrow*.

The incident was trivial in itself. Under an ordinance passed in Hong Kong in 1855 Chinese owners of ships who had registered their ships with the colonial authorities were allowed the protection of the British flag as if their ships were British-owned. One ship which took advantage of these considerable benefits was the *Lorcha Arrow*, which had a British captain but was Chinese-owned.

At this time piracy was rife in the area and the Chinese authorities in Canton (Guangzhou) suspected that the *Arrow* was being used for questionable purposes. They boarded the ship in the Autumn of 1856, arrested the crew, charged them with piracy, and imprisoned them. The British quickly responded by demanding an apology from the Chinese and, in the absence of a response, took an imperial junk hostage. The Chinese authorities pointed out that no British flag was flying when they boarded the *Arrow*—a point endorsed later by the crew. They also established that the registration of the ship had expired and nowhere in the Treaty of Nanking (Nanjing) did the navy have a right to take Chinese ships hostage. These justifiable protests could not, however, avert the outbreak of hostilities which are often referred to as the Arrow War. (See Convention of Peking (Beijing); Nanking (Nanjing), Treaty of; Tientsin (Tianjin), Treaty of.)

ASSESSMENT OFFICES. It has always been difficult to gauge public opinion in Hong Kong largely because of the absence of direct elections and the refusal of the authorities to countenance referenda on major issues. In the period 1984/1985 the government set up an Assessment Office to try and measure the reactions of the public to the agreements concerning the future of Hong Kong. The Assessment Office, which was staffed by civil servants, was subject to independent monitoring. The small number of submissions received from individuals and organizations showed a cautious acceptance of the proposed agreements. In 1987 another assessment exercise was undertaken by the Survey Office to measure reaction to the proposals for the future development of representative government in Hong Kong. In the future such devices are unlikely to be developed further, as the People's Republic of China does not favor such formal means of measuring public reaction to political initiatives. (See Joint Declaration.)

ATTORNEY GENERAL. A position in the administration of Hong Kong as the principal adviser to the government on legal matters. The position was established in the

1840s following the accepted pattern of colonial administration. Since that time the Attorney General has been an
ex-officio member of the Executive Council and the
Legislative Council. He is also the head of the Legal
Department of the government and is responsible for all
prosecutions in Hong Kong. (See Executive Council;
Legal System; Legislative Council.)

AUTONOMY. Hong Kong is not, and never will be, a
sovereign state. Its status is that of a subordinate entity to
a larger sovereign organization. In formal terms, Hong
Kong has had little autonomy over its domestic affairs,
and none in its foreign affairs. In reality, however,
particularly since the Second World War, the territory
has been allowed to run its own domestic policy and has
even been allowed limited independence in certain
economic aspects of foreign policy. The agreements on
the future of Hong Kong allow the future Special
Administrative Region a high degree of autonomy in
many areas such as the economy, its political institutions,
way of life, currency, laws and, to some extent, the
pursuit of its economic interests in the wider international community. Indeed, the agreements even stipulate
that socialism will not be practiced in Hong Kong for fifty
years, even though on the mainland no other political
system is allowed! There has been general agreement
that without a high degree of autonomy granted by the
Chinese authorities the territory could not continue to
function as one of the great financial, banking, and
economic centers of Asia. (See Basic Law; Constitution;
Joint Declaration; Political System.)

-B-

BANKS. Hong Kong's first bank, a branch of the Oriental
Bank, was opened in 1845 shortly after the colony was

acquired by the British. This bank issued its own notes which 12 years later were recognized as legal currency. Other banks quickly followed, such as the Chartered and Mercantile Bank in 1857 and the Hongkong and Shanghai Bank in 1864. The latter was locally based, and did much to smooth financial transactions both within the colony, and between Hong Kong and China throughout the nineteenth and twentieth centuries. As the colony expanded in importance after the Second World War the banking sector assumed great significance. In 1955 there were 34 incorporated banks in the territory, but by 1970 this had grown to 70. With the opening up of the People's Republic of China under the "Four Modernizations," the number increased further, thus reinforcing the reputation of Hong Kong as a major financial and banking center. The number of licensed banks rose from 88 in 1978, to 113 in 1980, and to 165 in 1989.

In the absence of a central bank the Hongkong and Shanghai bank and the Standard Chartered Bank issue the local currency. Under the agreements between the British government and the government of the People's Republic of China, concluded in 1984, the territory will still be allowed to authorize designated banks to issue the local currency. (See Currency; Economic System; Hongkong and Shanghai Banking Corporation.)

BASIC LAW. A document of considerable constitutional significance to Hong Kong. It grew out of the Joint Declaration signed by the governments of Britain and Hong Kong in September 1984. It was agreed that the British would continue to administer the territory until June 30, 1997 after which Hong Kong would become a Special Administrative Region (SAR) under Chinese sovereign control. The Joint Declaration stipulated that a Basic Law would be drafted and eventually promulgated. Such a document would outline and expand upon certain matters stipulated in the Joint Declaration and form the basis of the territory's political, economic, social, and judicial arrangements for the next fifty years. It also had the function of outlining more precisely the relationship between the central government in Peking (Beijing) and the local system. A Basic Law Drafting Committee was set up in April 1985 with a membership of 59, of whom 23 were from Hong Kong and the remainder from the mainland. Another committee, called the Basic Law Consultative Committee, was established in December 1985 to collate Hong Kong opinion. The latter committee was much larger (180) and drawn from a broad cross section of the community. After two draft proposals in April 1988 and February 1989, the final version was ratified by the National People's Congress on April 4, 1990. It is scheduled to come into operation as of July 1, 1997.

The Basic Law covers the following areas:

1. General principles.
2. Relationship between the central authorities and the Hong Kong Special Administrative Region.
3. Fundamental rights and duties of residents.
4. The political structure, including the roles of the Chief Executive, the executive authorities, the legislature, the judiciary, the district organizations and public servants.
5. The economy including public finance, monetary affairs, trade, industry and commerce, land leases, shipping and civil aviation.
6. Education, science, culture, sports, religion, labor and social services.
7. External affairs.
8. Interpretation and amendment of the Basic Law.
9. Supplementary provisions.
10. Three annexes relating to the selection of the Chief Executive, the formation of the Legislative Councils and Executive Councils and the national laws to be applied in the Hong Kong SAR.

11. Various other decisions relating to the methods of formation of the first government and the first Legislative Council of the SAR. (See Bill of Rights; Constitution; Economic System; Joint Declaration; Sovereignty; Special Administrative Region.)

BELCHER, SIR EDWARD. Captain Edward Belcher was in charge of the detachment of sailors sent by Commodore J. J. Bremer to claim Hong Kong Island for the British crown in 1841. He landed from HMS *Sulphur* on 25 January at Possession Point. The possession was formally celebrated the next day by Commodore J. J. Bremer when the flag was raised on the slopes of what was later to be known as Victoria Peak. (See Anglo-Chinese Wars.)

BILL OF RIGHTS. The Basic Law for Hong Kong which was adopted in 1990 and which becomes operative in 1997 contains certain provisions relating to rights in Articles 24–41. However, it was argued by jurists and others in the territory that this was an insufficient safeguard for the people of Hong Kong. The Hong Kong government came to share this view and in October 1989 the Governor, Sir David Wilson, announced that a Bill of Rights would be introduced into the territory which would entrench the provisions of the International Covenant on Civil and Political Rights, the International Covenant on Economic, Social and Cultural Rights, and the International Labor Conventions. Such a Bill of Rights would also be superior to all other Hong Kong law. However, the People's Republic of China argued that entrenchment and superiority were not applicable to Hong Kong and that the Bill of Rights could not be binding upon the Basic Law. Accordingly in March 1990, following the publication of the Basic Law, the Hong Kong government announced that the Bill of Rights would be neither superior nor entrenched. The Bill of

Rights, entitled in Hong Kong the Human Rights Ordinance, was finally approved in 1990. The articles of the Ordinance covered the following rights:

1. Entitlement to rights without distinction.
2. The right to life.
3. No torture or inhuman treatment.
4. No slavery or servitude.
5. Liberty and security of person.
6. Rights of persons deprived of liberty.
7. No imprisonment for breach of contract.
8. Liberty of movement.
9. Restrictions on expulsion from Hong Kong.
10. Equality before the courts and the right to a fair and public hearing.
11. Rights of persons charged with, or convicted of, criminal offence.
12. No retrospective criminal offenses or penalties.
13. Right to recognition as person before the law.
14. Protection of privacy, family, home, correspondence, honor and reputation.
15. Freedom of thought, conscience, and religion.
16. Freedom of opinion and expression.
17. No propaganda for war or advocacy of national, racial, or religious hatred.
18. Right of peaceful assembly.
19. Freedom of association.
20. Rights in respect of marriage and family.
21. Rights of children.
22. Rights to participate in public life.
23. Equality before and equal protection of law.
24. Rights of minorities.

It must be added, however, that certain exemptions from the international covenants were included in the Ordinance. The most significant one makes it clear that neither the Legislative nor Executive Councils need necessarily be elected bodies. In addition after 1997 when the Letters Patent will no longer apply, the power vested in the Legislative Council by the Basic Law will make it possible to amend any of the provisions of the Ordinance by a simple majority. (See Basic Law; Executive Council; International Covenant on Civil and Political Rights; International Covenant on Economic and Cultural Rights; Legislative Council.)

BLACK, SIR ROBERT (1906–). Governor of Hong Kong from January 1958 to March 1964. He helped to oversee a period of rapid economic growth of the territory. In March 1958 he announced to the Legislative Council that, while Britain still exercised formal authority over the territory, there would be considerable autonomy granted in the administrative and financial fields. British authority would normally only be exercised in the conduct of foreign policy. (See Government, British.)

BLAIR-KERR REPORTS. Milestone reports in the attempts to counter the widespread corruption in Hong Kong society associated with the great economic expansion of the 1960s and early 1970s. The Reports, which were named after a High Court Judge who investigated a case of a senior police officer accused of accepting bribes, were published in September 1973. Corruption was recognized to exist on a wide scale in the community, and previous efforts to deal with it were seen as clearly inadequate. As a result of the reports, the police officer in question was eventually extradited from Britain, arrested, and imprisoned. More significantly, these Reports laid bare the extent of corruption and led to the creation in 1974 of the Independent Commission against Corruption, a body with considerable powers independent of the police, to investigate and prosecute corrupt persons. (See Godber Affair; Independent Commission Against Corruption.)

BLAKE, SIR HENRY (1840–1918). Sir Henry Blake was Governor of Hong Kong from November 1898–November 1903. He arrived a few months after the New Territories had been leased to Britain for 99 years by the Chinese government. He quickly stamped British authority by despatching troops to put down Chinese resistance in the New Territories and removed Chinese imperial troops from Kowloon City. He was also active in bringing about a major set of improvements in the standards of housing and sanitation in the colony. He was replaced by Sir Henry May. (see Health; Kowloon Walled City; New Territories.)

BLOCKADE. The "blockade" which took place between 1867 and 1886 reflected, and contributed to, the gradually worsening relations between China and Hong Kong. Its origins lay in the troubled questions of who was to control the burgeoning opium trade and who was to benefit from the profits made. Under the agreements reached between the British and Chinese authorities in 1860, foreign trade was confined to the Treaty Ports. But Hong Kong merchants were circumventing this agreement and acting as distributors of European goods with other areas along the coast. The Chinese complained to the Hong Kong government which replied that it was not their responsibility to suppress this illicit trade. Viewed in this light, the issue concerned control of the local distributive trade between Canton (Guangzhou) and the colony. The Chinese authorities levied a charge of $46 a chest of opium, from two sets of tax controls, and were unwilling to lose a potentially large sum. How large can be gauged by Chinese estimates that the smuggled opium into Hong Kong was in the region of 1,000 chests per annum. Even allowing for this to be an inflated figure, the sums involved must have been considerable.

Accordingly, in November 1867 Chinese revenue cruisers which had been operating at the entrance to

Hong Kong harbor seized a junk carrying opium. Despite strong objections from the Hong Kong Governor, MacDonnell, this was followed by the setting up of nine Chinese marine and land customs stations around the colony, with all native vessels being subject to search. The British government refused to support the Governor, who was under considerable pressure from the merchants in the territory, and a commission was eventually set up in 1876 which resulted in attempts to reach a compromise over the issue. During this period trade was increasing at a rapid rate: the number of ships entering Hong Kong grew from 1,896 in 1866 to 3,214 in 1881. The junk trade, however, began to decline after 1879 under the influence of the blockade, thus increasing pressure for some type of settlement. In 1886 another, and more realistic, compromise was reached with the Chinese entering an agreement whereby all opium entering Hong Kong harbor was to be controlled by the Harbormaster. None was to be exported except under rigid controls, and the revenues would be collected by the British and remitted to China. These revenues would be collected by the Chinese Maritime Customs, whose head was British, and an arrangement was to be set up in China itself to sell opium duty certificates at 100 *taels* per chest. This agreement was formalized by the Opium Ordinance in March 1887. (See Drugs).

BOAT PEOPLE. See Vietnamese Refugees.

BOGUE, TREATY OF. This refers to a supplementary treaty to the Treaty of Nanking (Nanjing, 1842), which was signed between the British and Chinese governments in 1843. The main provisions of the treaty were as follows:

1. British subjects accused of committing offenses in China were to be tried under British law.

2. A 5% tariff was to be placed on all goods.
3. The "most favored nation" status that might be granted to any other nation would also automatically apply to the British.

This treaty combined with the Treaty of Nanking (Nanjing), was regarded as extremely humiliating by the Chinese authorities. The provisions of the treaties were to prove a source of continual friction between the two governments and eventually led to the second Anglo-Chinese Wars. (See Anglo-Chinese Wars; Nanking (Nanjing), Treaty of.)

BONHAM, SIR SAMUEL GEORGE (1803–1863). Governor of Hong Kong from 1848 to 1854. He succeeded Sir John Davies as Governor and was immediately faced with a financial crisis arising from attempts by the previous governor to charge increased taxes to make the colony self-supporting. The Hong Kong government, faced with declining land prices and a depressed economy, was running a deficit, much to the annoyance of the British government which refused to increase its subsidy. Bonham reacted by stringently controlling government expenditure. All public works were suspended, government posts were cut, and major cuts in military expenditure were imposed. He did, however, manage to avoid the unpopular proposal to raise taxes in the colony. Some have seen his financial restraint and low taxation policies as the forerunner of government fiscal policy in later years. (See Governor.)

BOWEN, SIR GEORGE FERGUSON (1821–1899). Governor of Hong Kong between 1883 and 1885. He is best remembered in his short period of office for the introduction of improved sanitary services to the colony, the widening of a very narrowly based Legislative Council and Executive Council, the strengthening of Hong

Kong's garrison through local recruitment and the building of fixed defenses in the colony.

BOWRING, SIR JOHN (1792–1872). Governor of Hong Kong from 1854 to 1859. A fluent speaker of Cantonese who seems generally to have been regarded as a fair person by the local population. He was however inflexible on the question of the treaties agreed between the British and Chinese, and furthermore was determined to renegotiate them to gain further advantage for the British. In this sense his efforts can be seen as ultimately contributing, through the Arrow incident, to the outbreak of the second Anglo-Chinese Wars. (See Anglo-Chinese Wars; Arrow War.)

BRAIN DRAIN. Over the last 150 years Hong Kong has seen a constant flow of people emigrating from its shores. Since the Second World War the loosening of controls over immigration to such states as the United States of America, Canada, and Australia led to several thousand moving to those countries. The problem was largely alleviated by a net inflow of immigrants to the colony from the People's Republic of China.

In the mid-1970s some 38,000 persons per year left, but this dropped in the early eighties to 20,000. However, emigration began to rise as concern grew over the future of Hong Kong following the signing of the Joint Declaration between Britain and China which established the territory's return to Chinese sovereignty in 1997. In late 1987 and early 1988 it was noticed that the rate of emigration, particularly in the young, professional band was rising at an alarming rate. In 1987 some 27,000 people left, increasing to 46,000 in 1988. By 1989 the figure had moved to over 50,000, partly as a result of the suppression of the disturbances in Peking (Beijing).

Demands were expressed to grant a right of abode in Britain, and calls were made for greater access to preferred destinations in the U.S.A., Canada, and Australia. But the countries concerned largely practiced policies of accepting only the wealthiest and best qualified applicants.

Emigration was a challenge to the territory as its ever increasingly sophisticated economy required the skills of the very professionals who were leaving. The government's efforts both to tempt leavers back to the colony and to provide a safety net with the granting to selected groups of a right of abode in Britain for 50,000 heads of households and their families appeared to have little effect on the problem in the early 1990s. (See Basic Law; Emigration; Stability and Prosperity; T'ien-an-man (Tiananman).)

BRITISH ARMY AID GROUP. After the fall of Hong Kong to Japanese forces on December 25, 1941 a number of escapees set up a British Army Aid Group in that part of China not controlled by the Japanese. With headquarters in Kweilin (Guilin) they aided escapees, saved many lives by supplying medicines and gathered intelligence regarding conditions in Hong Kong. (See Second World War.)

BRITISH DEPENDENT TERRITORIES CITIZEN. Until 1963 persons who were born in Hong Kong, or were born to a permanent resident, or who had applied for naturalization having lived there for seven years, were defined as British Citizens. They were given the right of abode in the United Kingdom. However, in 1963, under the British Nationality Act, this right was taken away for any future persons registered in this category. In 1983 the British Immigration Ordinance, as a follow-up to the 1981 revised British Nationality Act, put further restrictions on those people allowed to hold a passport under this category. In 1990 there were 3.25 million people with such citizenship in the territory. (See British National Overseas; British Nationality Acts.)

BRITISH FORCES. See Armed Forces.

BRITISH GOVERNMENT. See Government, British.

BRITISH NATIONAL (OVERSEAS) (B.N.(O). This category of citizenship replaced the British Dependent Territories Citizen category discussed above. It was created by the Hong Kong Act of 1985. In effect it was a tidying up exercise after the signing of the Joint Declaration on Hong Kong's future status after 1997. It is useful as a passport and gives access to British Consular protection while abroad. It does not give a right of abode in the United Kingdom, and no person born on or after July 1, 1997 will be entitled to this category status. (See British Dependent Territories Citizen; British Nationality Acts.)

BRITISH NATIONALITY ACTS. Until 1948 persons born in countries owing allegiance to the British crown were entitled to British nationality. Quite simply this meant that they were able to live in Britain if they wished to do so with no hindrance. However, with the decolonization process and the creation of the new Commonwealth, made up of sovereign states (e.g., India, Pakistan), fears of huge immigration into the United Kingdom developed, and restrictions were placed on those who wished to live in Britain. Hong Kong, of course, was not, and is not, an independent state, and so the British Nationality Acts of 1963 and 1983 were introduced to clarify status and its associated rights. The Acts removed full British citizenship from those living in the colony. An interesting comparison can be made with two colonies still under British control in the late 1980s. In the case of both the Falkland Islands and Gibraltar full British Nationality, with right of abode, was granted. (See British Dependent Territories Citizen; British National Overseas.)

BRONZE AGE. This period marks the final stage of Hong Kong's prehistory. It appeared around the middle of the second millennium B.C. It does not appear that bronze was in wide use, but specimens of weapons (swords, arrowheads, and halberds) and working tools, such as axes and fish hooks, have been discovered. It appears that the bronze artifacts were made in Hong Kong as evidenced by the excavation of pottery molds which have been discovered at the Tung Wan site at Shek Pik on Lantau Island. The pottery of the Bronze Age is similar to that found in earlier periods. In addition some finds have been made of pottery fired at a higher temperature leading to vitrification. This latter is termed "hard geometric" and has a distinctive pattern known as "*Kui*-dragon" or "double-F." Also stone carvings have been found at a number of sites near to the sea shore which are unique to Hong Kong.

BUREAUCRACY. See Civil Service.

-C-

CABINET. The Cabinet is the most important decision-making body in the United Kingdom's political structure. It is there that the key British decisions relating to Hong Kong were made, and will continue to be made, until the end of the period of British administration. Until the 1960s specific responsibility for Hong Kong policy within the Cabinet lay with the Secretary of State for Colonial Affairs. Following the abolition of this post, the Secretary of Foreign and Commonwealth Affairs has taken over this responsibility. (See Government, British; Foreign and Commonwealth Office; Parliament, British.)

CALDECOTT, SIR ANDREW. (1884–1951). Governor of Hong Kong from December 1935 until April 1937. He made little impact on the colony in his brief tenure. He did, however, increase the number of Chinese at the senior levels of government, and was vigorous in his attacks on the *mui tsai (mei zi)* system which was prevalent in the colony at the time. (See Governor; *Mui Tsai (Mei Zi)*.)

CANTONESE. Immigration into the territory has always been dominated by movements from the adjacent province of Canton (Guangzhou). Despite the presence of many other Chinese groups (e.g., *Hakka,* Shanghainese) over 90% of the population is of Cantonese origin, and the territory has been greatly influenced by the culture of the region. The dialect spoken by the overwhelming majority has always been Cantonese and not Mandarin (*Putonghua*). (See Official Language Issue.)

CAPITAL PUNISHMENT. Until the 1960s, when hanging was effectively abolished in the United Kingdom, Hong Kong used capital punishment for certain crimes. The last hanging took place in 1966, but the punishment was still technically available in the territory until 1991. In 1973 the then Governor, Sir Murray MacLehose, supported by the Executive Council, refused to pardon an offender sentenced to death for murder. The Governor was, however, overruled by the British Government. Subsequently, convicted murders sentenced to death have had their sentences commuted to life imprisonment by the Governor. (See Autonomy; MacLehose, Sir Murray.)

CAPITALISM. The economy of the colony has always been largely organized on capitalist lines. Indeed much of its economic success has, particularly since the Second World War, been widely attributed to the virtues of a free market based on private ownership and the concept of profit. Government intervention in economy and society was certainly limited in the 1950s and 1960s. However, in the period since the early 1970s the degree of government intervention in the economy, in housing and in social welfare began to increase substantially. (See Economic System; *Laissez-faire;* Trade.)

CARRIAN AFFAIR. The Carrian affair was a major scandal which broke out in 1982. It resulted from the collapse of a company (Carrian) which had incurred debts running into billions of Hong Kong dollars which it could not meet. Criminal charges were brought against those in the company, but the case was dismissed by the presiding judge on questionable grounds. The senior crown prosecution officer later fled the territory, but was extradited back to Hong Kong where he was prosecuted and found guilty on a number of corruption charges. (See Independent Commission Against Corruption.)

CATHAY PACIFIC. Set up just after the Second World War, Cathay Pacific rapidly expanded to become the major air carrier in the territory. Another airline, Dragonair, was established in 1985, but did not seriously challenge the dominance of Cathay Pacific. In the Joint Declaration, signed between Britain and the People's Republic of China, there was provision for Cathay Pacific to continue to operate from the future Special Administrative Region.

CENSUS. Hong Kong held the first census in 1911, and with the exception of 1941, they have been held every ten years since. Partial censuses are also held every five years. As elsewhere, their function is to provide comprehensive information on Hong Kong's population for government use and for general information.

CENTRAL POLICY UNIT. This unit was set up in 1989 by the Hong Kong government. Often referred to as the "think tank," its major functions are to consider central problems facing Hong Kong in the future and to prepare papers for discussion by government. It reports directly and in confidence to the Governor, the Chief Secretary, and the Financial Secretary.

CERTIFICATE OF IDENTITY. A document made available to those not eligible for the British Dependent Territories Citizen or the British National (Overseas) passport. It signifies a right of abode in Hong Kong and is used as a passport for purposes of travel abroad. It has never been valid for right of abode in the United Kingdom. (See British Dependent Territories Citizen; British National (O).)

CHADWICK REPORT. The Chadwick Report, which was published in 1882, was named after Osbert Chadwick, a former engineers officer, who was sent by the British Colonial Office to look into the sanitary and health conditions in the colony. Despite the constant outbreaks of disease and the outrageously bad sanitation conditions, the government had taken little action even in response to major criticisms in the territory. The Report's provisions called for major improvements in such areas as drainage systems, water supply, building regulations, toilets, baths and markets. Its recommendations led to the creation of the Sanitary Board that was later to develop into the Urban Council. Unfortunately, much of the Report was not acted upon promptly, and cholera in particular continued to claim lives. Even more disturbing, bubonic plague was to break out in 1894. (See Health; Sanitary Board; Urban Council.)

CHAMBER OF COMMERCE, CHINESE GENERAL. The Chinese Chamber of Commerce began to operate in 1900. From its inception it was an organization of local firms, businesspeople, and professionals. After the 1949 revolution in China it developed close links with the mainland, particularly in the field of trade and in 1957 was authorized to issue invitations on behalf of the

Chinese Export Commodities Fair authorities. It was seen by the Hong Kong government as a predominantly pro-Peking (Beijing) organization, and it was given a functional constituency in the Legislative Council in 1985. (See Functional Constituencies; Legislative Council; Pressure Groups.)

CHAO TZU-YANG (ZHAO ZIYANG). Chao Tzu-yang (Zhao Ziyang) was General Secretary of the Communist Party of China from 1987 until his removal following the events of June 1989 and the T'ien-an-man (Tiananmen) massacres. He was widely regarded in Hong Kong as constituting part of the liberal wing of the Communist Party in the PRC, and consequently was seen as a force for progress. His removal from power was interpreted in Hong Kong as a victory for the more conservative elements opposed to political reform. (See Communist Party of China; T'ien-an-man (Tiananmen).)

CHARTER OF 1843. The Charter and Instructions formed the constitutional basis for the governance of the territory. The Charter was dispatched on April 5, 1843 to Sir Henry Pottinger who administered the Territory from August 1841 to June 1843 and was Governor from June 1843 to May 1844. It was read publicly on June 26, 1843, the date on which Hong Kong was proclaimed a British Colony with the ratification of the Treaty of Nanking (Nanjing). The basic Charter was complemented by two sets of instructions which expanded upon the original charter and which were sent on April 6 and June 3, 1843.

The Charter and its instructions laid down the following:

1. The establishment of Hong Kong as a Crown Colony.
2. The establishment of the position of Governor (a

Chief Executive), an Executive Council, and a Legislative Council.

3. The terms of appointment, powers, constraints, and membership of the bodies.
4. Legal provisions and grants of land and financial responsibilities.
5. The powers of the Hong Kong government in relation to the British government.

The Charter was the basic document relating to the establishment of the colony and was to be amplified by the Letters Patent, Royal Instructions, and by precedent over time. It ceases to be operative in any sense after June 30, 1997. (See Letters Patent; Nanking (Nanjing) Treaty of; Pottinger, Sir Henry.)

CHEONG AH LUM. The owner of the E Sing bakery in the 1850s. In January 1857 anti-British feelings were running high in the territory owing to the deterioration in relations between the British and Chinese. The British attack on Canton (Guangzhou) had been initially repulsed by the Chinese, and anti-foreign sentiment spilled over to the colony. At this time westerners eating bread suddenly became ill, and it was discovered that large quantities of arsenic had been added to the other ingredients. Ah Lum was tried and acquitted, but 52 of his Chinese employees were deported. The baking of bread was taken over by a British business. No westerners died because the large amounts of arsenic caused vomiting so quickly that little was absorbed! Cheong Ah Lum wisely quit Hong Kong before further claims for damages could be filed against him. (See Anglo-Chinese Wars; Arrow War.)

CHIANG KAI-SHEK (JIANG JIESHI) (1887–1975). Chiang Kai-shek (Jiang Jieshi) was a Chinese soldier and statesman who headed the Nationalist or Kuomintang

(Guomindang) government in China from 1928 until his defeat by the communists in 1949. He retreated to Taiwan where he set up a nationalist government in 1950, claiming that his regime was the *de jure* government of the whole of China. (See China, People's Republic of; China, Republic of; Kuomintang (Guomindang).)

CHIEF EXECUTIVE. In essence the Governor of Hong Kong exercised the function of a chief executive but was not referred to as such. The role of the Governor as *a* chief executive should not be confused with the post to be created after June 1997 which is formally entitled *the* Chief Executive. The details of appointment procedures and powers given to this latter post are set out in the Basic Law. (See Basic Law; Governor.)

CHIEF JUSTICE. The position of the Chief Justice and his office was outlined in the Letters Patent dated 14 February 1917, a document which was amended regularly as circumstances permitted or required. The role, which has remained largely unchanged since that time, is to act as the senior officer in Hong Kong responsible for the administration of the Judiciary and the Courts. The Chief Justice is appointed by the Governor on the instructions of the British Crown, but is given the usual safeguards accorded to the judiciary by the Letters Patent to minimize political interference. In 1988, the first local Chinese Chief Justice, Sir Ti Liang Yang, was appointed. Under the provisions of the Basic Law promulgated in April 1990 the post will remain in existence after the territory returns to the People's Republic of China. (See Basic Law; Legal System; Localization.)

CHIEF SECRETARY. The position of Chief Secretary was created in 1976 when the post of Colonial Secretary was abolished, although the change was more a change of title than of function. As head of the Civil Service, the Chief Secretary is in effect second only to the Governor in the administration of Hong Kong's affairs. He holds a seat as the senior official (government) representative in the Executive Council and the Legislative Council. He is also chair of the powerful financial committee of the Legislative Council and has since 1902 acted as the Governor's deputy in his absence. Although not mentioned in the Basic Law, it can be assumed that the office will remain in being after June 30, 1997.

CH'IN (QIN) DYNASTY (221–207 B.C.). This dynasty ruled China from 221 B.C. until 207 B.C. Under this dynasty China was unified, the Great Wall was completed and an efficient system of local government was introduced. The Hong Kong area was conquered by the Ch'in (Qin) in 214 B.C. with the region later divided into prefectures and counties. Coins from this period have been excavated in Hong Kong and it is believed by some that salt farms were put under imperial control. Imperial interest in the South was not concerned with the colonizing of the area, but rather used it as a base for traders with soldiers protecting imperial interests. With no permanent settlers the local inhabitants were left very much alone.

CHINA, PEOPLE'S REPUBLIC OF. The People's Republic of China (PRC) was proclaimed by Mao Tse-tung (Mao Zedong) on October 1, 1949 following the culmination of a long civil war and the expulsion from the mainland to Taiwan of the Nationalist or Kuomintang (Guomindang) government. In 1949 the new government announced that it was a socialist state under the leadership of the Communist Party of China. The People's Republic of China never accepted that Hong Kong was sovereign British territory and always claimed that they would resume sovereignty over the territory when the "time was ripe."

There was no diplomatic representation established between the colony and the PRC in 1949 but the unofficial representative of the PRC in the territory has been the New China News Agency (Xinhua). (See Basic Law; Joint Declaration; Kuomintang (Guomindang); Mao Tse-tung (Mao Zedong); Sino-British Negotiations; Sovereignty.)

CHINA, REPUBLIC OF. The Republic of China was first declared on January 1, 1912 at Nanking (Nanjing) following the revolution which had broken out in October 1911. Its first President was Dr. Sun Yat-sen (Sun Yixian). From 1928 to 1949 the Presidency of the Republic was held by Chiang Kai-shek (Jiang Jieshi). In 1949 the nationalist party Kuomintang (Guomindang) was defeated on the mainland and fled to Taiwan.

Although since 1949 the Republic of China has not had any representation in the colony, on October 10 of every year some supporters of the Republic of China fly the Nationalist flag as a sign of support for the Taiwan government. However, active membership of any Kuomintang (Guomingdang) party is probably minimal.

At the time of the negotiations over the future of Hong Kong the PRC hoped that the document might be used for a blueprint for the unification of the "two Chinas," but no immediate breakthroughs occurred.

Since 1949 there has been increasing trade between Hong Kong and the Republic of China. In addition, much of the trade between the Republic of China and the People's Republic is conducted through Hong Kong on an unofficial basis. Similarly all Taiwanese entering the PRC have had to pass through Hong Kong. (See Chiang Kai-shek (Jiang Jieshi); Kuomintang (Guomindang); Sun Yat-sen (Sun Yixian); Trade.)

CHINESE BURIAL CUSTOMS. The reverence of the Chinese for the dead was exemplified by the elaborate ceremonies held on a certain fixed day after the death, in order to provide comfort to the soul on its journey to its final destination. In the Chinese culture seven is thought to be a lucky number so that dates for the commemoration services were fixed on a multiple of seven times seven and lasted over 49 days. The most important ceremony took place on the 21st day (3 × 7). The eldest son paid for the first and third service and the woman of the family the second. The local system required a double burial with the body exhumed, the bones cleaned, and then placed in an urn after seven years.

CHINESE LANGUAGE ISSUE. The question of which language is to be dominant in Hong Kong has been a problem since the inception of the colony. For the purposes of law, government, and international business English has dominated. This was despite the fact that the vast majority of the population neither spoke nor understood English.

Following the riots of 1966 and 1967 a committee was set up by the government to look into the problem of language policy, but its progress was slow. Eventually the Official Language Ordinance was announced in 1974. This gave Chinese an official and equal status with English. After 1997 the Chinese language will prevail over the English in the case of any conflict. However, there is confusion on the question of whether the form of Chinese used will be Mandarin (*Putonghua*), the official Chinese language in the People's Republic of China, or the local Cantonese dialect spoken in Hong Kong. (See Basic Law.)

CHINESE TEMPLES. The oldest temple in Hong Kong is the Buddhist monastery at Tuen Mun which was founded in the fifth century. Other temples were founded in honor of different deities. The most famous and the oldest is the temple at Joss House Bay, built in the Sung (Song) period 969–1279 for the worship of Tin Hau, the goddess of the fishing community. Other famous temples include the Man Mo Temples dedicated to the gods of literature (Man) and war (Mo). The god of literature is worshipped by scholars and civil servants, and the god of war by police officers, pawnbrokers, and antique dealers. The position and orientation of temples is influenced by the principles of *fung shui* (literally translated "wind and water"). The roof is usually green or yellow with rounded tiles, and stone lions often guard the door. (See Tin Hau Festival.)

CH'ING (QING) DYNASTY (1644–1912). The Ch'ing (Qing) dynasty ruled China from 1644 until its overthrow and replacement by the Republic on January 1, 1912. Sometimes referred to as the Manchu dynasty, as the conquerors came from Manchuria, it replaced the Ming (Ming) dynasty which had ruled since 1368. In the South the supporters of the Ming continued to operate and attack coastal areas. In particular the pro-Ming figure Koxinga, based in Taiwan, threatened the important coastal areas around Kwangtung (Guangdong) province. The insecurity of these areas was further compounded by regular attacks by pirates.

Faced with this problem, the government decided to take drastic action. To consolidate their authority they ordered, in 1661, that all the coastal areas in the province should be evacuated to 50 *li* (approximately 12 miles) inland. All civilians were forcibly moved out and their houses destroyed. This caused starvation and death in the Hong Kong area but the draconian measures, combined with military expeditions removed the threat from the pro-Ming rebels. It also cut down on the predations of piracy, at least temporarily.

In 1669 the authorities felt safe enough to remove the

coastal evacuation order. The local inhabitants, in gratitude for the efforts of the Governor of Kwangtung (Guangdong) and the Viceroy, deified them. In the meantime the imperial revenues were in need of replenishment so settlers were encouraged to move back into the area. The new settlers provided badly needed income to the government from salt and agriculture. Many of the new settlers were *Hakka* people from further north, who entered the area along with the older *Punti* (local Cantonese).

The Ch'ing (Qing) dynasty continued to administer the Hong Kong area as part of the San On (Xin-an) County in the province of Kwangtung (Guangdong). This southern province was the first in which the European traders made their impact. In the eighteenth century attempts by the Chinese government to control the Europeans seemed reasonably successful but the nineteenth century proved to be disastrous for the dynasty. The numerous and unsuccessful wars, both civil and against the colonial powers led to concession after concession, each time undermining the legitimacy of the dynasty.

In the end, exhausted by the unequal struggle and faced by growing internal dissention, the dynasty simply collapsed and was replaced by a republic. (see Anglo-Chinese Wars; Arrow War; Blockade; Bogue, Treaty of; Convention of Peking (Beijing); Nanking (Nanjing), Treaty of; New Territories; Opium War.)

CHING MING CEREMONY. The Confucian festival observed in Hong Kong as one of the two occasions to honor the dead. Its origins can be traced back to the Han (Han) Dynasty (206 B.C.–220 A.D.).

CHINNERY, GEORGE (1774–1852). George Chinnery painted portraits and figures in landscapes in the early 19th century, and was the most influential of the "China trade" painters who worked in the region. He spent 27 years in or around Macau, and his works vividly capture the life and times of the period. Other painters painting in the East included W. J. Huggins (1781–1845); Auguste Borget (1808–1877); Thomas Boswall Watson (1815–1860); and Walford Thomas Bellairs (c. 1794–1850). Mention should also be made of the interesting works of Kuan Tso-lin (Guan Zuolin), and his two sons Kuan Ch'io-Ch'ang (Guan Qiochang) (1830–1860) and Kuan Lia-ch'ang (Guan Liachang), all of whom were often imitative of Chinnery's style.

CHOU EN-LAI (ZHOU ENLAI) (1898–1976). The first Premier of the People's Republic. Chou En-lai (Zhou Enlai) was more pragmatic than Mao Tse-tung (Mao Zedong) and was the main architect of Chinese foreign policy until his death. It was he who mitigated the worst effects of some of Mao's policies such as the "Great Leap Forward" and the Cultural Revolution. He also introduced the Four Modernizations (although today most people ascribe the idea to Teng Hsiao-p'ing (Deng Xiaoping)). Chou (Zhou) was largely instrumental in opening negotiations for the normalization of relations with the United States of America and for better relationships with European countries and, later, Japan. Nearly all his policies have been followed by his successors. He was, and still is, seen as a major and popular figure in Hong Kong—much more so than Mao Tse-tung (Mao Zedong). (See Cultural Revolution; Four Modernizations; People's Republic of China; Teng Hsiao-p'ing (Deng Xiaoping).)

CHOU NAN (ZHOU NAN). Mr. Chou Nan (Zhou Nan) replaced Hsu Chia-t'un (Xu Jiatun), as the head of the New China News Agency in 1990. He has an extensive knowledge of the territory gained from his experiences as head of the Chinese team in the negotiations over the territory's future which led to the Joint Declaration of

1984. He was also an influential member of the Basic Law Drafting Committees for both Hong Kong and Macau. Finally he was a member of the Central People's Government of the People's Republic of China to whom the Chinese team on the Joint Liaison Group reported. (See New China News Agency.)

CHRISTIAN INDUSTRIAL COUNCIL. Established in the early 1970s and made up of protestant Christian organizations, the Christian Industrial Council has been active in attempting to improve the conditions of labor and labor legislation. On a wider front it has allied itself with reformist movements arguing for more representative government in Hong Kong. (See Pressure Groups.)

CHRISTIANS. See Religion.

CHUANPI (CHUANBI), CONVENTION OF. An agreement signed on January 20, 1841 between Britain and the Viceroy of Kwangtung (Guangdong)—Kwangtzu (Guangzi) following the defeat of Chinese forces at the forts of Bocca Tigris. The terms were humiliating to the Chinese particularly in the demands for six million dollars to be paid to the British by the Chinese as indemnity; for Hong Kong to be ceded to Britain; for British merchants to be allowed to return to trade in Canton (Guangzhou); and for British and Chinese authorities to have official contact on an equal basis. These terms were repudiated by the Emperor, and the Viceroy was dismissed from his post and deported. Hostilities then resumed. (See Anglo-Chinese Wars; Elliot, Captain Charles; Nanking (Nanjing) Treaty of.)

CIVIC ASSOCIATION. A group created in 1955, with a predominantly expatriate membership, to promote the economic, social, cultural, and political welfare of the people of Hong Kong. Membership today is mostly local and middle class, but it has been overtaken in terms of influence by newer and more vociferous groups. (See Pressure Groups.)

CIVIC EDUCATION. The idea of civic education stemmed largely from the initiatives of the Hong Kong Education Department in the early 1980s. Its function was to promote civil awareness in the community in general, and in schools in particular. The underlying rationale was to help to foster an identification with the territory and its institutions and an understanding of its relationship with the People's Republic of China. (See Education.)

CIVIL RIGHTS. Civil rights are a subgroup of human rights. In the case of Hong Kong, these in the past have been influenced by the British tradition. In Britain, unlike the United States for instance, the supremacy of Parliament forbids an entrenched system of civil rights. However, the Basic Law, which will be active in 1997, constitutionally defines the rights of the citizens of the Special Administrative Region. These rights are further reinforced in the Human Rights Ordinance of 1990. However, this latter document is not entrenched, and the People's Republic of China has retained the right to amend or annul this ordinance after 1997 if it is deemed necessary. Also the terms of the civil rights in the Basic Law are subject to change, should this be required by the legislative body in the People's Republic of China. (See Basic Law; Bill of Rights; Joint Declaration; International Covenant on Civil and Political Rights; International Covenant on Economic, Social and Cultural Rights.)

CIVIL SERVICE. The branch of government which normally performs the function of administering and executing policy in government. However, Hong Kong's colonial status has enhanced the power of the civil service considerably. Its senior officers have held considerable power in the role of executive decision-making as well as in the formulation, implementation and administration of policy—not least through their membership of the Legislative Council and the Executive Council. The Basic Law still provides for considerable political power to be left in the hands of the civil service.

For much of Hong Kong's history the size of the civil service was small, reflecting the government's preference for minimal intervention in the economy and in the provision of services to the community. At the same time, the recruitment into the higher levels of the civil service was limited to European officers. It was not until 1946 that local officers were enlisted. The first Chinese to enter the administrative class (the top band) was appointed in 1946, and it was not until 1961 that a Chinese appointee reached a position as head of a Department. In 1951, 54 members or 10.75% of the administrative and senior professional classes were Chinese.

In the postwar period the growth of the civil service was considerable. It rose from 17,500 in 1949, to 45,000 in 1959 and almost 80,000 in 1979. This growth was continued under the Governorship of Sir Murray MacLehose (1971–1982). Between 1973 and 1983 it grew by a further 71.3% (from 101,793 to 173,788). Such growth was inevitably accompanied by problems of efficiency and coordination. The problems were approached by the use of a United Kingdom firm of consultants who were to advise on how to reorganize and restructure the civil service to accommodate the more complex tasks asked of it. The McKinsey Report, entitled the "Machinery of Government; a New Framework for Expanding Services" was published in 1973, and led to a radical overhaul of governmental organization. Its main provisions were to form the basis of civil service structure for the next three decades.

In the 1970s and 1980s localization of the civil service continued, and by 1989 the service was 98% localized. At the most senior levels progress was slower, but locals formed a narrow majority (50.7% to 49.3%). Under the provisions of the Joint Declaration and the Basic Law it was established that all the top posts in the civil service would be reserved for locals after 1997. (See Basic Law; Executive Council; Legislative Council; Localization; McKinsey Report; Political System.)

CLEMENTI, SIR CECIL (1875–1947). Governor of Hong Kong from 1925 until 1930. Clementi was one of the colony's most accomplished administrators, whose diplomatic skills were instrumental in normalizing the strained relationships with the Chinese government in the period following the First World War. Internally, he was active in clearing the slums in the colony and in improving the water supply. He was also anxious to integrate the Chinese more than his predecessor and appointed the first Chinese member, Sir Shouson Chow, to the Executive Council in 1926. (See Disturbances; Executive Council; First World War; General Strike.)

CLOSED CAMPS. "Closed camps" were set up in July 1982 to contain the increasing number of Vietnamese refugees entering the territory. Run by the Correctional Services Department, they were primarily intended as a deterrent to any further refugees from Vietnam. The closed camps were still in existence in 1992 despite attempts to either resettle their inmates in other countries, or to persuade them to return as voluntary repatriates to Vietnam. (See Vietnamese Refugees.)

CLUBS. Many of the informal contacts which underpin business affairs in the territory have traditionally taken place in its clubs. One of the most influential is still the

Hong Kong Club, founded in 1846. Initially it excluded "shopkeepers, Chinese, Indians, women and other undesirables." Although these criteria no longer apply, membership is still very exclusive.

Almost as exclusive and influential is the Royal Hong Kong Jockey Club (first established under a different title in 1884) which traditionally has also been the largest charitable benefactor in the territory. Other clubs of more recent origin include the Foreign Correspondents Club, the American Club, and the Chinese Recreation Club.

COLONIAL LAWS VALIDITY ACT. An Act passed in the United Kingdom in 1865 to remove any doubt about the validity of laws passed in any of the colonies. Its most important provision was that any laws passed by the Hong Kong Legislative Council which contradicted an act of the British Parliament applicable to Hong Kong had no legal effect. (See Capital Punishment.)

COLONIAL OFFICE. When Britain acquired Hong Kong the Colonial Office was combined with the War Office, with its head being referred to as the Secretary of State for War and the Colonies. This office was split in 1854 so that a Secretary for the Colonies was created with a Colonial Office. The Secretary of State was responsible for the administration of crown colonies and was the official point of communication between the United Kingdom and the overseas possessions. In 1907 the office was divided into three units: the Dominion Department; the Colonial Department; and the General Department. Within this framework Hong Kong came under the wing of the Colonial Department. With the dissolution of the British Empire after the Second World War, the necessity for a Secretary of State for the Colonies gradually became redundant and the responsibilities of the post were taken over by the Foreign and

Commonwealth Office in 1967. (See Foreign and Commonwealth Office.)

COLONIAL SECRETARY. The post of Colonial Secretary was established in Hong Kong in 1843 and remained in force until 1976 when the position was renamed Chief Secretary. The Colonial Secretary was the head of the civil service and was, after the Governor, the second most important administrator in the territory. (See Chief Secretary.)

COLONY. Hong Kong was declared a colony of Great Britain and accepted as such by the Ch'ing (Qing) dynasty under the various treaties signed and ratified between the two governments in the treaties of Nanking (Nanjing) 1843 and Tientsin (Tianjin), 1860.

In 1972 at the request of the People's Republic of China, Hong Kong was removed from the United Nations list of colonies. Given the overtones of the term "colony," the practice in Hong Kong over the last two decades has been to refer to the possession as a "Dependent Territory"—although its legal status remains until 1997 that of a colony. (See Letters Patent: Political System; Royal Instructions.)

COMMANDER BRITISH FORCES. A position established in 1843 to oversee military affairs in the territory. The first commander of British forces was Major General D'Aguilar, who was given the title of Lieutenant Governor and allowed to act as Governor if required. Under the Royal Instructions of 1917 the Commander British Forces was given a seat on the Executive Council, and he retains that position under the present administration until the cessation of British administration in 1997. The Commander is responsible to the Chief of Defence Staff in the United Kingdom and his function has been to advise the Governor on any matters affecting the security of Hong Kong. (See Armed Forces; Executive Council.)

COMMANDER IN CHIEF, HONG KONG. Under the provisions of the Letters Patent of 14 February 1917, the Governor of Hong Kong holds the position of Commander in Chief of the armed forces in Hong Kong. (See Governor.)

COMMERCE AND INDUSTRY. See Economy; Industry.

COMMISSIONER FOR ADMINISTRATIVE COMPLAINTS. The Commissioner for Administrative Complaints was set up in 1988, and is commonly referred to as the "Ombudsman." The post involves investigating complaints made by individuals in Hong Kong relating to possible maladministration by public bodies. The office had been under active consideration since 1969, but it took nearly 20 years to bring it into being. The position is not mentioned in the Basic Law for the future Special Administrative Region after 1997.

COMMONWEALTH, BRITISH. The Commonwealth was an associative arrangement known in 1939 as the British Commonwealth of Nations. Its original members were Australia, Canada, Newfoundland (until 1949 when it became a province of Canada), New Zealand, and South Africa. It had no constitution or charter, placed few obligations upon its members, and the only document describing its nature was the Statute of Westminster drawn up in 1931. As decolonization gathered momentum, many of the old colonies voluntarily joined the Commonwealth. A number of informal rules applied to the members, such as noninterference in the internal affairs of other members. Consultations between member states took place on an occasional basis. In 1992 there were 50 self-governing independent nations in the Commonwealth. It continues to hold meetings attended by the Prime Ministers of the states involved and has its own permanent secretariat. Hong Kong was not a member but its interests were formally represented by the United Kingdom. Formal links with the organization will cease after 1997.

COMMUNIST PARTY OF CHINA. The Communist Party of China was established in 1921. It fought intermittently with the nationalist government, ultimately defeating it in 1949. It was the founder and power behind the People's Republic of China which was established in that same year. The Communist Party of China was from the beginning a party based on Marxist-Leninist principles. There has never been a registered arm of the party in Hong Kong, although it has been active through several front organizations. The party's activity is centered and coordinated through the New China News Agency (*Xinhua*). (See Kuomintang (Guomindang); New China News Agency; People's Republic of China.)

CONFUCIANISM. Confucius lived in China from 551–479 B.C. and has had a marked influence upon Hong Kong's culture. In broad terms Confucianism emphasized a paternalistic mode of rule, demand for obedience from the ruled, combined with strict hierarchical government and social relationships. Principles of public and private conduct were overlapping and based on the family. Rule was based on moral example, with the ruled expected to apply deferential obedience.

These precepts are widely seen as underlying the attitudes to social, economic, and political affairs. Some explanations of the territory's economic success emphasize the acceptance of Confucian values of hard work, thrift, the importance of saving and investing in the future, and the role of the family. However, there is considerable argument about the extent to which Confucian values were significant explanations of past trends and over the degree to which they are being undermined by the modernization and secularization of society. (See Familism.)

CONSERVATION. An area of little concern until recently. For much of the postwar period economic growth was emphasized with little consideration of environmental impact. By the early 1970s the deterioration of the environment was such that the issue could not be ignored. The first government interventions came in 1976 with the establishment of country parks. In 1981 the strengthened Environmental Protection Agency helped introduce positive steps to legislate against some of the worst manifestations of pollution. (See Environment.)

CONSTITUTION. The Constitution of Hong Kong has been that of a colony throughout its history. Its legal authority was based on prerogative, that is, the unrestricted right of the British monarch. Queen Victoria used her prerogative to establish the colony by Order in Council, which was followed by the Royal Charter in 1843. There followed a series of further constitutions from further Orders in Council when Britain acquired Kowloon in 1860, and the New Territories in 1898 and when the Kowloon Walled City was annexed in 1899. These later documents did not, however, alter the constitutional structure of the colony.

The content of the Royal Charter was passed from Governor to Governor in the Letters Patent and the Royal Instructions and much of its original content is still operative.

Under the provisions of the Charter, the Governor is primarily answerable to the British Crown rather than to Hong Kong. He is obliged to inform and consult the

Executive Council and the Legislative Council, but is not obliged to respect their wishes.

The Royal Instructions expanded on the duties of the Governor and, despite occasional slight modifications, the structure remained broadly the same. Within the Royal Instructions there were gaps relating to such areas as the composition of the legal system, the civil service, the structure and powers of local government, taxation, human freedoms, and the size and scope of government. Some of these gaps were filled by ordinances and such subsidiary documents as the Colonial Regulations.

The partial coverage of these various documents allows considerable powers to lie formally in the hands of the Governor. He could, for example, disregard the advice of the Executive Council providing he had the consent of London. In practice, however, the Governors of the territory rarely, if ever, used the formidable powers granted to them. Restraints, such as Common Law and the power of the British Parliament, plus the prudence of the Governor in his relations with other actors in the colony, ensured that the formal powers were not abused.

In 1984 the Joint Declaration between the United Kingdom and the People's Republic of China allowed for considerable constitutional changes in 1997. These changes were set out within a Basic Law eventually published in April 1990. The major changes outlined within that document were as follows:

1. British administration of Hong Kong would cease in 1997. The superior constitution would become that of the People's Republic of China and the subordinate written constitution would be the Basic Law.
2. The Basic Law was far more detailed in its content than its predecessor and attempted to cover such

areas as basic freedoms, the Chief Executive, the Legislative Council, the Judiciary, and the civil service.

3. Formally the Basic Law was also more democratic than its predecessor, more unitary than federal, and also is subordinate to the state constitution of the People's Republic of China. (See Basic Law: Joint Declaration; Letters Patent; Political System; Royal Instructions.)

CONVENTIONS OF PEKING (Beijing). The first Convention of Peking (Beijing) ended the Second Anglo-Chinese War (Opium or Arrow War), and was signed in 1860. The agreement provided for the cession of Kowloon and Stonecutters Island to Britain in perpetuity. These were added to Hong Kong Island, which had been acquired by Britain under the Convention of Chuanpi (Chuanbi).

The second Convention of Peking (Beijing) was signed on June 9, 1898. Under its provisions, Imperial China leased the New Territories to the United Kingdom for 99 years. This Convention followed Japan's defeat of China in the First Sino-Japanese War, (1894–1895) which resulted in the Treaty of Shimonoseki, and created a general enthusiasm among the great powers for making territorial claims on China. Strategically, the reason for the taking of the New Territories was to make Hong Kong and Kowloon easier to defend. However, the leasing of the New Territories under this Convention also meant that the British Administration there had to cease on June 30, 1997. In fact, this was the complicating factor that brought about the need for the United Kingdom to negotiate with the People's Republic of China about the territory's future, which in turn resulted in the Joint Declaration of 1984. (See Anglo-Chinese Wars; Arrow War; Chuanpi (Chuanbi), Convention of; Joint Declaration; New Territories; Stonecutters Island.)

CULTURAL REVOLUTION. At the Party Congress of 1969 the Cultural Revolution was officially ended, and the power of the party and state structures reestablished. However, in the official Chinese version of these events the Cultural Revolution lasted beyond this period right up to 1976, culminating only with the fall of the "Gang of Four," which had tried to seize control of power after Mao's death.

The major impact of the Cultural Revolution on Hong Kong was its encouragement of major riots, demonstrations, and bombings in 1967. British military reinforcements were brought into Hong Kong although they were not directly used to quell the riots. Following so closely upon the Star Ferry riots of the previous year, these events led the Hong Kong government to introduce major reforms aimed at increasing public involvement in policy making and execution. (See Disturbances; Gang of Four; Mao Tse-tung (Mao Zedong); Star Ferry Riots.)

CURRENCY. With the acquisition of Hong Kong there was a need to regularize the currency. In 1844 equal legal tender was accorded to the major currencies in circulation, and it became possible to deal in dollars, English currency, and Indian gold and silver coins. However, the growth in trade and population resulted in the virtual elimination of English and Indian coins in favor of the dollars used by the Chinese. Therefore in 1862 the silver dollar, minted in Spain, Mexico and South American states was declared the legal tender in tandem with coins minted in England. This was further extended in 1864 by the colony issuing its own one dollar as well as cent and ten-cent pieces.

The value of the dollar gradually decreased from its original approximate value of four shillings and two pence to the pound sterling to about one shilling and eleven pence and one halfpenny in 1898. Its price fluctuated with the value of silver which continually declined. In 1935, in order to stabilize the currency, the Hong Kong dollar was linked to the pound sterling at one shilling and 3 pence. This gave an exchange rate of HK$16 to 1 pound sterling. This provided stability and an exchange rate that was to last until 1967.

In that year sterling was devalued by 14.3%, and the Hong Kong government decided that the old relationship with sterling was becoming counterproductive. The Hong Kong dollar was allowed to break free of sterling and from 1974 until 1983 became a floating currency. The major economic and political uncertainties generated during the negotiations between Britain and the People's Republic of China in 1983 led to a near collapse of the currency, and the government introduced a revised system which pegged the Hong Kong dollar to the United States dollar at an exchange rate of US$1 = HK$7.8. That rate has been in force since that time. After the resumption of Chinese sovereignty in 1997, Hong Kong will continue to have the Hong Kong dollar as its legal tender. (See Economic System; Economy.)

CUSTOMS BLOCKADE. See Blockade.

-D-

DAVIS, SIR JOHN FRANCIS (1795–1890). Governor of Hong Kong from May 1844 to March 1848. He assumed the position on the departure of Sir Henry Pottinger, and saw his main function as increasing order in the colony. He improved internal policing and the control of piracy. He also increased the application of British law and systems of punishment.

Amateurs in the government were replaced by the more competent team which he recruited. However, his attempts to increase the size of the Executive Council and the Legislative Council to make them more effective were overruled by London. Most significantly he attempted, against major opposition from the merchants, to raise revenue for the governance of the territory in order to reduce the subsidy reluctantly granted from Britain. His methods included selling monopolies on opium, granting licenses, and levying taxes on all property. Although this had a marginally depressing effect upon trade and profit, it did put the financial system on a firmer long-term footing.

On his own initiative he ordered the attack on Canton (Guangzhou) in April 1847 and forced concessions from the Chinese on the treatment of British citizens in that city. (See Governors.)

DAVISON REPORT. This Report, published in 1988, was undertaken by Mr. Ian Hay Davison to investigate the collapse of the Hong Kong stock exchange in October 1987. The Report was highly critical of the running of both the stock exchange and the futures exchange in the territory and of the relevant regulatory bodies. Its major recommendations were to:

1. make the stock market a non-profit making organization;
2. rename the Stock Exchange Committee the Council;
3. extend the powers of this Council and its membership, particularly by including some international stockbrokers and some nonbrokers;
4. tighten up the rules and regulations relating to dealings; and
5. establish a new seven-member Securities Commission which would be responsible for the administration of the Stock and Futures Exchanges. Although this body would be nongovernmental, its members could be dismissed by the Governor.

DAYA BAY. Daya Bay, situated some 50 kilometers from Hong Kong, was chosen in 1982 as the proposed site for a nuclear power station. The project was a joint venture between Hong Kong electrical interests and the Kwangtung (Guangdong) Electric Company. Given the proximity of the site to Hong Kong, there was considerable opposition to its construction on environmental grounds. Despite considerable pressure group activity by an umbrella group known as the Joint Organization for the Concern for Nuclear Energy and by the Friends of the Earth, the project was approved. The joint venture named the "Kwangtung (Guangdong) Nuclear Power Joint Venture Company" was established in December 1983. Intense lobbying by both sides continued and the opposition case was strengthened in April 1986 by the Chernobyl disaster. Although opposition to the project rose to 70% in opinion polls, the contracts on the Daya Bay nuclear station were signed in September 1986 and construction began. A further problem emerged in October 1987 when it was discovered that the number of reinforcement bars installed was substantially below the planned number.

In 1991 the Peking (Beijing) authorities announced that they were considering building a second nuclear power station near to Daya Bay. (See Harwell Report.)

DEFENCE COSTS. The question of how much Hong Kong should contribute to its own defence costs and how much the British government should pay has been one which has been hotly debated since the founding of the colony. The British government was anxious to minimize its contribution and has generally tried to persuade the Hong Kong government to increase its share. For its part the colonial government, anxious not to increase taxes, has tried to minimize payment.

Initially the cost of the armed forces was born entirely by the British government, but by 1848 it was established that the local government should make a contribution to defence costs, pay for fortifications and defence works, and provide the necessary land. Total defence expenditure was gradually increased so that in 1885 the colony voted 56,000 pounds sterling to defence and this was increased in 1886 by an additional 60,375. Expenditure continued to grow particularly in the early years of the twentieth century: the figures tripled between 1898 and 1913.

On the eve of the First World War the military contribution was fixed at 20% of government recurrent revenue. In the interwar years this meant that the cost to the colonial government of defence was HK$ 2,319,645 in 1921 rising to HK$ 6,051,926 in 1939.

Between 1965 and 1975, the British government continued to meet the majority of military costs in the territory. In 1975, however, in response to major re-thinking in the United Kingdom, it was decided that the ratio of costs for the defence of the colony would be shared more equally. In 1975 the ratio of defence costs was fixed at Hong Kong: 50% and the United Kingdom: 50%. However, this soon shifted to Hong Kong: 75% and the United Kingdom: 25%. That figure was to remain constant until the late 1980s when, after considerable argument between the Hong Kong and London, the ratio was changed to 65% Hong Kong and 35% British. As a proportion of the territory's GNP this was under 1% of the total, and less than 5% of total government revenue.

After 1997 the British armed forces will no longer remain in Hong Kong. Under the provisions of the Joint Declaration the People's Liberation Army will take the responsibility for defence, and will meet all costs. (See Armed Forces; Basic Law; Joint Declaration; Second World War.)

DEMOCRACY. Hong Kong has never been democratic in the western pluralist sense of the concept. If democracy is taken to mean a system where there is universal suffrage, competitive elections, popular sovereignty, and the legal and political equality of individuals regardless of race, language or religion, then the colony does not emerge with a particularly good record. Universal suffrage was only granted to the legislative body in the last days of British administration, and even then to a limited number of seats in the legislature. In addition, the Governor was appointed rather than elected. The colony has a reasonable record of religious toleration. However, although the formal position regarding racial equality is relatively strong, the minority expatriate community has enjoyed privileges incommensurate with its actual numbers.

Pressure from the more articulate members of the community to increase the pace and expression of institutional democratization was intense during the period 1984 up to the publishing of the Basic Law in 1990. The final document, however, while allowing for the continuing introduction of a limited number of directly elected seats to the central legislative body, refused to countenance a fully elected legislature. At the same time, the Chief Executive of the future Special Administrative Region is to be made more accountable to the people in so far as he or she is to be elected. While this disappointed those who had hoped for a political structure on western lines, many conservative elements argued that such a model of democracy was inappropriate for Hong Kong. This position was evidently shared by the government of the People's Republic of China. (See Elections; Executive Council; Legislative Council; Political System.)

DENG XIAOPING See Teng Hsiao-p'ing.

DEPOLITICIZATION. A term widely used to describe Hong Kong society, particularly in the period between the Second World War and the disturbances during the

Cultural Revolution in 1967. It suggested that the people of the colony did not wish to involve themselves in the affairs of government. Nor were they encouraged to do so by a colonial government which saw itself as benevolently paternalistic.

Explanations of the reluctance of the population to involve themselves in the political process include:

1. The political culture of the Hong Kong population which militated against positive identification with the government or the concept of the civic society.
2. The argument that the majority of the population came from the mainland where political involvement was a precarious activity.
3. A governmental system where the idea of popular participation was seen as unnecessary in the governance of what the colonial government saw as an efficient and well-run system.

The events of 1966 and 1967 raised doubts with these assumptions. Society in general, and a growing Chinese elite in particular, seemed to be looking for greater participation in the public affairs of the territory. Since 1967 levels of political participation have increased, manifesting themselves in constitutional debates, the growth of pressure groups as well as the civic-education programs, and the gradual, though limited, democratization of the political system, in the period leading up to the ending of colonial rule in 1997. (See Familism; Localization.)

DEPORTATION. Deportation was introduced in the colony's early years in the attempt to control crime. Those Europeans convicted of crimes were deported either to the Straits Territories or later to Australia. Criminals of Chinese origin were deported back to China. This system was perceived as having the added advantage of removing the costs of potential incarceration. However, many of the deported Chinese returned, and were often arrested again having committed further crimes. They were therefore "painlessly" branded as criminals to facilitate subsequent redeportation if they attempted to return. In 1857 the transportation of criminals ceased but deportation continued with the active support of both the local and European populations. In 1882 a Banishment Ordinance was introduced which allowed for banishment of five years. This was followed by the Peace Preservation Ordinance in 1884 which allowed for the banishment of persons who, although not convicted, were "dangerous to the peace and good order of the colony." This particular piece of legislation was intended primarily for emergencies.

Under the present regulations, deportation involves the removal of persons who have no right of abode in the territory. This means that only Hong Kong permanent residents are immune from deportation. The term is distinguished from "removal" which is applied to any illegal immigrants who might enter the territory. (See Illegal Immigrants; Permanent Resident; Snake Heads; Touch Base Policy.)

DEPUTY CHIEF SECRETARY. A now-defunct post in the civil service created in 1985 and abolished in 1989. The post largely involved constitutional developments and was replaced by the post of Secretary for Constitutional Affairs.

DES VOEUX, SIR WILLIAM (1834–1909). Governor of the colony from October 1887 until May 1891. In his comparatively short period of tenure he was often out of the colony. His biggest problem lay with the Chinese opposition to the new powers of the Sanitary Board. This Board had the powers to improve health standards by inspection of housing, disinfecting premises, and, if necessary, removing any persons suffering from contagious diseases. It could also demand the upgrading of property to provide more ventilation in the overcrowded areas. The Chinese population strenuously objected to these proposals denying the existence of health problems, claiming that the new regulations would drive up rents, and insisting that their homes were private. Compromise was reached by compensating the owners of houses for the improvement of living conditions. However, the effectiveness of the reforms was limited. A report published in 1890 showed that in some city areas the population density was often in excess of 1,500 persons per acre, and in one particular block it was over 3,235 per acre.

The other achievements during Des Voeux's period of office were the vastly improved water supply and the ending of the Blockade with China. However, by general consent, the impact of Des Voeux upon the affairs of the colony was marginal. (See Blockade; Health; Water Supplies.)

DIRECT ELECTIONS. See Elections.

DISTRICT ADMINISTRATION SCHEME. The District Administration Scheme was introduced in 1981, with the publication of a White Paper entitled, "District Administration in Hong Kong." Its aim was to "provide an effective forum for public consultation and participation in administration at the district level." It was, in effect, a means of bringing the administrative system into line with the more sophisticated needs of a fast-developing territory. The system was further developed in 1987 with another White Paper entitled, "The Development of Representative Government: The Way Forward." Under the new arrangements the territory was divided into 19 districts: four on Hong Kong Island, six in Kowloon, and nine in the New Territories.

Prior to these changes the local administration system

had been complex. Effectively the urban and the rural areas of the colony were administered separately. The former were run by the City District Committees and the latter by the District Advisory Boards. Both were totally nonelected, comprising official and appointed members.

In 1982 the first elections were held for office in the reorganized District Boards, and in 1985 all officials were removed from membership. Presently two-thirds of the membership is elected and the remainder appointed.

The District Boards are seen as advisory in capacity and their responsibilities restricted to their own district. (See Constitution; Local Government; Political System.)

DISTURBANCES. A term used in Hong Kong to describe minor or major disruptions in society. In the 19th-century there were sporadic disturbances, but for the most part they presented no challenge to the authority of the government. Usually the disturbances were a reflection of relationships with the Chinese government. Examples would include the E Sing Bakery incident in 1857, and the disturbances in the colony in 1884 following the Franco-Chinese Wars.

In the post-World War I period there were a number of disturbances, some provoked by local causes, others arising from the turmoil on the mainland. Examples of the former type occurred in 1919 when widespread strikes occurred in response to the rising price of rice. This was followed by a Seamen Union strike in 1922, which eventually spread and became a nationwide strike.

The strike and boycott of 1925–1926 lasted almost 16 months and was anti-British in intent. It followed an incident in Shanghai where British police had opened fire on a crowd demonstrating against the Japanese in particular and foreigners in general. A general boycott of British goods was declared, and all Chinese workers went on strike. The strike only ended after it had substantially damaged the local economy.

Since World War II there have been a number of disturbances. The most important were in 1956, 1966, 1967, 1984, and 1989. The 1956 disturbances developed into a riot and involved clashes between the pro-Nationalist and pro-Communist factions. The rioting was largely confined to Kowloon and Tsuen Wan, but it left 59 people dead.

There followed nearly ten years of relative tranquillity ended by the Star Ferry riots. These were triggered by an increase in fares across the harbor in the Star Ferry. No sooner had this riot died down than the colony suffered its most violent demonstrations. The 1967 riots were a spill-over from the Cultural Revolution within the PRC. Fifty-one people were killed. These included 10 police officers, and 15 people killed by bombs.

The years from 1967 until 1984 were relatively peaceful. The economy boomed, reducing the significance of many of the underlying causes of previous disturbances. The worst aspects of poverty had been largely eradicated and the government had spent large amounts of public money on public housing, education, and health. The system of greater consultation which had emerged as a consequence of the 1966 and 1967 riots had also reduced the extent of political alienation of the populace. It was therefore a surprise when a taxi drivers' dispute escalated into a full-scale riot. The taxi drivers had gone on strike in opposition to an ill-considered attempt by the government to increase license fees. The tension erupted into an outbreak of rioting and looting in the Mongkok area. The prompt action of the police and the limited scope of the grievances led to the rapid collapse of the disturbance.

The 1989 disturbance occurred on the night of June 7 following the events of T'ien-an-man (Tiananmen) Square, Peking (Beijing). It began and ended very quickly and was of no political significance. Since that time there have been no major disturbances. (See Cultural Revolution; E Sing

Bakery Incident; General Strike; Star Ferry Riots; Taxi Drivers' Dispute; T'ien-an-man (Tiananman).)

DRUGS. The most important drug in Hong Kong's history has been opium and its derivatives. The smoking of opium was probably introduced to China by the Dutch in the 18th-century, although it had been used in China as a pain-killing drug since the eighth century A.D.

In 1729 the Chinese authorities introduced an edict prohibiting its use, but this failed to curb the importation of opium increasingly supplied by the British from India. Opium imports were forbidden in 1796, but smuggling saw the number of imported chests increase from 2,000 in 1800 to 40,000 in 1839.

Attempts by Governor Lin to stamp out the importation of drugs into China led to the outbreak of the Opium War in which British military force triumphed and China was forced to open up to trade with the West. The trade in opium through the treaty ports subsequently increased further. After the second Opium War (1856–1860) the Chinese officially recognized the importation of opium and were allowed to levy a tax on it.

From 1840–1860 Hong Kong was a significant entrepôt for both the official movement of opium and its smuggling. After 1860 the amount of smuggling increased in the attempt to avoid Chinese taxes. In response the Chinese authorities imposed a blockade on the colony which was not lifted until 1886.

Hostility among the educated classes in China led to major pressure to rid China of all opium, both locally grown and imported. At the same time British missionaries and other liberals pressured the British government to cease the trade. In 1906 an imperial edict was passed which demanded that opium use should be eradicated within ten years and passed punitive regulations to set the plans in motion. The election of the Liberal government in Britain in 1906 brought about an agreement between the Chinese authorities and the British government to reduce the importing of opium from India and to eradicate its importing completely by 1917.

There is clear evidence that much of the early prosperity of Hong Kong was related to narcotics. As late as 1905 it was estimated that 10% of the value of goods shipped through Hong Kong were based on opium. As a source of revenue for the government the opium monopoly established in 1858 provided between 9% and 29% of the total between 1886 and 1906. The table below gives further details.

Proportion of Government Revenue Derived from the Opium Monopoly, 1886–1913.

Year	Total Revenue (HK$)	Opium Monopoly (HK$)	(%)
1886	1,367,977	178,500	13
1896	2,609,914	286,000	11
1906	7,035,011	2,040,000	29
1913	8,512,308	1,183,200	14

In 1908 the British government decided, despite opposition from the Hong Kong government, that all smoking divans were to be closed in Hong Kong.

The Chinese revolution of 1911 produced a new government even more hostile to the importation of opium, and regulations were more strictly applied. This led in 1913 to the ending of exports to China of Indian opium. However, the government's monopoly on opium consumed in the colony continued to provide a steady revenue through its sale in both government shops and other retail outlets.

Following World War I the newly formed League of Nations put great pressure upon the British government to end the government monopoly on opium and to make its consumption illegal. Pressure from the United States was particularly strong. In this period there was a reversal of smuggling activity with large amounts of cheaper opium now being smuggled from China into Hong Kong. Official revenue from the legal sale of opium to the public in the colony still yielded the government over three million Hong Kong dollars in 1931.

With the fall of Hong Kong to Japan in 1941, the influence of a colonial government upon the Colonial Office disappeared and that of the United States became paramount. Slowly the British were edged towards the acceptance of prohibition which they accepted in September 1945. The government monopolies in Hong Kong (and Singapore) were abolished and the desirability of suppressing the consumption of opium in the colony was accepted.

Since that time behavior and laws relating to narcotics in the territory have conformed to that of the West. The use of narcotics has been illegal and the law enforcement agencies have been active in suppressing the consumption and movement of narcotics both within and through the territory. (See Opium Wars.)

-E-

E SING BAKERY INCIDENT. The E Sing Bakery Incident refers to an abortive attempt to poison the European population in Hong Kong by putting arsenic in the bread produced by the E Sing Bakery. The incident occurred in January 1857 when anti-British feelings were running high in the colony. The owner of the bakery, Cheong Ah Lum, was acquitted of the crime but 52 of his employees were imprisoned and later deported. (See Cheong Ah Lum.)

EAST INDIA COMPANY (1600–1858). The East India Company was established in 1600 and was given the monopoly of trade with India. It eventually gained effective administrative control over the whole of India, which it maintained until 1858 when India was made an imperial possession by the British crown.

For a time it also held a monopoly of British trade with China. However, this was lost in 1833 following opposition from other British merchants. (See Anglo-Chinese Wars.)

ECONOMIC AGREEMENTS. With the increasing economic autonomy granted by the British government to Hong Kong and the awareness that the trading interests of the metropolitan power and that of the territory did not necessarily coincide, the colony was allowed to become a member of the Multi-Fibre Arrangement with the U.S.A. from 1973 onwards and the General Agreements on Tariffs and Trade (GATT) in 1988. Under the Joint Declaration of 1984 it is accepted that GATT membership will continue after Hong Kong's hand-over to the People's Republic of China in 1997. This was endorsed in Article 116 of the Basic Law. (See Basic Law; Economic System; GATT; Multi-Fibre Arrangements; Trade.)

ECONOMIC SYSTEM. The development of the economic system of Hong Kong has been affected by the long-standing government acceptance of the principles of *laissez-faire.* In the nineteenth century such an approach was endorsed by the British entrepreneurs, but it was also accepted by the Chinese as they gradually entered into the colony's economic system. Trade unionism or collectivist ideas had little impact upon the general consciousness.

Until World War II, Hong Kong's economy depended almost entirely upon entrepôt trade. This had in the early stages been conducted between Britain, India, and the United Kingdom, although in the interwar years trade with Japan, the United States, and other European countries had increased.

Largely dependent on the entrepôt sector, service industries had also grown up in such areas as ship repairing yards, ships' victuallers, insurance companies, merchant houses, and banks. The population of Hong Kong had gradually grown from an estimated 24,000 in 1845 to about one million in 1936.

The Japanese occupation from 1941 until 1945 saw the collapse of the traditional economy, but after the Second World War Hong Kong experienced extremely rapid economic growth. It had few conventional advantages, but it exploited to the full its abundant supply of cheap labor (provided by a constant influx of refugees from China) and the ample credit provided by the banking system. In the event structural change was almost made necessary by the disruption to the traditional entrepôt trade arising from the civil war in China.

The triumph of the communists on the mainland led to another bonus for the colony—the immigration of many industrialists from the mainland China. In particular, many of the owners of the great cotton mills of Shanghai moved to Hong Kong, bringing with them their expertise, knowledge of export markets, and capital. They were to be followed in many cases by skilled workers from those factories. The Korean War, which broke out in 1950, also boosted demand for textiles and clothing. By 1960 employment in textiles and clothing provided over 40% of total manufacturing employment in the territory. Another indicator of the growing importance of manufacturing can be seen in the changing balance between exports and re-exports. In 1953 only 30% of all Hong Kong's exports were of local origin and 70% were re-exports, but by 1959 the situation was reversed to 70% exports of local origin and 30% re-exports. Other forms of manufactures grew even more rapidly including plastic toys, plastic flowers, shoes, gloves, torches, torch batteries, vacuum flasks, enamelware, aluminum ware, and rattan ware. Again the demand for labor was satisfied

by the continued influx of immigrants from the mainland. By 1961 the population had grown to over 3.1
million—an increase of over 50% in only 11 years.

The 1960s and 1970s saw a continuing growth of the
economy. For 20 years the Gross Domestic Product
(GDP) grew at an average annual rate of around 10%.
Throughout this period the government allowed the
forces of supply and demand for goods and services to be
largely unrestricted. Few barriers to trade within or
without the territory were allowed. The government's
general stance was termed "positive non-interventionism" and received wide support among businesspeople
and the influential bureaucratic sector.

The period from 1980 to 1990 also showed a steady
growth in the economy of Hong Kong, but this was
accompanied by a substantial restructuring of the economy itself. Textiles, the vehicle by which the territory
launched itself into the international market, showed a
marked decline in importance. They were increasingly
replaced by the growth of electronics. Those textile
manufacturers who remained increasingly moved to
higher value-added products. In the period 1973–1985,
the share of the textile industry in net output fell from
27% to 15% and in manufacturing employment from
21% to 13%. Meanwhile, clothing expanded from 20%
to 23% and electrical and electronic goods from 9% to
14%. Overall, manufacturing showed a significant decline, but the service sector—chiefly banking and financial services, transport and communications, retailing,
and the hotel and catering sectors—showed a dramatic
expansion.

One of the reasons for the decline in manufacturing in
the territory is that the comparative advantages in labor
costs have been whittled away. The other newly industri-
alized countries in the region had lower labor costs and
this applied in particular to the People's Republic of
China. By the late 1980s, for instance, the average

factory wage per month in Hong Kong was US$685 compared to US$45 in the People's Republic of China. With the introduction of the policy of the "Four Modernizations" in the People's Republic of China in 1978 it became much easier to establish manufacturing units in that country. The creation of Special Economic Zones (SEZ's), especially Sham Chun (Shenzhen) across the border from the New Territories, attracted considerable investment from Hong Kong. By the late 1980s over two million workers were employed in joint venture companies established between Hong Kong and China. At the same time the opening up of the People's Republic of China to international trade saw the reemergence of Hong Kong as a center for the redistribution of goods and services to and from the mainland. The integration of the two economies and the mutual reciprocity between the two systems has been massively underlined in the last ten years and this trend appears likely to continue in the next few years.

Real GDP growth has been maintained at between 6% and 7% over the decade 1977–1988. Employment has also remained high with official records showing the worst year since 1960 to be 1983 with an unemployment rate of 4.5%. Strikes in Hong Kong have been rare. Membership of the trade unions has decreased. Registered membership of trade unions in the late 1980s was only just over 13% of the total workforce.

Hong Kong is heavily reliant upon the rest of the world for its economic prosperity. Its strongest links are with the United States and the People's Republic of China. In the latter case reliance is increasing, not only for the importation of essential food and water, but also due to the ever-growing integration of the two economies. The need to export to the U.S.A. (and other economies such as Japan and western Europe) lies behind the territory's commitment to free trade. But in order to promote the idea of free trade and to counter protectionist policies, the territory has remained open to foreign investment and trade. In 1986 the major sources of foreign investment (apart from the People's Republic of China) were:

U.S.A.	24%
Britain	14.7%
Japan	11.9%
Singapore	5.7%

The Joint Declaration on the future of Hong Kong states that the economic system will remain the same for 50 years. This was endorsed in the Basic Law. Articles 105–119 basically allow the government of the future Special Administrative Region (SAR) autonomy to pursue the largely capitalist, free market, noninterventionist set of economic policies that have been practiced since the Second World War. (See Basic Law; Joint Declaration; Sham Chun (Shenzhen); Special Economic Zones; Trade.)

EDUCATION. Prior to the arrival of the British in Hong Kong there was little formal educational provision except for the small village schools. The majority of the population was illiterate. The private schools tended to be traditional and of variable quality. In 1843 the beginnings of a structured and free education system was established by the Morrison Educational Society under the presidency of the American missionary Dr. E.C. Bridgman. This was followed by an Anglo-Chinese College, and a Catholic college in the same year.

In 1845 eight Chinese schools were set up by the Chinese community of which three were given HK$10 per month grant from the government. By 1845 the total given from public sources towards education in the colony was HK$120.

The provision of public education was slow in expanding, and it was estimated that out of a total of over 22,000 children in Hong Kong in 1865 only just over 1,800 were being given an opportunity for schooling. The situation gradually improved as the government became aware of the benefits of education. By 1883, there were a total of 180 schools in Hong Kong with a total of 7,758 registered pupils. Of these 39 were government funded, 48 were given grants by the government, and 103 were outside government supervision. It is noteworthy that until 1890 the expansion was intended primarily for boys; it was not until the last decade of the century that any girls' schools were established.

Development of the tertiary sector was equally late to start. A college of medicine was set up in 1887, later to be incorporated into the Hong Kong College of Medicine in 1907. In 1911 the University of Hong Kong was established.

The post-Second World War period saw a dramatic expansion in the provision of education at every level. From the 1970s onwards free education for nine years was provided for every child. Total government expenditure increased from HK$327 million in 1970 to over HK$13,000 million in 1989.

However, tertiary education was one area which continued to be underprovided until relatively recent years. The University of Hong Kong was complemented by the Chinese University of Hong Kong in 1963, and a third university, the University of Science and Technology, was opened in 1991. In 1973 the Polytechnic of Hong Kong was established and complemented by the opening up of the City Polytechnic in the 1980s and the upgrading to degree-awarding status of the Hong Kong Baptist College. In 1970 the total number of students in the two universities was just over 5,000, but by 1989 they had nearly 18,000 students at undergraduate and graduate level. Moreover, this was complemented by nearly

19,000 students studying for degrees or other advanced qualifications at other institutes of tertiary education.

Success in the highly competitive education system is highly prized by the general population. Within a system of examinations modelled on the British system, students at secondary level have had to compete for places in the best schools and need the local Hong Kong Certificate of Education (HKCEE) taken at the age of 16 to proceed to the Advanced Level of Education if they wish ultimately to enter University. Over the last ten years increasing numbers are studying abroad at both secondary and university levels.

Under the Basic Law, Articles 136 and 138, the education system is promised freedom from external interference after 1997. (See Education Commission; Universities.)

EDUCATION COMMISSION. A body set up in November 1984 to advise the Governor on future community needs in education. It published major reports in 1985, 1986, and 1988. The first two dealt mainly with the appropriate language of instruction in schools (Chinese versus English); and the last recommended that general degree programs at the university level should—in the case of the Chinese University of Hong Kong—be reduced from four to three years. (See Education; Universities.)

ELECTIONS. Although elections at the central level of Hong Kong government are a relatively recent innovation, they have a longer history at the local level. The first elections for public office in Hong Kong were for two positions on the Sanitary Board in 1887. This elected element continued until the Sanitary Board was renamed the Urban Council in 1936. Eligibility for office and access to the franchise were, however, limited.

Under the terms of the Young Plan attempts were made between 1946 and 1949 to widen the base of political representation through the creation of a Municipal Council, which was to be fully representative and deal with certain internal administrative functions. The proposal allowed for an elected majority on the proposed council to be elected by a fairly wide franchise. The council was to have powers and autonomy over all urban services, education, social welfare, town planning, and other functions. The Plan also proposed indirect elections to the Legislative Council at the central government level. However, in the face of considerable opposition by members of the Legislative Council, the Plan was effectively killed. Apart from the limited and slowly increasing numbers elected to the Urban Council—a body with restricted powers—little progress was made at the local level and none was made in the provision of elected members to the central government legislative body, the Legislative Council.

In 1982 direct elections were extended to the District Boards, and the franchise was broadened to include all citizens who had been resident in Hong Kong for seven years or more and who were over 21. However, the District Boards had little real political power, their role being to safeguard the interests of the citizens living in small constituencies, to advise central government on their community needs, and to spend a small amount of money on minor local amenities. They had no financial autonomy.

Direct elections were subsequently applied to the Urban Council elections and to the newly created Regional Council in 1986. More significantly, steps were taken to introduce an elected element into the Legislative Council. In 1985 elections for membership of the Council took place for the first time although only a minority of the seats were elected, and none were elected by universal suffrage. This was the result of an extremely complex system whereby the legislature was made up of official members (nonelected government officials); members appointed by the government; members elected by the District Boards and the Urban and Regional Councils; and finally, members elected by functional constituencies. In 1987 a Government proposal suggested further extensions of the system to allow direct elections for a number of directly-elected seats on the Legislative Council in 1991. Under the terms of the Basic Law it is anticipated that in the Legislative Council to be chosen in 1995, 20 members will be returned by direct elections from geographical constituencies, 30 members by functional constituencies (e.g., the financial constituency), and 10 by an election committee. In other words, only one-third will be directly elected in the chamber. The plans for the Council's second and third terms provide for the directly-elected membership to rise to 50% of the total in the year 2003.

Membership of the Executive Council has never been subject to elections, and there are no plans to change this. Similarly, the Governor has never been elected, but has been appointed by the Crown. The proposals in the Basic Law of April 1990 for the future Chief Executive suggest that direct elections to that post are not anticipated in the foreseeable future. (See Basic Law; District Administration; Electorate; Joint Declaration; Legislative Council; Regional Council; Urban Council; Young Plan.)

ELECTORATE. Historically there was no electorate of any note in Hong Kong until after the Second World War. Even until the 1980s, the franchise was extremely limited. With the more recent extension of the franchise and expansion of elected membership on the District Boards, Municipal Councils and Legislative Council, the total eligible electorate has increased to about 3.4 million. However, the total who had actually registered to vote was only 1.9 million in 1991. (See District Administration; Elections; Legislative Council.)

ELECTRONIC ROAD PRICING (ERP). The growth in affluence in Hong Kong during the period 1960–1980 led to a huge growth in the number of vehicles using the roads. In 1970, for instance, there were just over 144,000 vehicles registered in the territory, but by 1983 this had increased to 327,000. To meet the problems of congestion, the government invested heavily in improvements to the communications infrastructure while simultaneously increasing fees for licenses and first registration of vehicles. But when these measures proved insufficient, the government in 1983 proposed a scheme to fit road vehicles with electronic number plates. In conjunction with fixed recorders at various sites, these would record the road use of each vehicle. The road users would then be presented with bills at the end of each month according to road usage. The charge for entering the urban areas was to be higher than in the more outlying areas. The scheme was tried out on an experimental basis, but was abandoned in the face of considerable opposition to it by motorists and those concerned about the government's potential ability to monitor people's movements.

ELLIOT, CAPTAIN CHARLES (1801–1875). Charles Elliot was appointed by the British government as Superintendent of Trade in December 1836 with orders to press for the expansion of trade between the home government and China. His express instructions were to maintain a friendly policy as far as possible with the Chinese authorities and win recognition of the diplomatic equality for Britain, which the Chinese government had refused to grant. However, relations between the two sides deteriorated rapidly. The seizure of opium stocks owned by British merchants by Governor Lin in 1839, his demand that any individual importing opium suffer the death penalty, and the detention of British merchants in their factories in Canton (Guangzhou) all contributed to the worsening situation. While Elliot requested permission from Britain for military intervention, Commissioner Lin was putting pressure on the Portuguese to remove the British from Macau. In the face of this pressure, Elliot withdrew the British community to Hong Kong.

When the British government demanded the cessation of an island for the purposes of providing more security for British merchants, Captain Elliot was instructed to occupy "one or more islands . . . (to be) conveniently situated for commercial intercourse, not merely with Canton (Guangzhou), (which shall) have good harbors, afford natural facilities for defence, and be easily provisioned." On his appointment as Plenipotentiary he was instructed to blockade the Canton (Guangzhou) and surrounding areas. Elliot moved against the Canton forts and negotiated the Convention of Chuanpi (Chuanbi) in 1841. Under its provisions Hong Kong was to be ceded to Britain. Hong Kong was duly occupied on January 26, 1841 and recognized by Britain as a colony some two-and-a-half years later.

In the event Elliot was seen by Lord Palmerston, the British foreign minister, as having disobeyed his orders and neglected his instructions. Accordingly, in August 1841, after eight months as administrator in Hong Kong, he was replaced by Sir Henry Pottinger. (See Anglo-Chinese Wars; Chuanpi (Chuanbi), Convention of; Palmerston, Lord; Pottinger, Sir Henry.)

EMERGENCY REGULATIONS AND POWERS. A number of laws were passed in the interwar years in response to various crises. Under the Emergencies Powers Ordinance the Governor in Council was empowered to issue regulations of very wide scope. They were, for example, used by the Governor on the outbreak of the Second World War to introduce controls relating to censorship, mining of the harbor approaches, the requisitioning of ships and aircraft, interning of enemy aliens, and trade and exchange control. They were last brought into force in the disturbances of 1967 when detention without trial was permitted under the Emergency Regulations Ordinance. (See Disturbances; Second World War.)

EMIGRATION. Hong Kong has experienced emigration throughout its history. Large numbers have migrated to other parts of Asia, and more recently to Canada, the United States, Britain, Australia, and New Zealand.

Emigration began to be a major problem after the signing of the Joint Declaration between the British and Chinese governments in 1984. Many are clearly anxious about the post-1997 situation despite the guarantees so far given. The level of emigration from Hong Kong rose inexorably in the years 1984–90 particularly among the young, professional groups that Hong Kong could least afford to lose. Whereas the annual level of emigration was estimated to be around 20,000 in the early 1980s it rose to 30,000 in 1987, 42,000 in 1989, and 60,000 in 1990. (See Joint Declaration.)

ENVIRONMENT. The increase in the colony's population to over 5.8 million in 1989 has given Hong Kong the highest density of population in the world at 5,130 persons per square kilometer. (In Mongkok, a particularly congested area, the density was estimated in 1988 at 139,594 per square kilometer.) At the same time the government's policies of limited intervention, coupled with industrialization and economic growth, have led to increasing problems of environmental pollution. Inadequate sewage disposal, and a lack of effective laws against industrial effluent and noise and airborne emissions have also been evident. Housing provision was dense, the streets overcrowded, and the increasing use of vehicles led to further air pollution.

Increasing public awareness led in the 1970s to some limited tightening of government regulations in the areas of air, water, and noise pollution, and the creation of an administrative framework to monitor the environmental deterioration. This was gradually expanded and given greater, but still limited, powers over the next twenty years. An Environmental Protection Agency was established in 1981 and was upgraded to a department in the 1989. (See Health.)

EXECUTIVE COUNCIL. The Executive Council was created on April 5, 1843 under the provisions of the then Hong Kong Charter. Its role was to assist and advise the Governor on the governance of the colony. It was kept deliberately small with no more than three members (excluding the Governor) until 1872. It was then expanded to four members.

The actual role and powers of the Executive Council were further spelled out in the Letters Patent and the Royal Instructions of 1917. These two documents, which outline the constitution of the colony, stated that, "There shall be an Executive council in and for the Colony, and the said Council shall consist of such persons as We direct by Instructions under our Sign Manual and Signet, and all such persons shall hold their place under our pleasure" (Letters Patent, Article 5). It also provided for the removal of members "upon sufficient cause," which would have to be provided to the home government. The actual minimum number was spelled out in the Royal Instructions where it was specified that the membership would include:

1. The Commander of British Forces
2. The Chief Secretary
3. The Attorney General
4. The Secretary for Home Affairs
5. The Financial Secretary

The above were to be collectively known as the *ex-officio* members. However, provision was made to increase the numbers if deemed necessary. They were to be known as "Official" members if they held office under the Crown, or "Unofficial" members if they did not. The unofficials, unlike the officials, were obliged to vacate their seat after five years in office, but were not debarred from reappointment. The Council has always been nonelected, with members being appointed by the Governor—although formally the actual appointments were made by the government in Britain. Until 1926 when the then Governor appointed Sir Shou-son Chow, there were no Chinese on the Executive Council.

Throughout the interwar years the Executive Council met once a week, and much of its business dealt with largely administrative matters. However, despite being an advisory body, it did occasionally provide a restraint on the Governor's power. The records show that members often disagreed, and votes were taken on controversial decisions which were then often modified as a result. The Governor was allowed to override the advice of the Executive Council, but this was only done twice by the then Governor May (1912–1919), and not at all by any other interwar Governor.

As the table below indicates, the membership has gradually increased with the unofficials assuming greater significance. The unofficials on the Executive Council are mostly composed of members of the Legislative Council. The Chairman of the Hongkong and Shanghai Bank is by convention a member, also as an unofficial.

	Governor	Officials *ex officio*	Other	Unofficials
1843	1	0	3	0
1844	1	0	4	0
1845	1	0	3	0
1865	1	3	0	0
1872	1	3	1	0
1875	1	3	2	0
1884	1	4	2	0
1896	1	4	2	2
1921	1	4	2	3
1928	1	5	2	3
1946	1	5	2	4
1948	1	5	1	6
1966	1	5	1	8
1978	1	5	1	9
1984	1	4	2	10
1990	1	4	1	9

The ratio between expatriates and local people has also changed—particularly over the period 1965–90.

	Expatriate	Local
1965	10	5
1971	11	4
1975	8	7
1982	9	7
1985	6	9
1990	7	9

However, the significance of these changes in ethnic composition may be less significant than the absolute dominance of the Council by the civil service and business *elite*. The business dominance of the Executive Council has persisted to a greater extent than is the case of the Legislative and Municipal Councils. The composition of the Council in recent years has been:

	Civil Service	Business & Finance	Professional	Other
1965	7	6	3	0
1971	7	6	2	0
1975	7	6	2	0
1982	7	6	3	0
1985	7	7	1	0
1990	7	5	4	0

In the early 1990s the Executive Council met once a week and could still be loosely described as the Governor's Cabinet. However, with the increase in the administrative load, there has been an increasing use of subcommittees. The Council's most important task remains to advise the Governor, and to approve legislation to be put to the Legislative Council.

The Basic Law established that an Executive Council would continue to exist after 1997. Although no details were provided, it is assumed that its powers, duties, and functions will probably be similar to those under the British administration. However, the position of Commander, British Forces must disappear, and the Basic Law does not mention whether the individual holding this post will be replaced by a counterpart from the People's Liberation Army. The Basic Law does stipulate that all future members of the Council will be Chinese nationals who are permanent residents of Hong Kong. (See Basic Law; Constitution; Joint Declaration; Letters Patent; Localization; Officials and Official Members; OMELCO; Political System; UMELCO.)

-F-

FAMILISM. A term used in the Hong Kong context to denote the persisting significance to contemporary Hong

Kong of traditional Chinese values concerning the family. Often the term utilitarianistic familism is used to indicate the mixture of traditional values with the colonial and materialistic culture. Its main assumptions are that:

1. People in the territory have become more concerned with the acquisition of wealth and status.
2. The traditional emphasis on family support which was to be found in the original rural system remains. Other social groups or the community's needs as a whole have less significance.

To a large extent social structure is therefore based on the self-sufficient family, and a downgrading of interaction with the government or nonfamily social affairs. This is widely seen as having contributed to a weak civic identity and low levels of political participation.

FEDERALISM. Under the colonial administration there was always a bias towards central power. Given the small size of the colony and the attitude of the British colonial masters this was hardly surprising. Local subdivisions in Hong Kong were more for administrative convenience with the real political power being concentrated in central government. In some quarters it was hoped that after 1997 a federal system might evolve with regard to Hong Kong's relationship to the People's Republic of China. However, the PRC has always been a unitary system, and the Basic Law made it clear that, although the Special Administrative Region might have a relatively high level of autonomy over its own affairs, its powers were limited to those granted by the central government in Peking (Beijing). Moreover, powers granted to the government of the Special Administrative Region after 1997 could be removed by Peking (Beijing) if deemed necessary. (See Autonomy; Basic Law; District Administration; Political System; Special Administrative Region.)

FINANCIAL SECRETARY. A position in the Hong Kong government with responsibility for the colony's financial affairs. Under the Letters Patent and Royal Instructions, updated in 1917, the Financial Secretary was to be an ex-officio member of the Executive and Legislative Councils. The position was guaranteed under the Basic Law. (See Basic Law; Executive Council; Legislative Council.)

FIRST WORLD WAR. In August 1914 Britain's declaration of war against Germany automatically involved Hong Kong as part of the British Empire. All German women and children were therefore required to leave the colony and German men of military age were interned for the duration. All German businesses were taken over by the government, liquidated, and their assets sold off. When China declared war on Germany in 1917 German operations in China, which hitherto had not been constrained, were closed down. Although Hong Kong was not involved in any hostilities during the war, there was some commercial dislocation because of the embargoes on trade with the enemy and some controls on the export of strategic goods. As was the case in most parts of the Empire, a large proportion of the expatriate male community (nearly 25%) volunteered their services to the Crown.

FIVE DYNASTIES (907–960). During the five dynasties the Hong Kong area fell within the control of the Nan Han kingdom. That kingdom established a pearl monopoly at Tai Po in 907, salt commissions, and set up a naval station at Kowloon. It also built a new fort at Tuen Mun which was visited by one of the Nan Han emperors. (See Forts.)

FLAG AND BADGE. Under British administration the flag representing the territory has the Union Jack placed in the top left-hand corner, against a blue background with the emblem in the lower-right corner. The national flag of the territory was the Union flag of the United Kingdom (often referred to as the Union Jack). As the territory ceases to be administered by Britain after 30 June 1997, a new flag and emblem will be used. Under the Basic Law it was declared that the national flag would be that of the People's Republic of China. The flag of the Special Administrative Region was announced in February 1990 and endorsed in the Basic Law. It is to be a pink bauhinia flower in the center on a red background. Each of its five petals is to be adorned with a star.

FOREIGN AFFAIRS COMMITTEE. The Foreign Affairs Committee is a select committee of the British House of Commons first set up in its present form in 1979. Its main function is to scrutinize the conduct of British foreign policy by the executive branch. Its powers, given the nature of the British Parliamentary system, were far less than those of its counterpart in the United States Congress, and there was no obligation for the government to act on any of its recommendations. The committee made occasional visits to Hong Kong, made recommendations on policy and criticized certain policy decisions relating to the territory.

The committee itself was bipartisan and had a membership of 11 with five subcommittees. It published a major report in 1989 following a visit to the colony. Among the recommendations were: a faster pace of democratization; forced repatriation of Vietnamese refugees; quick action for the introduction of a Bill of Rights; and renegotiation of the question of the presence of the People's Liberation Army after 1997. The proposals were debated in the House of Commons, but led to no significant changes of policy. (See Government, British; Parliament, British.)

FOREIGN AND COMMONWEALTH OFFICE. The Foreign and Commonwealth Office (FCO) is the ministry in the British government responsible for advising on and implementing foreign policy. It was created from the amalgamation of the Foreign Office and the Commonwealth Office. In 1967 it took over the responsibilities of the old Colonial Office which ceased to function. At its head is the British Foreign Secretary who is a member of the government and sits in the British Cabinet. With regard to Hong Kong its duties are:

1. to convey and explain to the colonial administration the decisions of the British Government;
2. to safeguard the interests of Hong Kong in negotiations with other governments—in particular the People's Republic of China;
3. to liaise with other departments in Whitehall concerning any policies affecting Hong Kong.

Given the PRC's refusal to deal directly with Hong Kong or its government, the FCO is the sole authority with whom the mainland deals on questions relating to the territory. Consequently, the FCO played a large part in the negotiations over the future of Hong Kong between 1982 and 1984. Under the agreements reached in 1984 the FCO was to be represented on the Joint Liaison Group to monitor the agreements until the hand-over of power, and was also to provide personnel for the Land Commission. Under the provisions of the Basic Law the FCO will cease to represent the territory once Hong Kong reverts to the People's Republic of China as a Special Administrative Region. However, the Joint Liaison Group which monitors the progress of the handover of power will continue to function with an FCO contingent until 1 January 2000. (See Basic Law; Constitution; Foreign Relations; Government, British; Joint Liaison Group.)

FOREIGN RELATIONS. Hong Kong's foreign relations were conducted by the Foreign Office (later to be renamed the Foreign and Commonwealth Office). One major exception to this occurred when, as a consequence of the Joint Declaration between the People's Republic of China and the United Kingdom, the colony was allowed membership of the General Agreements on Tariffs and Trade (GATT) in its own right.

At the more informal level Hong Kong has increasingly assumed greater independence in economic foreign affairs. Since the Second World War it has become a member of over 132 international nongovernmental organizations. It has set up Hong Kong government offices in London, Geneva, Brussels, Washington, New York and San Francisco, and industrial promotion offices in Brussels, New York, San Francisco, Tokyo and London. Trade development offices which are not governmental have been established in nearly all the world's great cities.

The Basic Law states that after 1997 Hong Kong's external relations will be the responsibility of the mainland authorities, although in certain important commercial and cultural areas, a high degree of autonomy may be maintained. (See Basic Law; Economic System; GATT; Multi-Fibre Arrangements; Trade.)

FORTS (CHINESE). Although the earliest written records date only from the early ninth century, it is thought that a naval base had been established at Tuen Mun by the middle of the Han (Han) dynasty (206B.C.–220A.D.). Protection of the entrances to the Pearl River was a major strategic factor from that time onwards. Forts had been built at the Kap Shui Mun Channel, and probably in

Kowloon and elsewhere by the thirteenth century. The 15th and 16th centuries saw the further construction of small forts around Hong Kong to guard the coasts and to deal with local pirates. There are four surviving forts dating from the Ch'ing (Qing) dynasty (1664–1912), all constructed during the early 18th century to guard the strategic passages through the Hong Kong harbor. One is situated on Tung Lung Island and the other three on the west and east side of Lantau Island.

FOUR MODERNIZATIONS. The Four Modernizations were first announced in 1964 by Chou En-lai (Zhou Enlai), but were not made official policy in the People's Republic of China until adopted under that name in December 1978. They were associated with the reforms proposed by Teng Hsiao-p'ing (Deng Xiaoping). The Four Modernizations concerned the role of agriculture, industry, national defence, and science and technology in national development. Hong Kong's role in the People's Republic of China's modernization process was seen as crucial by Chinese leaders from the first adoption of the program. (See Economic System; Special Economic Zones; Teng Hsiao-p'ing (Deng Xiaoping); Trade.)

FRANCHISE. See Elections

FREE PORT. See Economic System; Trade

FREE TRADE. See Economic System; Trade

FUNCTIONAL CONSTITUENCIES. Functional Constituencies were first introduced into the Legislative Council elections in 1985. The principal justification advanced for the system is that members of influential groups in the territory should be guaranteed representation in the legislative assembly. Initially twelve such constituencies were created, many with highly individual and complex electoral processes. Areas of functional representation included industrial interests, commercial interests, labor interests, and the social services. The number of functional constituency seats was increased in 1988 to 14 and in 1991 to 21. The Basic Law allows functional constituencies to play a major part in the future Legislative Council. In its first three terms after 1997, 50% of the membership of the Legislative Council will come from these constituencies. (See Legislative Council; Pressure Groups.)

FUNG SHUI (FENG SHUI). (Wind and water). Concerned with the rudiments of natural science and of Chinese origin, *fung shui* involves manipulation of the supposed divine powers of nature which are thought to govern the actions of people. The method and practical application of modern *fung shui* are primarily based on the teachings of Chu Hai, who lived during the Sung (Song) dynasty. He traced the Creation from one abstract principle, called "absolute nothing" which evolved out of the "great absolute." When this was in motion its breath and vital energy produced the active, or male element, and, when it rested, the female element was born. The "supreme cause" divided things above to become heaven and that which was below to become the earth. As motion and pause succeeded one another, humans and animals, vegetation, and minerals took their place in nature. The perpetual energy produced by these two contending principles is *Chi* or breath of nature. This works according to two sets of laws, known as *Li* and *Shu* which could be traced mathematically and illustrated in diagrams and numerical proportions. *Li* and *Shu,* acting in nature, produce forms which are recognizable to the human eye called *Ying* and these four manifestations constitute the system of *fung shui.*

Every hill and tree influences the *fung shui* of the locality. One of the principal duties of those adept in *fung shui* is to locate suitable locations for tombs, as the belief is that one of the souls of the deceased inhabits the grave, and, unless it is disposed of comfortably, it will not be sympathetic towards any petitions by its descendants.

Today *fung shui* experts are consulted regularly by a wide cross section of the population in the colony, and are usually brought in to advise on the correct layout of houses or offices.

-G-

GANG OF FOUR. A term given to a group of people who were highly influential in Mao Tse-tung's (Mao Zedong's) declining years and who tried to take over power after his death in 1976. The four were Chiang Ch'ing (Jiang Qing) (Mao's second wife), Chang Ch'un-ch'iao (Zhang Chunqiao), Yao Wen-yuan (Yao Wenyuan), and Wang Hung-wen (Wang Hongwen). They made a major attempt to seize power in 1974 using the mass media and attacks on other political leaders and were protected by Mao. However, Hua Kuo-feng (Hua Guofeng), Mao's named successor had them arrested in October 1976 to foil what many believe was an imminent coup. They were subsequently expelled from the party and put on public trial in 1980 along with ten others. Chiang Ch'ing (Jiang Qing) and Chang Ch'un-ch'iao (Zhang Chunqiao) were sentenced to death but later reprieved, and the other two were sentenced to long terms of imprisonment. (See Cultural Revolution; Mao Tse-tung (Mao Zedong).)

GATT. The General Agreement on Tariffs and Trade began operations in 1948. Its objectives were to expand and facilitate international trade and to minimize protectionism by member nations. Throughout its history it has been a major forum for resolving trade disputes, reducing tariffs, quotas, and other trade barriers and preferential trade agreements. Hong Kong was allowed to become a full contracting member of GATT in 1986. The Basic Law allows for the territory's continued membership after the reversion of Hong Kong to Chinese sovereign control in 1997. (See Economic System; Trade.)

GAZETTE, THE GOVERNMENT. *The Government Gazette* has been published regularly since 1841. It lists proposed legislation, government appointments and any other matters of official business which are required to be officially promulgated. It also contains many other items of nongovernment information. From 1862 the *Gazette* has been published in Chinese as well as English.

GENERAL STRIKE. In the years 1925–1926 the unrest in the colony culminated in a general strike and a general boycott of British goods. Discontent was encouraged by the growth of nationalist sentiment throughout China and popular resentment of privileges accorded to foreigners. During May 1925 an anti-Japanese demonstration in Shanghai expanded into a more general antiforeign sentiment. The size of British interests in Shanghai also made them a clear focus for unrest. As discontent spread the labor unions in Kwangtung (Guangdong) province demanded a strike against the British in Hong Kong and South China. The seamen came out first in June 1925 and other trades quickly followed suit. On June 23 a mass demonstration in Canton (Guangzhou) was fired on by British and French troops in Shamien (Shamian) island which left 52 dead. This inflamed the situation further and the strike intensified. Its effects were, however, mitigated by contingency plans drawn up by the Hong Kong government. The Volunteer Defence force was called out, emergency regulations were activated, essential services were maintained by volunteers, and higher pay offered for those who wished to work. By September the worst of the strike was over, but the boycott remained a serious threat to the colony. It was actively supported by the Kwangtung (Guangdong) government which stopped all British and Hong Kong Chinese shipping from entering Canton and other southern ports. These ports were manned by pickets who enforced the boycott. The boycott ended in October 1926 partly because the Canton government balked at the strike's effects on their revenue, partly because of a show of force by the British when naval troops sailed up the river to Canton and cleared the strike pickets from the wharfs, and partly because of the Hong Kong government's refusal to discuss compromise.

The costs to the trading companies were estimated by one source to be in the region of $500,000,000, and it took many years for the colony as a whole to recover from the effects of the dispute.

GIS (GOVERNMENT INFORMATION SERVICES). The formal title of this branch of government is the Informational Services Department. It was set up after the Second World War as a press relations office. It became a department in the early 1950s, and, particularly after the disturbances of the 1960s, began to be seen as a potentially important means of informing the press and the media of government policy and proposed legislation. (See Cultural Revolution; Disturbances; Star Ferry Riots.)

GODBER AFFAIR. A major incident in the postwar history of Hong Kong which led to major changes in the systems for the control of corruption. In 1970 an investigation was launched into the case of Chief Superintendent Peter Godber who had amassed financial assets far greater than his official salary. Godber escaped to the United Kingdom, possibly with the collusion of government officials. A commission of enquiry strongly criticized existing procedures and allowed the then Governor Sir Murray MacLehose to create in 1974 a new body, the Independent Commission against Corruption which had considerable power to deal with cases of public and private corruption. (See Independent Commission Against Corruption; Royal Hong Kong Police Force; MacLehose, Sir Murray.)

GOVERNMENT, BRITISH. From its inception as a colony the constitutional position of Hong Kong *vis a vis* the British Government has remained relatively constant. For Hong Kong the British government was technically the Crown with the monarch advised by his or her ministers. All colonies were acquired by the Crown, which then created their governmental systems. However, effective control over the territory's government was held by the Cabinet and the department of state responsible for administering Crown territory. This was originally the Colonial office, but, on the abolition of that office, the functions were taken up by the Foreign and Commonwealth Office. At the formal and constitutional level the Crown can divest itself of its colonies and can adopt any policy it wishes towards those possessions without reference to Parliament. But in practice and through convention Parliament is a regulator of policy and its approval is essential.

The practical consequences of all this were as follows:

1. The Hong Kong government was answerable to the Crown through the Colonial Office and after 1967 to the Foreign and Commonwealth Office (FCO).
2. All senior Hong Kong government appointments had to be ratified by the Crown.
3. The Governor had to make regular reports to the Crown via the Colonial Office and the FCO.
4. All direct, formal representations had to go via the Colonial Office or later the FCO. (See Constitution; Foreign and Commonwealth Office; Governor; Parliament, British.)

GOVERNMENT HOUSE. Government House was built in 1855 near to the Cathedral and the residence of the Commander of British forces. It has since been the official residence of the Governor of Hong Kong except for the period of the Japanese occupation (1941–45).

GOVERNMENT INFORMATION SERVICES. See GIS.

GOVERNOR, THE. Since 1841 there have been 28 Governors and two Administrators. They have been:

Capt. Charles Elliot	Administrator	1841*
Sir Henry Pottinger	Administrator	1841–1843*
Sir Henry Pottinger	Governor	1843–1844
Sir John Davis	Governor	1844–1848
Sir Samuel Bonham	Governor	1848–1854
Sir John Bowring	Governor	1854–1859
Sir Hercules Robinson	Governor	1859–1865
Sir Richard MacDonnell	Governor	1866–1872
Sir Arthur Kennedy	Governor	1872–1877
Sir John Pope Hennessy	Governor	1877–1882
Sir George Bowen	Governor	1883–1885
Sir George Des Voeux	Governor	1887–1891
Sir William Robinson	Governor	1891–1898
Sir Henry Blake	Governor	1898–1903
Sir Matthew Nathan	Governor	1904–1907
Sir Frederick Lugard	Governor	1907–1912
Sir Francis May	Governor	1912–1919
Sir Reginald Stubbs	Governor	1919–1925
Sir Cecil Clementi	Governor	1925–1930
Sir William Peel	Governor	1930–1935
Sir Andrew Caldicott	Governor	1935–1937
Sir Geoffrey Northcote	Governor	1937–1940
Sir Mark Young	Governor	1941–1947
Sir Alexander Grantham	Governor	1947–1957
Sir Robert Black	Governor	1958–1964
Sir David Trench	Governor	1964–1971
Sir Murray MacLehose	Governor	1971–1982
Sir Edward Youde	Governor	1982–1986
Sir David Wilson	Governor	1987–1992
Mr. Christopher Patten	Governor	1992–

*The term "Administrators" was used prior to Hong Kong becoming a colony, until 1843. Although not mentioned here, the term "Administrator" ("Officer Administering the Government") was also used for persons acting for the Governor during his temporary absence.

The powers of the Governor were set out in the Letters Patent and the Royal Instructions, documents which were updated from time to time as circumstances required. The post involves considerable formal powers granted by these and other documents such as the Colonial Regulations. In the Colonial Regulations the post is described as, ". . . the single and supreme authority responsible to and representative of, Her Majesty . . . entitled to obedience, aid, and the assistance of all military, air force, and civil officers . . ."

The Governor is the Chief Executive of the Hong Kong government, President of the Legislative Council, the person who appoints all judges and magistrates. Governors also act as leaders of the Executive Council, a body which they appoint to act in an advisory capacity. The Governor is, however, subordinate to the British Crown and to the laws of Hong Kong, and is normally restrained by convention and common sense.

Under the terms of the Basic Law, the office of governor will cease to exist after the resumption of Chinese sovereignty. In its place will be a Chief Executive, whose formal powers will be less extensive and more subject to restraint. (See Basic Law; Constitution; Governors (Various); Letters Patent; Royal Instructions.)

GRAND ELECTORAL COLLEGE. An arrangement first drawn up in 1987 to elect indirectly members of the Legislative Council and the first Chief Executive after 1997.

The Basic Law stipulates that 10 members of the first Legislative Council would be elected by a Selection Committee, which in turn would be selected by a Preparatory Committee, composed of 50% of members from the mainland and 50% from Hong Kong. The Selection Committee would be made up entirely of permanent residents of Hong Kong, with a total membership of 400 from various sections of the community. The same Selection Committee was empowered to select the first Chief Executive.

For subsequent Legislative Council assemblies, it was stated that an Election Committee would be formed with 800 members. These would be drawn from industrial, commercial and financial sectors (200); the professions (200); labor, social services, religious organizations and other sectors (200); and members of the Legislative Council, district organizations, Hong Kong deputies to the National People's Congress and Hong Kong members of the National Committee of Chinese People's Committee of the Chinese People's Political Consultative Conference (200). In the second term the number of Legislative Councilors elected in this way would fall to six, and by 2003 the system would have ceased. The Election Committee would, however, remain responsible for the election of the Chief Executive. (See Basic Law.)

GRANTHAM, SIR ALEXANDER (1899–1978). Governor of Hong Kong from 1947 to 1957. He came to office with considerable experience of the colony, having previously served 13 years there in another capacity. His main role was to guide the colony through the difficult postwar years particularly following the establishment in 1949 of the People's Republic of China, and the years of the Korean war. His policies were avowedly *laissez-faire* in economic affairs, but were coupled with the continuation of strong central government authority. During his term of office the development of the textile industry and the export-led economy began to take shape. (See Economic System.)

GREAT LEAP FORWARD. A policy launched by Mao Tse-tung (Mao Zedong) in 1958 in an attempt to increase rapidly industrialization in the People's Republic of

China. The aim was to achieve an economic growth of 25% per annum. Based on the idea of self-sufficiency, it aimed at the expansion of small local socioeconomic units. The policy failed completely and was abandoned in 1961, at an estimated cost, *inter alia,* of approximately 14 million people who died mostly of starvation. (See China, People's Republic of; Mao Tse-tung (Mao Zedong).)

GREEN PAPERS. See White Papers.

GROUP OF 89. A conservative pressure group, drawn mainly from the business and professional sectors, which was active during the drawing up of the Basic Law. It favored minimum changes in the political system of Hong Kong after 1997. More specifically it stressed the need for a limited franchise, the avoidance of party politics, and the maintenance of an independent judiciary. (See Pressure Groups.)

GROUP OF 190. This group was formed after the Joint Declaration on the future of Hong Kong as a counterweight to the more conservative Group of 89. It was liberal in outlook and attempted to widen the franchise, increase direct elections to the Legislative Council, and to push for maximum autonomy for the future Special Administrative Region after 1997. (See Political System; Pressure Groups.)

GUANGDONG. See Kwangtung Province.

GUOMINDANG. See Kuomintang.

GURKHAS, BRIGADE OF. A mercenary force recruited from Nepal and originally raised by Britain in the mid-19th century for service in India. After Indian independence from Britain in 1948, Gurkha regiments continued to serve in the British army. For much of the post-Second World War period Gurkha infantry battalions were stationed in Hong Kong as part of the British military garrison. They will remain in Hong Kong until the handover to the People's Republic of China. (See Armed Forces.)

-H-

HADDON-CAVE, SIR PHILIP. One of Hong Kong's longest serving Financial Secretaries. He coined the term "positive non-interventionism" to describe the government's minimal role in the economy. During his period of office (1971–1981) he helped oversee a period of substantial economic growth. He was later made Chief Secretary in 1981 and held that office until 1985. (See Chief Secretary.)

HAKKA. Until 1669, most people in Hong Kong area and the Pearl River estuary had been Cantonese speaking. After 1669, however, the depleted Cantonese clans who returned after the military campaigns against Koxinga were unable to bring back into cultivation all the lands they had previously controlled. The Imperial Government, anxious not to lose the taxes from these lands, urged the old families to sell off land to new settlers. These were mostly *Hakka* speakers from the northeast. Between 1669 and the mid-18th century hundreds of *Hakka* groups moved into the area, taking up the more marginal lands in the mountains, particularly in the east. It was this mixed society, of old Cantonese clans in the fertile west, newer *Hakka* families in the less fertile east, plus a few groups of *Tanka* and *Hoklo* boat people, that characterized the area when the British first appeared on the scene. (See Ch'ing (Qing) Dynasty.)

HAN (HAN) DYNASTY (206 B.C.–220 A.D.). The Han (Han) Dynasty ruled China from 206 B.C. until 220 A.D. It was divided into the Eastern and Western Han (Han) periods. The Hong Kong region was effectively independent as part of the Kingdom of Nan Yueh from 208 B.C. until 111 B.C., when it was conquered by the armies of the Eastern Han (Han). Eastern Han (Han) occupation of the area is evidenced by the excavation of a tomb discovered at Lei Cheng Uk, thought to date from the early to middle Eastern Han (Han) period. The region was part of the Nan-Hai prefecture under the Han (Han). There was no real attempt to colonize the region during this period. It was used as a base for trade in valuable commodities with military and naval occupation. It is thought that a naval base at Tuen Mun may have been constructed at this time. (See Forts; Lei Cheng Uk Tomb.)

HANSARD, HONG KONG. The Hong Kong Hansard has provided an official record of Legislative Council debates from the 19th century to the present day. Debates in the Executive Council have remained confidential.

HARWELL REPORT. The Harwell Report was commissioned as a consequence of the public unease over the building of a nuclear power station in Daya Bay, in close proximity to Hong Kong. Its findings, published in 1988, recommended appropriate contingency measures to be taken by the Hong Kong government in preparation for any emergency. (See Daya Bay.)

HEAD OF GOVERNMENT. The head of government in Hong Kong since 1843 has been the Governor. He is the head of the executive branch and President of the Legislative Council. Hong Kong's colonial status rules out the role of a separate head of state. The Basic Law identifies the Chief Executive as the head of government from 1997 on. (See Basic Law; Constitution; Governor; Letters Patent; Political System.)

HEAD OF STATE. Because of its colonial status the head of state for Hong Kong has always been the Crown of the United Kingdom. Since 1952 Queen Elizabeth II (1926-) has been head of state for the colony. Under the Basic Law, the head of state for the Special Administration Region will be the President of the People's Republic of China. (See Basic Law; Queen.)

HEALTH. From the first days of the occupation of the colony there were periodic outbreaks of communicable diseases. Records indicate that in the year 1843 over 100 men of a British regiment lost their lives to "fever." Indeed the colony gained the reputation of being a particularly unhealthy place. As the population grew, the absence of any measures to regulate building and sanitation, led to typhus, typhoid, and cholera becoming endemic in the colony. Hospital provision was limited, as were the medical means to deal with the sick. With the cholera outbreaks in Britain in the mid-19th century and the connection being made between health and living conditions, attempts, at first half-hearted but later more positive, were made to promote public health. In 1866 an Order and Cleanliness Ordinance was passed forbidding the housing of pigs and other similar animals in dwellings, as well as the creation of a Sanitation Board. The Chadwick Report of 1882 recommended the proper disposal of waste and night soil, the provision of clean water, the reduction of overcrowding, and other similar measures. The problem came to a head, however, with the outbreak of bubonic plague in the spring of 1894 and in each of the next six years. In 1896, 1,088 fatal cases were reported; in 1898, 1,175; in 1899, 1,428; and in 1900, 1,434. Further outbreaks continued until 1920.

During the 20th century tighter regulations on sanitation and housing, combined with improved preventative and curative measures led to a dramatic decrease of communicable diseases in the colony. During the post-Second World War era better education, nutrition, and the provision of improved medical services has virtually eradicated malaria, cholera, typhus, typhoid, leprosy, and amoebic dysentery. Rabies was eradicated except for minor imported cases from time to time. Tuberculosis remained a problem in the 1950s and 1960s with the numbers averaging 25,000 under treatment in any given year. Infant mortality was reduced from 37.7 per 1000 live births in 1961 to 19.6 by 1970. The major hazards to health increasingly became those associated with those of developed countries. By 1990 tuberculosis cases were down to 382 with no other major communicable diseases recorded. Life expectancy at birth in 1990 was 74.6 years for males and 80.3 years for females, figures which compare favorably with any country in the world. (See Chadwick Report; Housing.)

HENNESSY, SIR JOHN POPE. Governor of Hong Kong from April 1877 to March 1882. Generally regarded in retrospect as a liberal and farsighted Governor of the colony. He alienated the more conservative members of the European community in the territory. In particular his promotion of more lenient punishment of Chinese criminals, campaigning against branding and deportation and flogging, led to him being unfairly accused by the expatriates of encouraging crime.

He also attempted to reform the Legislative Council, argued for the inclusion of a Chinese member on the Legislative Council, and had considerable success in expanding the educational system. However, he was frequently in dispute with the colonial administration. By the time he left the colony in 1882 he was widely seen in the colony as an inefficient administrator, unable to delegate authority, and he was not on speaking terms with most of his administration except for official business. (See Governor; Legislative Council.)

HEUNG YEE KUK. An organization first established in 1926 in the New Territories. Its original role was to provide advice and guidance to the District Commissioner. It had a fairly simple structure in its early days, but this was made more complex and formal in 1948 when elections were introduced for village representatives to replace the old system of appointment of village elders. In 1957, as a result of a major dispute within the leadership, the government withdrew its recognition of the organization. It was, however, reconstituted in 1959 as a corporate body and its structure was laid down in an appropriate government ordinance. It was to be based on some 900 representatives of the 500 or so villages in the New Territories. Each village was to have up to three representatives, each representing some 50 families. These representatives, in turn, formed 27 Rural Committees, which with one exception elected a Chairman, two Vice Chairmen, and an Executive Committee every two years. The *Heung Yee Kuk* sat at the top of this complex structure and is composed of the 54 Chairmen and Vice Chairmen of the Rural Committees, plus others. These, in turn, elect the Chairman of the *Heung Yee Kuk* along with the Vice Chairmen. Women play a limited role in the choice of representatives.

In the 1970s, with the massive expansion of the population of the New Territories and the growth of the New Towns there, the power of the traditional rural representation of the *Heung Yee Kuk* waned. For instance by the end of the 1970s it was estimated that only 10%-to-12% of the population were native to the area. However, the *Heung Yee Kuk* managed to gain representation on the Regional Council and the Legislative Council in the 1980s, thus regaining some political power. By implication the Basic Law guaranteed a degree of political power to the *Heung Yee Kuk* under article 40 where it is stated that, "The lawful traditional rights and interests of the indigenous inhabitants of the 'New Territories' shall be protected by the Hong Kong Special Administrative Region." (See Basic Law; Legislative Council; New Territories; Regional Council.)

HIGH COURT. See Legal System.

HO KAI, DR. (1857–1914). Sir Kai Ho Kai was the first Chinese to qualify in medicine in Hong Kong. He was admitted as a barrister in the Supreme Court and became the third Chinese member to serve on the Legislative Council. He served on the Legislative Council for 24 years, founded the Hong Kong College of Medicine, and helped to found the University of Hong Kong in 1912. He was closely associated with the reform movement in China and worked with Sun Yat-sen (Sun Yixian) towards the overthrow of the Ch'ing (Qing) dynasty. He is still regarded as one of the most influential Chinese in Hong Kong's history and is highly regarded in the community as a reformer and champion of Chinese rights. (See Ch'ing (Qing) Dynasty; Sun Yat-sen (Sun Yixian); Universities.)

HOKLO. A people from the eastern parts of Kwangtung (Guangdong) province and Fukien (Fujian) province who settled in Hong Kong from the late 17th century, to be found in fishing villages.

HOMOSEXUALITY. In 1901 the Criminal Law Amendment Act of 1885 was adopted in the colony. Its provisions were far harsher than the previous laws relating to homosexuality which had been laid down in 1865. The new law created the offence of gross indecency between males regardless of whether the act was committed in public or private or with the consent of those involved. The law remained in force with amendments under the Offenses Against the Person Ordinance (1981) with punishments that ranged from two years for gross indecency to life imprisonment for acts of sodomy. In 1981 the Law Reform Commission was asked to consider the decriminalization of homosexuality but its recommendation to decriminalize homosexual acts between consenting adults over the age of 21 was largely ignored. Eventually, in 1991, this change in the law was approved.

HONG KONG ACT. The act passed by the British parliament to provide for the change of sovereignty over Hong Kong from 1 July 1997. (See Joint Declaration; Parliament, British.)

HONG KONG AND MACAU OFFICE. Two offices in the People's Republic of China bear this title. The first comes under the PRC's State Council and the second is controlled by the PRC's Foreign Ministry. The former was created in 1978 and is the more important. Its role is to report on the economic and political situation in the two territories and report on public opinion; to help to form the policies of the Chinese government on the territories; to look after the affairs of Hong Kong and Macau; and to coordinate with other interested departments in the People's Republic of China. The Hong Kong and Macau office has wielded considerable influence over the future of Hong Kong and Macau. It was instrumental in arranging the details of the Basic Law and since that time has promoted Chinese interests in Hong Kong in the run up to 1997. After the creation of the Special Administrative Region in 1997 the State Council's Hong Kong and Macau office will be a major conduit in relations between the SAR and the central government in Peking (Beijing). (See New China News Agency.)

HONG KONG GENERAL CHAMBER OF COMMERCE. An industrial and trade association founded in 1861. Its main functions were to promote trade and to attract investment from abroad. It expanded massively in the postwar period and had a membership of over 2,700 companies in 1990. In 1985 its importance was recognized by the granting to the association of one seat on the Legislative Council as a functional constituency. (See Functional Constituencies; Legislative Council.)

HONG KONG OBSERVERS. The Hong Kong Observers were a powerful and influential pressure group set up in 1975 to promote change in Hong Kong's political system. They were highly critical of what they saw as a patronizing central government. The membership was overwhelmingly Chinese, middle class, and university educated. They were particularly active in the late 1970s and early 1980s, but were overtaken by the creation of larger political groups in the late 1980s. (See Pressure Groups.)

HONG KONG PERMANENT RESIDENT. A term introduced in 1987 as a consequence of the Joint Declaration of 1984. It defined who was a Hong Kong citizen by stating the right of abode. The status of permanent resident and nonpermanent resident was further elucidated in the Basic Law in Articles 24–26.

HONG KONG SPECIAL ADMINISTRATIVE REGION. Under the provisions of the Joint Declaration it was agreed that from midnight on 30 June 1997 Hong Kong would cease to be a British Colony and would become a Special Administrative Region (SAR) under the sovereignty of the PRC. The Declaration allowed for a high degree of autonomy for the SAR which was to last for at least 50 years. The detailed political, economic, and cultural details relating to the proposed SAR were to be found in the Basic Law promulgated in April 1990. (See Autonomy; Basic Law; Joint Declaration.)

HONGKONG AND SHANGHAI BANKING CORPO-RATION. Founded in 1864 and incorporated some two years later the Hongkong and Shanghai Bank has always been the most prominent bank in the colony. It was the banker for the government, one of the two note-issuing banks, and in nearly all respects the central bank for the colony. Its Chairperson has been a member of the Executive Council since the end of the Second World War. Its influence is waning as 1997 approaches, and it has in the last few years deliberately reduced its reliance on the territory by various means. The Bank of China, a PRC-controlled bank, may well challenge the preeminence of the HKSBC in the coming years. (See Banks; Currency.)

HOUSE OF COMMONS. The House of Commons is part of the British Parliament. Parliament is bicameral with the House of Lords making up the second part. Of the two houses the Commons is by far the most powerful. Its membership is 651 and is directly elected from geographical constituencies on a universal adult franchise. It traditionally performs the functions of providing the majority of the executive (including the prime minister), and is the guardian against the abuse of executive power. It also has the power to scrutinize, change or reject legislation, and it is normally seen as enhancing the legitimacy of the government. Since the Second World War the House of Commons has rarely interfered in the autonomy of Hong Kong to run its own affairs. It has debated issues, passed necessary legislation pertaining to the colony, and has received annual reports on the state of the territory. (See Anglo-Chinese Parliamentary Group; Constitution; Foreign Affairs Committee; Government, British; Parliament, British.)

HOUSE OF LORDS. The House of Lords is the second and weaker chamber in the British Parliament. Its powers were curtailed in the 20th century by a series of acts (e.g. 1911 and 1948). It has always been a nonelected chamber made up of hereditary peers and, since 1958, life peerages. It again debates issues relating to Hong Kong and plays a formal though not influential role in passing legislation relating to the territory. (See Government, British; House of Commons; Parliament, British.)

HOUSING. Until the postwar period all housing in the colony was private and subject only to controls relating to health and sanitation. Even in this area the controls were fairly lax. However, with the major growth in the population after the Second World War a huge number of squatter areas grew up in the colony. Much of the housing stock was also of poor quality without running water, electricity, proper cooking facilities, or sanitation. In 1953 it was estimated that 13% of the population lived in these squatter areas. In that year a major fire broke out in the Shek Kip Mei squatter settlement which left over 58,000 people homeless. The government intervened and a program was announced to provide basic public housing for the poorer sections of the community. The public housing schemes proved successful and by 1963 over 620,000 people were living in public housing. A Housing Board was set up in 1965 which set the number of apartments to be built and established improved standards for their construction. Since that time the number of public housing units has been increased both in quantity and quality. However, by American or British standards the size allowance of 3.3 sq. meters per adult might seem meager. Rental costs have averaged about 7% of family income on rent which indicates a high degree of subsidy from an avowedly "noninterventionist" government. In 1990 nearly 3 million people out of a total population of 5.8 million lived in public housing. (See Chadwick Report; Health; MacLehose, Sir Murray.)

HSU CHIA-T'UN (XU JIATUN). Hsu Chia-t'un (Xu Jiatun) was the director of the New China News Agency, Peking's (Beijing's) *de facto* embassy in Hong Kong from July 1983 till February 1990. He was previously the Party First Secretary in the Province of Chiang Su (Jiangsu). As director, he was far more inclined to make political statements than his predecessors. For example, as early as November 1985 he accused the Hong Kong Government of breaching the Joint Declaration, an accusation that was quickly retracted following a protest from the Governor. Under his leadership, the New China News Agency increased both in size and importance.

He defected to the United States of America after his retirement in February 1990. He was replaced by Chou Nan (Zhou Nan), previously the Vice Minister in the Foreign Ministry of the Central People's Government. (See New China News Agency.)

HUMAN RIGHTS. See Bill of Rights.

HUNGRY GHOSTS FESTIVAL. An annual festival (Fifth Lunar Month) of long standing in Hong Kong where an attempt is made to placate ghosts who have become dispossessed and could be dangerous on earth. At this time the gates of the underworld are opened and ghosts are free to wander at will. Large numbers of Hong Kong people burn offerings, such as paper money, for use in the underworld.

-I-

ILLEGAL IMMIGRANTS. A term used to refer to persons who entered Hong Kong illegally by sea or by land.

Although the vast majority came from the People's Republic of China, others arrived from other politically turbulent parts of South East Asia. Prior to 1949 there was free immigration into the colony from the mainland (with exceptions such as those who had been deported from the territory). However, this policy was revised as the numbers increased rapidly at the same time as relationships between the governments of the United Kingdom and the People's Republic of China deteriorated badly.

This did not stop large numbers of Chinese, particularly Cantonese, from attempting to enter the colony illegally. The numbers increased dramatically during the Cultural Revolution in the late 1960s, and even in the 1970s the number entering the colony illegally was estimated at 20,000 per year. The "touch base" policy (also called the "reached base" policy) at the time meant that if the illegal immigrants could reach an urban area they were permitted to stay, but if apprehended in the rural areas they were deported.

For Hong Kong the major advantage was an influx of cheap and unorganized labor for the emerging manufacturing industry. The major disadvantages were the strain on the health system, education, social services, and housing. In the period 1979–1980 a surge of 100,000 was experienced with a peak of over 450 a day. In response, the Hong Kong government, in concert with the authorities in the People's Republic of China, came to an agreement ending the "touch base policy."

All existing illegal immigrants in the territory were required to register within a three-day period for an identity card which it would be compulsory to carry on the person. Since that time any person without an identity card (or, in the case of a visitor, a passport) has been liable for deportation. Despite this policy, substantial numbers of illegal immigrants still enter the territory to work on construction sites, and in small manufacturing firms.

Finally, with the arrival of the Vietnamese people the term "illegal immigrant" was extended to cover those who were not defined as genuine political refugees. In particular, a distinction was drawn between those who were seen as genuine political refugees and those who were perceived to be merely economic migrants. The latter group were classified as illegal immigrants. This policy of screening all Vietnamese was formally adopted by the Hong Kong government in June 1988. (See Economic System; Immigration Ordinance; Reached Base Policy; Snake Heads; Vietnamese Refugees.)

IMMIGRATION ORDINANCE. Immigration control in Hong Kong was not applied until 1923 when all persons entering the colony were required to have travel documents. Non-British were also required to have visas. The major exception were people deemed to be of Chinese race, upon whom no restrictions were placed. However, in 1949, with the imminent success of the communists on the mainland and the huge upsurge of immigration into the territory, legal controls were placed upon Chinese entering Hong Kong. These controls were followed by the issuing of entry permits in 1950 which applied to all those of Chinese race, with the minor exception of a few groups in Kwangtung (Guangdong) province. Essentially this situation has remained with a few additions relating to restrictions on Commonwealth citizens which were introduced in September 1969. (See Illegal Immigration.)

INDEPENDENT COMMISSION AGAINST CORRUPTION (ICAC). The Independent Commission Against Corruption, commonly referred to in Hong Kong as the ICAC, was established in the territory in 1974 to counter widespread corruption in the public domain. Although laws against corruption had been in existence as early as 1898 they were increasingly felt to be ineffectually administered. New ordinances, particularly the 1948

Anti-Corruption Ordinance, did little to improve the deteriorating situation. The Advisory Committee on Corruption was established in 1958 and recommended in 1961 that an independent group be set up to deal with corruption. Its recommendations, however, were opposed by the Commissioner of Police and not acted upon.

In 1973 a major corruption scandal involving a high-ranking police officer (see Godber Affair) led to an inquiry, and the production of the Blair-Kerr Reports. This strongly recommended the establishment of an independent group to tackle corruption. The Governor, Sir Murray MacLehose, endorsed the Reports and the Independent Commission Against Corruption was set up in 1974. It was given wide powers to deal with corruption with policing, consultative, and educational functions within its brief. In its policing role it was extremely active concentrating initially on the Royal Hong Kong Police Force. In 1977 it prosecuted 121 members of the police force, 20 from other parts of the public sector and 96 from the private sector. As a body it gained increasing support from the public and was successful in reducing the incidence of corruption in the territory. There are no indications that the ICAC will cease to operate after Hong Kong returns to Chinese administration. (See Advisory Committee on Corruption; Blair-Kerr Reports; Godber Affair; MacLehose, Sir Murray; Royal Hong Kong Police Force.)

INDEPENDENT MONITORING TEAM (IMT). The Independent Monitoring Team (IMT) was set up in 1984 by the Secretary of State for Foreign Affairs to monitor the work of the Assessment Office. This was established in the same year to test public opinion on the proposed Joint Declaration on the future of Hong Kong up to and beyond 1997. The IMT was to ensure that the Assessment Office discharged its duties impartially and within its terms of reference. Its report largely endorsed the methods and findings of the Assessment Office. (See Assessment Office; Joint Declaration.)

INDIRECT ELECTIONS. Indirect elections to the Legislative Council were introduced in 1985, whereby a series of electoral colleges were formed from District Boards and Municipal Councils. These returned 12 members to the 56 member Legislative Council. Under the Basic Law, there is provision for the indirect election of the Chief Executive by an electoral college after the handover of the territory. Also, in the first Special Administrative Region Legislative Council there will be 10 members out of a total of 60 elected indirectly by an election committee. The indirectly-elected members will be reduced to six in the second term and phased out completely in the third term. (See Basic Law; Functional Constituencies; Legislative Council.)

INFORMATION SERVICES DEPARTMENT. See GIS.

INSTRUMENT OF SURRENDER. The document signed on 16 September 1945 which formally declared that Japan surrendered to British Forces. The document simply stated: "We, Major General Umekichi Okada and Vice Admiral Huitaro Fujita, in virtue of the unconditional surrender to the Allied Powers of all Japanese Armed Forces and all forces under Japanese control wherever situated, as proclaimed in Article Two of the Instrument of Surrender signed in Tokio [sic] Bay on 2nd September 1945, on behalf of the Emperor of Japan and the Japanese Imperial Headquarters, do hereby unconditionally surrender ourselves and all forces under our control to Rear Admiral Cecil Halliday Jepson Harcourt, C.B., C.B.E., and undertake to carry out all such instructions as may be given by him or under his authority, and to issue all necessary orders for the purpose of giving effect to all his instructions.

"Given under our hands this 16th day of September, 1945, at Government House, Hong Kong." (See Second World War.)

INTEREST GROUPS. See Pressure Groups.

INTERNATIONAL COVENANT ON CIVIL AND POLITICAL RIGHTS. The International Covenant of Civil and Political Rights (ICCPR) was adopted by the United Nations in 1966, thus codifying in treaty form the Universal Declaration of Human Rights which was first issued in 1948. Britain was a signatory to the ICCPR except for the protocol issued in 1976. However, with respect to Hong Kong, the United Kingdom ratified the ICCPR with certain reservations. These will remain until the 1997 handover, and relate to such matters as free elections to the elected legislature and executive, the question of self-determination, right of abode, nationality, legislation, deportation of aliens, and mixing of juveniles and adults in prisons. In April 1990 the Basic Law stated that the provisions of the ICCPR "as applied to Hong Kong will remain in force and shall be implemented through the laws of the Hong Kong Special Administrative Region" (Article 39). It is widely presumed that the British reservations will continue to apply to the SAR. (See Basic Law; Bill of Rights; International Covenant on Economic, Social and Cultural Rights.)

INTERNATIONAL COVENANT ON ECONOMIC, SOCIAL AND CULTURAL RIGHTS. The International Covenant on Economic, Social and Cultural Rights was the second covenant relating to human rights which was ratified by Britain on May 17, 1976. By virtue of Britain's signature they applied to Hong Kong also until

1997. However, as in the case of the International Covenant on Civil and Political Rights (ICCPR) there were reservations pertaining to Hong Kong and other dependent territories. In particular Britain had reservations relating to equal pay for men and women, the right of trade unions to form confederations and precluding the imposition of restrictions, based on place of birth or residence qualifications, on taking employment in any particular region or territory. The Basic Law stipulated in Article 39 that as in the case of the ICCPR, the provisions would remain in force after 1 July 1997. (See Basic Law; Bill of Rights; International Covenant on Civil and Political Rights.)

INTERNATIONAL LABOR ORGANIZATION (ILO). The International Labor Organization (ILO) was first established in 1919 and was affiliated to the United Nations in 1946. Although Hong Kong was not a member, Britain made declarations on behalf of the territory. By 1990 Hong Kong had recognized 29 of the total 169 ILO conventions and a further 18 with reservations. Those reservations applied to such areas as equal pay for men and women, unemployment benefits, and contracts of employment. Under the Basic Law the future Special Administrative Region (SAR) will be permitted to abide by the provisions of the ILO although the document makes no mention of any separate membership for the SAR. (See Basic Law).

-J-

JAPAN. Japan's significance for Hong Kong increased substantially with its invasion of the colony in December 1941. The build-up to this event can be traced first to the outbreak of the undeclared war between Japan and China in July 1937. The Japanese quickly took Peking (Beijing), Tientsin (Tianjin), Shanghai, and Nanking (Nanjing) and in October 1938 Canton (Guangzhou) also fell to the Japanese. Britain's position on the war was one of sympathy with the Chinese while not overtly alienating the Japanese. This position did not change with the outbreak of war in Europe in September 1939. However, on December 8th shortly after the Japanese attack on Pearl Harbor, Japanese troops, which had massed on the borders of Hong Kong, attacked in strength against an ill-prepared British defence. The British resistance to the Japanese lasted only two weeks with the British surrendering on 25 December 1941. The Japanese occupation of Hong Kong lasted until 14 August 1945 and the formal surrender took place on 16 September 1945.

During this period the colony came under direct Japanese military rule under the title of, "The Captured Territory of Hong Kong." Lt. General Rensuke Isogai was appointed as Governor. The period of occupation saw a huge reduction in the population from 1,600,000 just before the invasion to under 600,000 by the end of the war.

In the post-Second World War era Hong Kong's relations with Japan have been on a more friendly footing. Trade between the two increased rapidly as they both underwent their individual economic "miracles." By 1970 Japan was the number one exporter to Hong Kong, exceeding both China and the United States of America. In 1990 China again overtook Japan. Japan was the fourth most important destination for Hong Kong's exports after the United States of America, the United Kingdom and the Federal Republic of Germany. Japan has also become a major investor in the territory. Although it is difficult to obtain precise figures of current investment in the territory it is thought that Japan has overtaken the United States of America. (See Second World War; Trade.)

JARDINE MATHESON AND COMPANY. A famous company which was founded in Canton (Guangzhou), acting in its early years both as an agent and a private trader. The company was established by William Jardine (1785–1843) and James Matheson (1796–1878) in 1832. Initially, Jardines were heavily involved in the opium trade, but the company gradually expanded into trading and commerce. The company has retained a major role in the economic affairs of the territory.

JOINT DECLARATION. The term often used to refer to the agreements between Britain and the People's Republic of China over the future of Hong Kong. The full title of the Government White Paper containing the Joint Declaration is: "A Draft Agreement between the Government of the United Kingdom of Great Britain and Northern Ireland and the Government of the People's Republic of China on the Future of Hong Kong." The agreement was initialled on 26 September 1984, and formally signed by the British Prime Minister Mrs. Margaret Thatcher and the Chinese Prime Minister Chao Tzu-yang (Zhao Ziyang) on 19 December 1984. It was published in two languages, namely Chinese and English.

The English version was a lengthy document which was divided into six major sections. It began with an introduction from the British perspective and then moved into a text of the Declaration itself. There were three annexes: an elaboration by the People's Republic of China on its basic policies towards Hong Kong; details of the setting up of a Sino-British Joint Liaison Group; and details of land leases. It then proceeded to the Exchange of Memoranda with a British memorandum and a Chinese memorandum. The final part dealt with the British Government's explanatory notes. The provisions of the agreement were as follows.

1. On July 1, 1997 Hong Kong would become a Special Administrative Region (SAR) of the People's Republic of China.
2. The SAR would be directly under the ultimate authority of the Central Government of the People's Republic of China. At the same time a high degree of autonomy would be granted to the SAR except in the fields of defence and most areas of foreign policy.
3. The SAR would have its own government and retain its existing laws.
4. Local people would govern Hong Kong but foreigners would be allowed to continue in government service in all but the most senior positions.
5. The socioeconomic system would be allowed to continue and basic freedoms were to be guaranteed.
6. Hong Kong would be institutionally and economically independent of China.
7. The autonomy of the SAR would be allowed in cultural, economic and other areas, and it would, in its relations with other states, be referred to as "Hong Kong, China."
8. Public order would remain the responsibility of the SAR and not the central government of the People's Republic of China.
9. All the agreements mentioned above would be included in a Basic Law which would be passed by the National People's Congress and which would guarantee the Hong Kong way of life for fifty years after 1997. (See Basic Law.)

JOINT LIAISON GROUP (JLG). The Joint Liaison Group (JLG) was set up in 1985 as a result of the Joint Declaration. It was to oversee the transition from British to Chinese control, and is to cease to exist in the year 2000. It met alternatively in Peking (Beijing) and London until 1988, when it became substantively based in Hong Kong. However, it has continued to meet occasionally in the two capital cities. Although it has no clearly specified powers, it has discussed a range of key issues, such as constitutional reform and the developing of a new airport in the territory. Its membership was drawn from the respective foreign ministries. Its terms of reference were:

1. To conduct consultations on the implementation of the Joint Declaration.
2. To discuss matters relating to the smooth transfer of government up to 1997.
3. To exchange information and consult on certain matters. (See Foreign and Commonwealth Office; Foreign Relations.)

JOINT VENTURES. With the adoption of the "Four Modernizations" as official policy in the People's Republic of China in the late 1970s, there was provision for the establishment of Joint Ventures with foreign firms wishing to set up businesses on the mainland. Hong Kong companies have been heavily involved in these ventures. (See Economy; Four Modernizations; Trade.)

JOURNALISM. See Mass Media.

JUDICIARY. See Legal System.

-K-

***KAIFONG* ASSOCIATIONS.** The *Kaifong* associations, literally meaning people of the same street, were a traditional form of self-administration, especially in the old market towns. New associations were encouraged by the Hong Kong government after the Second World War. The government's enthusiasm can be best understood in the context of the rapidly growing population which increased from about half a million in 1945 to 1.6 million by the end of 1946 and nearly 2.4 million by 1950. The idea was to encourage a degree of local self-help princi- pally to reduce the demand on central government. The *Kaifongs* were encouraged to become responsible for such areas as recreation, education, local welfare, the resolution of family disputes and keeping the central government in touch with local needs. They were pro- vided with small budgets. Their potential success rested on the ability of traditional Chinese society to operate at a neighborhood level. However, from the early 1970s the importance of the *Kaifongs* has dwindled in response to social change, the introduction of new levels of government, and the extension of government interven- tion associated with rapid economic growth. (See District Administration; Political System.)

KENNEDY, SIR ARTHUR (1810–1883). Governor of Hong Kong from 1872 until 1877. He was particularly concerned with the state of law and order in the colony and encouraged the use of Chinese recruits into the police force. He also increased the extent of public works such as constructing reservoirs and new hospitals. He encouraged a grant in aid system whereby voluntary schools received financial support. He also made some changes in central government administration by strengthening the powers of the Legislative Council in areas of debate and financial control, increasing the membership of the Executive Council to five, and establishing the practice of having the Colonial Secretary as Acting Governor in the absence of the Governor himself. He failed to redress the problem of the blockade and did little to ameliorate the appalling sanitary conditions of the colony. (See Colonial Secretary; Education; Executive Council; Governor; Health; Legislative Council.)

KOREAN WAR. The Korean War lasted from June 25, 1950 to June 26, 1953. The United Nations, under the leadership of the United States, sent forces to repel an invasion of South Korea by North Korea. When United Nations forces pushed back the invading forces they moved into North Korea, and even advanced towards the border with the People's Republic of China. Chinese "volunteers" then crossed over into North Korea on October 26, 1950 and pushed back the United Nations forces almost to the border that had existed before the war.

The effect of the Korean War upon the economy of Hong Kong was quite dramatic. In the early part of the war, and before the Chinese military intervention, Hong Kong had supplied Peking (Beijing) with war-related materials such as petrochemical supplies, rubber, machinery and electrical appliances. However, with the imposition of the American embargo on all Chinese goods in the December of 1950 and a United Nations embargo in 1951, Hong Kong's traditional role of entrepôt almost collapsed. At the same time the United States, now no longer receiving any textiles from China, found new supplies from a Hong Kong textile industry expanding with the influx of entrepreneurs and cheap labor from China. In this sense the war acted as a major catalyst for economic restructuring and growth in the colony. (See Economic System; Trade).

KOWLOON PENINSULA. Part of China which, along with Stonecutters Island, was ceded to Britain in perpetuity by the Treaty of Peking (Beijing) in 1860. The Treaty extended the colony as far as what is now known as

Boundary Street. (See Convention of Peking (Beijing); Stonecutters Island.)

KOWLOON WALLED CITY. The Kowloon Walled City existed from the Sung (Song) (960–1279) and under both the Ming (Ming) (1368–1644) and Ch'ing (Qing) (1644–1912) dynasties. It had grown quite significantly during the period 1841–1898 in response to its proximity to the British colony which at that time covered Hong Kong Island, the Kowloon Peninsula, and Stonecutters Island. In 1898, when the Chinese government ceded the New Territories to Britain it was agreed that the Kowloon Walled City would remain under Chinese administration. However in 1899, after skirmishes with Chinese armed troops protesting against the establishing of British administration in the New Territories, Kowloon Walled City was occupied by British troops. The city was then declared to be no longer under Chinese jurisdiction. From that point the British government consistently rejected continual Chinese claims for jurisdiction both under the period of the Nationalist government and later that of the People's Republic of China. Britain, while having formal authority over the Walled City, was careful not to assert it too obviously. In 1947 there were riots in Walled City following British attempts to administer the area more actively. Further objections to any similar moves occurred in 1963, 1973–1975, and 1983. The problem was eventually solved in 1987 when the British and Chinese authorities agreed to clear the Walled City for development into a public park. (See Convention of Peking (Beijing); New Territories.)

KOWLOON-CANTON RAILWAY. The Kowloon-Canton Railway (KCR) was completed in 1911. It runs from the eastern side of New Territories, to the border with China at Lowu, and on to Canton (Guangzhou).

After 1949, passengers moving into the People's Republic of China would have to get off the train at Lowu and walk across into the PRC. This practice was discontinued with the easing of relations between governments of Britain and the PRC after the introduction of the Four Modernizations. The increase in passenger traffic both to the rapidly developing New Territories and to the mainland itself, combined with the huge increase in the movement of goods between Southern China and Hong Kong, led to the need to modernize the rail connection. With the electrification of the line and the construction of double tracking, this was achieved in Hong Kong by 1983. In consequence the average number of passengers using the KCR increased from 53,000 per day in 1980 to 422,000 in 1988. Inbound freight did not show a huge increase in the period 1980–1988, but exports to China via the KCR during this same period increased from 6,762 tons to 484,152.

KUOMINTANG (GUOMINDANG). The Kuomintang (Guomindang) (KMT) party rose to significance after the downfall of the imperial dynasty in 1912, and competed for power in the Republic of China. Its modern form is usually seen as arising from the leadership of Dr. Sun Yat-sen (Sun Yixian), the father of modern Chinese republicanism. After an uneasy spell of cooperation with the Chinese Communists where they combined to restore order in the war-ridden republic by the launching of the Northern Expedition, the KMT turned on the Communists in 1927 and attempted to liquidate them. General Chiang Kai-shek (Jiang Jieshi) who had led the military expedition, and who represented the right wing of the party emerged as the leader of the whole party. In 1949, after a prolonged civil war, the KMT was ousted from the mainland by the Communists under the leadership of Mao Tse-tung (Mao Zedong). It fled to Taiwan where it established a dominance over the island's politics, which still persists.

Relations between the KMT and Hong Kong were uneasy for long periods. The strains showed over trade relations in the 1920s, over the jurisdiction of the Walled City (1934), and over the attempts by the KMT to acquire the colony from Britain at the end of the Second World War. After 1949 many KMT supporters fled to Hong Kong. There were riots between the supporters of the Communists and the KMT in 1956, and many supporters most notably in the New Territories still fly the Nationalist flag on certain days. (See Chiang Kai-shek (Jiang Jieshi); China, People's Republic of; China, Republic of; Disturbances; General Strike; Kowloon Walled City; Sun Yat-sen (Sun Yixian); Taiwan.)

KWANGTUNG (GUANGDONG) PROVINCE. The province of the People's Republic of China of which Hong Kong is technically a part. The capital of the province is the historically important trading city of Canton (Guangzhou).

The links between Kwangtung (Guangdong) and Hong Kong are extremely powerful. It was the trade with the province and the wider area of southern China that led the British to acquire Hong Kong as a colony in 1843 as a secure base to conduct business. Immigration from China into the colony was overwhelmingly from the province. This has led to strong cultural links and to the adoption of Cantonese rather than Mandarin as the common spoken language. Links with Kwangtung (Guangdong) became even more compelling with the introduction of a Special Economic Zone in Sham Chun (Shenzhen), adjacent to Hong Kong. Set up in 1980, along with Chu Hai (Zhuhai), it attracted large amounts of Hong Kong investment particularly in the manufacturing sector.

The Basic Law places Hong Kong under the direct authority of the Central People's Republic after 1997, rather than the authority of the Kwangtung (Guangdong) government. However, functional cooperation between Hong Kong and Kwangtung (Guangdong) increased greatly in the 1980s particularly in matters of trade and commerce. (See Basic Law; Illegal Immigration; Sham Chun (Shenzhen); Trade.)

-L-

LAISSEZ-FAIRE. Hong Kong has for the greater part of its history been wedded to the concept of *laissez-faire*. This was the predictable corollary of the colony's dependence upon trade as an entrepôt until the late 1940s, and the later development of an economy which was dependent upon both trade and the exporting of its goods. The belief that, as far as possible, economic activity should be free from government interference or regulation has led to the status of the colony as a free port, to minimal government interference in the economy and to an aggressive stance against protectionism in the international community. In the postwar period, however, the pure concept of *laissez-faire* has been eroded insofar as the Hong Kong government has intervened in the economy more actively with vast increases in spending on public housing, hospitals, education, social services, and infrastructural development. (See Economic System; Trade.)

LAME DUCK. Originally a term used in U.S. politics to describe the declining influence and power of an American President during the last year or so of that final term of person's office. Mistakenly used in the period after the signing of the Joint Declaration in 1984 to describe the declining powers of the Hong Kong government. The implication is that the increasing powers of the

People's Republic of China over the affairs of the territory during the transitional period up to 1997 has led to a decline in the legitimacy of the territory's government. (See Basic Law; Joint Declaration.)

LAND LEASES. Since the founding of the colony all land has been owned by the government. One consequence of this was that the government could obtain valuable revenue by releasing land for sale under lease. In 1843 leases were granted for a maximum of 75 years. This period was extended to 999 years in December 1848, but that decision was rescinded in May 1898 reverting back to the old 75 years with a concession that they were renewable for one more term.

In the New Territories, ceded to Britain by China in 1898, all land became Crown land, but the inhabitants who were farming land there were immediately given a leasehold title to the land they occupied. Under the Convention of Peking (Beijing), it was established that land in the New Territories could not be leased for longer than 99 years *in toto*. From that time onwards Crown leases, that is land owned by the government, have been sold for any period until 28 June 1997, three days before the New Territories revert back to Chinese sovereignty.

Under the provisions of the Joint Declaration of 1984 it was agreed that leases in any part of Hong Kong could straddle 1997 and cover any period up to, but not beyond the year 2047. These conditions were repeated in the Basic Law for Hong Kong which comes into force on July 1, 1997. (See Joint Declaration.)

LANGUAGE. See Official Language Issue.

LEASEBACK. Leaseback was one of the options considered by the British in the early stages of the negotiations about the future of Hong Kong after 1997. This option, which was favored by the British negotiators, envisaged that

Hong Kong would be returned to the sovereignty of the People's Republic of China, but in return the Chinese authorities would allow the British to administer the territory for an agreed fixed term. The idea was quickly rejected by the Chinese government and the idea was dropped. (See Sino-British Negotiations.)

LEE CHU-MING, MARTIN. Mr. Martin Lee, a successful lawyer, rose to prominence in the 1980s as the most outspoken champion of the liberal position in the territory. He has been a member of the Legislative Council since 1985, initially representing the Legal functional constituency, but later as a directly elected representative. Mr. Lee campaigned heavily for the widest possible franchise for the territory, and for a Bill of Rights for Hong Kong. He was for a time a member of the Basic Law Drafting Committee, but his criticism of the Communist Party of China, particularly during the disturbances in the People's Republic of China in May and June 1989, led him to be expelled from the Basic Law Drafting Committee in July 1989. He was instrumental in forming the United Democrats of Hong Kong political party in 1990. (See Basic Law; Bill of Rights; Functional Constituencies.)

LEE PENG-FEI, ALLEN (1940–   ). Lee Peng-fei became the senior member of the Legislative Council in 1988. A successful businessperson, he first became a member of the legislature in 1978 and was made a member of the Executive Council in 1985. Mr. Lee was active during the drafting of the Basic Law. In the earlier stages, he was clearly in favor of limited representational reforms. After the events in Peking (Beijing) in May and June 1989 he tried to develop a consensus among OMELCO members attempting to bring together the more conservative proposals. However, the OMELCO document was rejected by the Chinese authorities. (See Basic Law; Executive Council; Legislative Council; OMELCO.)

LEGAL REPUGNANCY. Prior to Britain's assuming control over the territory the legal system was based on Chinese law, and questions soon arose over the degree to which traditional laws would be allowed to pertain in the colony. The general rule laid down in 1843 was that the "laws and customs of China should supersede those of England" except where the Chinese law was in conflict with the "immutable principles of morality which Christians must regard as binding on themselves in all places and at all times."

Until 1986 Ordinances passed by the Legislative Council which were repugnant to the Acts of Parliament, and specifically applicable to Hong Kong, were null and void to the extent of their repugnancy. However, under the Hong Kong Act (1985) the Legislative Council is given the power to amend or repeal any Act of Parliament so far as it was applicable to Hong Kong. (See Colonial Laws Validity Act; Legal System.)

LEGAL SYSTEM. There are several historical sources of Hong Kong law. The Treaty of Nanking (Nanjing), the Hong Kong Charter, and the subsequent Letters Patent and Royal Instructions form one major source. Another is to be found in constitutional and legal conventions, and a third in English and Hong Kong common law. Finally, there are traces of customary law from Ch'ing (Qing) China, although this is usually overridden if it contradicts British law. Formally, all Hong Kong law was subordinate to British law. British Parliamentary law was superior to any laws passed in the colony and could hence overrule any ordinances passed by the Legislative Council. Equally the British Crown could enact any laws which would apply to the colony irrespective of whether the territory objected or not (although this has occurred only rarely on domestic matters).

Institutionally the most important legislative agencies for Hong Kong were the Crown, the British Parliament and the Hong Kong legislature. In practice, however, the Executive Council was of great significance in identifying areas where legal changes were required, and the Legislative Council has been important in approving proposals for change. Also significant have been the Legal Department of the Civil Service, together with the enforcement agencies of the Royal Hong Kong Police, the Correctional Services Department, and the Independent Commission against Corruption.

The judicial system has a clear hierarchy, being headed by the Chief Justice, followed by Justices of Appeal, Deputy Judges and District Court Judges. The vast majority of cases were heard by Magistrates. The Final Court of Appeal lies not in Hong Kong but in London with the British Judicial Committee of the Privy Council.

The basis of the system operates on the assumption of the independence of the judiciary from the other branches of government. It also assumes traditional principles such as: the equality of the individual in the face of the law; limited government; the absence of any arbitrary law; the public nature of the law; consistency; predictability of outcome of the process; no retroactive measures; the protection of the rights of the citizens; and a law which is understood by its citizens.

From its inception the law was conducted largely through the medium of English rather than Chinese. All ordinances, legal opinions, and legal documentation were written in English. In the higher courts all cases are held in English, although this is occasionally relaxed in the magistrates court.

The return of sovereignty to the PRC will bring several changes. The major constitutional document will be the

Basic Law which sets out the revised basis of the legal system as follows:

1. Article 80 stated that the courts of the Hong Kong Special Administrative Region at all levels should be the judiciary of the region, exercising the judicial power of the Region;
2. Articles 81 and 82 established a set of legal institutions, mostly similar to those under British administration. They also confirmed that the existing judicial system should be maintained. It also, however, established a Court of Final Appeal in Hong Kong with final powers of adjudication;
3. Articles 81 to 87 prescribed the powers of the courts by law, established common law jurisdiction, judicial independence and trial by jury as practiced previously in Hong Kong; and,
4. Articles 87 to 93 established the right to a fair trial and to be presumed innocent, established rules to safeguard the independence of the Judiciary, and established that the Chief Justice of the Court of Final Appeal and the High Court had to be Chinese Citizens.

The major concern expressed in Hong Kong after the promulgation of the Basic Law was that the authorities on the mainland would have the power, if they so wished, to abrogate the Basic Law. There were also concerns about potential grey areas surrounding the extent of the Final Court of Appeal's jurisdiction. (See Basic Law; Chief Justice; Constitution; Letters Patent; Nanking (Nanjing), Treaty of; Parliament, British; Royal Instructions.)

LEGISLATIVE COUNCIL. The first Legislative Council (LEGCO) was established in January 1844 with an original membership of three as stipulated in the Hong

Kong Charter. Under that document the Governor was to make laws for peace, good order, and good government on the advice of the Legislative Council. The powers of the body were to include the administration of civil law, police and prisons, land and its transfer, and the authority to levy taxes. The legislative body would be nonelected, small, and appointed by the Governor, but with the powers of confirmation resting in the United Kingdom. It remained nonelective until the 1980s. Until 1880 it was also composed exclusively of non-Chinese. It has generally been supportive of the Governors, and for the most part noninterventionist.

The size and the composition of the Council have changed considerably over the years as can be seen from the accompanying table. After the early years when the Council was very small indeed, more government officials were included as well as increasing numbers of appointees from outside the government who were included principally as representatives of business interests.

| | | Officials | | | Unofficials | | | Total |
| | | ex- | | | Elected | | | |
	Gov.	officio	Other	Appt'd	FC	EC	DE	
1843	1	3(2)[a]	0	0	0	0	0	4(3)
1844	1	4	0	0	0	0	0	5
1845	1	3	0	0	0	0	0	4
1850	1	3	0	2[b]	0	0	0	6
1857	1	3	2	3	0	0	0	9
1858	1	3	3	3	0	0	0	10
1865	1	5	1	3	0	0	0	10
1884	1	5	1	5[c]	0	0	0	12
1896	1	5	2	6	0	0	0	14
1929	1	5	4	8	0	0	0	18
1946	1	5	4	7	0	0	0	17
1947	1	5	3	7	0	0	0	16
1951	1	5	4	8	0	0	0	18
1964	1	5	7	13	0	0	0	26
1966	1	4	8	13	0	0	0	26
1973	1	4	10	15	0	0	0	30

		Officials ex-			Unofficials Elected			Total
	Gov.	*officio*	Other	Appt'd	FC	EC	DE	
1976	1	4	18(15)[a]	23(22)[a]	0	0	0	46(42)[a]
1977	1	4	20(16)[a]	25(24)[a]	0	0	0	50(45)[a]
1980	1	4	22(18)[a]	27(26)[a]	0	0	0	54(49)[a]
1983	1	4	24(14)[a]	29	0	0	0	58(52)[a]
1984	1	3	25(13)[a]	32(30)[a]	0	0	0	61(49)[a]
1985	1	3	7	22	12	12	0	57
1988	1	3	7	20	14	12	0	57
1991[d]	1	3	0	18	21	0	18	60(61)

FC = functional constituency

EC = electoral college

DE = directly elected

a = the numbers in parentheses ( ) are actual numbers where this differs from possible permitted numbers.

b = a convention was instituted in 1849 whereby one of the appointed Unofficial Members was 'elected' by Hong Kong's unofficial Justices of the Peace. The practice was discontinued in 1973. It never had formal constitutional standing.

c = a convention was instituted in 1883 whereby one of the appointed Unofficial Members was 'elected' by the Hong Kong General Chamber of Commerce. The practice was discontinued in 1973. It never had formal constitutional standing.

d = includes a Deputy President appointed by the Governor to chair the Council in his absence.

The evolution of the Legislative Council speeded up in the post-Second World War period. As can be seen in the figures above the numbers were increased overall and the number of nonofficial members increased, eventually outnumbering the government officials. At the same time, there was a gradual localization of the membership with the ratio of 13 expatriate and four local in 1946 changing to 14 expatriate and 47 locals by 1984. However, there were still no elected members.

This situation changed following the White Paper of 1984, and members were elected for the first time in 1985. The electoral method employed was that of indirect elections with some members being elected by an electoral college made up mainly of members of the

District Boards and other members elected by functional constituencies (e.g., the medical and teaching professions). In the White Paper of 1988 it was announced that from 1991 the composition of the council would for the first time include a directly elected element and at the same time the number of appointed members would be reduced. In their place the numbers returned by functional constituencies which were indirectly elected would be increased. With an expanded Council of 60 members, 50% would now be either directly or indirectly elected.

The Basic Law promulgated in April 1990 stated that after July 1, 1997 the composition of the Legislative Council would be changed yet again. The Chief Executive (the replacement for the Governor) would not sit on the Council, but a President would be elected from among the members. Nonresidents could comprise up to 20% of the membership. The total membership would be 60 with the composition as follows:

	Functional Constituency	Directly Elected	Grand Electoral College	Total
1997	30	20	10	60
1999	30	24	6	60
2003	30	30	0	60

Other significant aspects of the Council dealt with in the Basic Law were as follows:

1. Articles 68 stated that the Legislative Council would be constituted by elections (but not necessarily direct elections) and that the terms of office would be two years for the first term but four years thereafter;
2. Article 71 specified that a President would be elected from among the members of the Council

and that he or she would have to be not less than 40 years old, have resided in Hong Kong for at least 20 years, and be a Chinese citizen and permanent resident of the Special Administrative Region;

3. Article 72 spelled out the powers of the President of the Council;

4. Article 73 specified the powers and functions of the Council. These include the functions of enacting, amending, and repealing laws; examining and approving budgets; taxation and public expenditure; receiving and debating policy addresses by the Chief Executive; scrutinizing government administration; debating issues of public interest; endorsing the appointment and removal of judges; and receiving and handling complaints from the public. It also provided for an investigation of the Chief Executive should he or she be charged with dereliction of duty or a breach of the law. In these circumstances the Council would have powers to summon persons to give testimony; and,

5. Articles 74 to 79 outlined the procedures for introducing bills; the quorum; rules of procedure; how bills become law; immunities for legislators when in session or going to a session; and the circumstances under which a member might lose office (e.g., serious illness, prolonged absence without consent, renunciation of status as permanent resident, acceptance of government appointment or becoming a public servant, bankruptcy, serious criminal offenses, and misbehavior in the Council).

After the promulgation of the Basic Law in April 1990, the Hong Kong government announced that the 1991 Legislative Council would be composed of: the Governor, three *ex officio* officials, 18 appointed unofficials, 18 directly-elected members, and 21 functional constituencies. The Government also announced the creation of the post of Deputy President of the Legislative Council starting in 1991. The Deputy President would normally chair the meetings in all sessions except the Governor's annual address.

LEI CHENG UK TOMB. A tomb discovered in 1955 and believed to be from the Eastern Han (Han) period (A.D. 25–220). Inside the tomb were found 58 bronze and pottery objects. Many of the pottery objects were models of pigsties, wells and stoves used in the period.

LETTERS PATENT. The Letters Patent have their origins in the Hong Kong Charter of April 5, 1843 establishing Hong Kong as a colony. They gave the first Governor, Sir Henry Pottinger, powers to establish, "the Island of Hong Kong into a separate colony and to create a Legislative and Executive Council in the said colony and for granting certain powers and authorities to the Governor for the time being of the said colony." They were, in effect, a public direction from the British monarch to one of his or her servants. Amendments were occasionally made through the 19th century, and a major revision was drawn up in 1917, which provides the basis for the present Letters Patent. They have been frequently amended since that time.

What was significant about the first Letters Patent was the degree of formal power to be vested in the Governor. Although some of this power was whittled away with the changes in the Letters Patent, the original model was still extant in the colony. The Letters Patent also clarified the relationship between the branches of government and between the Hong Kong government and the colonial power in London. The independence of the judiciary was also clearly spelled out in the Letters Patent. The document itself will cease to have any validity at midnight on June 30, 1997 when Hong Kong is handed over to the

People's Republic of China and becomes a Special Administrative Region. (See Basic Law; Constitution; Executive Council; Functional Constituencies; Governor; Joint Declaration; Localization; Political System; Royal Instructions.)

LI HON HING. Li Hon Hing unsuccessfully attempted to assassinate Governor Sir Henry Blake on 4 July 1912. At first it was thought that a connection existed between the act and turmoil across the border in China. However, Mr. Li bore only a personal grudge against the Governor for an earlier altercation when Sir Henry had been Captain Superintendent of the Hong Kong police.

LIN TSE-HSU (ZEXU) (1785–1850). Lin Tse-hsu (Zexu) was appointed the special Imperial Commissioner for the suppression of the opium trade and arrived to take up his office in Canton (Guangzhou) on 10 March 1839. He came prepared for drastic action and only eight days later he ordered not only all opium possessed by foreign merchants to be given up, but also that the British traders sign a bond promising not to import further opium on the pain of death. Europeans were subsequently detained in their factories, until the opium chests were eventually handed over. However, Charles Elliot, the United Kingdom's Superintendent of Trade, refused to accept the use of these agreements and the merchants were evacuated to Macau. Lin then put pressure on the Portuguese government in Macau to expel the British, leading Elliot to withdraw the British community to Hong Kong harbor. With the onset of military action between the British and the Chinese, Lin was made a scapegoat and was scolded by the Emperor. He was dismissed from his post, and exiled to Sinkiang (Xinjiang) in 1841. He died in 1850. (See Anglo-Chinese Wars; Chuanpi (Chuanbi), Convention of; Elliot, Captain Charles; Opium Wars.)

LOCAL GOVERNMENT. Traditionally the British administration in Hong Kong has been highly centralized with little power granted to more local institutions.

In Hong Kong Island and Kowloon there was virtually no effective local government at the district level until well after the Second World War. The administration was based on the functional distribution of work among the specialist services. The main disadvantage of this was that there was little coordination of planning and the particular needs of a local area were often overlooked. However, in 1967, following the disturbances in the colony a City District scheme was set up by the government. Its main purpose was to provide a recognizable "government" representative in each area. Ten City District Officers were created who were required to make themselves accessible to the people in their districts and keep in touch with local organizations. They were to explain government policies, coordinate services, initiate new policies, and receive complaints and representation arising from government activity. However, there was no intention of giving these District Officers any statutory power or authority.

In the New Territories, where the population was much smaller and traditional Chinese practices were much more deeply rooted, a district scheme was adopted from the very beginning. With the lease of 1898 it was seen that the long-settled rural area with its close-knit community was already provided with a number of administrative and social services. Accordingly, the government presence took the form of the district officer and the police officer, and these worked in tandem with the existing structure provided by the traditional *Heung Yee Kuk*. The district officer was concerned mainly with political, administrative, and judicial matters while the Police office was concerned with law and order. In any event, the District Officers shed many of their responsibilities as the New Territories were developed.

In the 1980s as the distinctions between the New Territories and the more urbanized Hong Kong Island and Kowloon became more blurred, a new and unified system for the whole territory was introduced. District Advisory Boards were formally established to advise the central government on local needs. They were not, however, given any fiscal powers and their role was heavily circumscribed.

At the next level of local government were to be the two Municipal Councils: the Urban Council and the Regional Council. The Urban Council had been formed in 1936 with a responsibility for Hong Kong and Kowloon taking over those previously performed by the Sanitary Board. Its role was the provision of municipal services such as street cleaning; refuse collection; environmental hygiene; the provision and running of public sporting facilities; museums; public libraries; and cultural events. The Regional Council was created in 1986 to fulfil similar purposes in the New Territories.

District Boards were established in all 18 districts in 1976 and elections were held for part of their membership from 1982, but real power in most areas continued to lie with the central government. The same overall judgement applied to the Municipal Councils. Under the provisions for the post-1997 period the same basic system of a powerful central government with a weaker set of sublocal government units looks likely to continue. (See District Administration; Heung Yee Kuk; New Territories; Political System; Regional Council; Urban Council.)

LOCALIZATION. For much of the period of British colonial administration the Chinese were largely excluded from key positions in the political and bureaucratic systems. The first Chinese was appointed to the Legislative Council only in 1880. Even in the early part of the twentieth century the percentages of Europeans in the public service were much higher than in other colonies such as Ceylon. For example, although in 1913 there were 175 European police officers, 472 Indians and 576 Chinese, all the top positions were limited to the Europeans and similar patterns were found in all the other public departments. Surprisingly, there was little pressure for change among those Chinese who were appointed to the Legislative Council.

It was not until the 1930s that the pressures began to mount for greater selection of local people for senior positions and for equal pay between people doing similar jobs. (For example, at this time a European doctor working for the Medical Department earned an equivalent of HK$10,266 on first appointment whereas his Chinese equivalent was paid only $4,500.) In 1946 the government adopted a policy of replacing Europeans with Chinese wherever possible. There was, however, little pressure to bring salaries into parity between expatriates and locals, and the impetus faltered as time progressed.

The situation changed gradually until by 1983 there were 394 locals and 484 expatriates in the most senior positions of the bureaucracy (a 55% majority for the expatriates). With the Joint Declaration of 1984 localization accelerated slightly so that by 1989 the ratio in the top posts was 635 locals to 493 expatriates (a local majority of 56.2%). At present rates of change, locals are likely to occupy 85% of these posts by 1997. In addition, the Basic Law guarantees that all posts at Secretary rank and above will be held by Chinese nationals who have lived in Hong Kong for at least 15 years.

At the highest levels of government the Legislative

Council reflected this trend. In the Executive Council, however, the trend was less marked. The figures for the Legislative Council were:

	Expatriates	Locals
1965	16	10
1971	13	13
1975	16	14
1986	9	48

The Basic Law stipulates that expatriates will still be allowed to be members of the Legislative Council, but that the numbers will be limited to no more than 20%.

In the Executive Council there were five locals to 10 expatriates in 1965 which changed to nine locals to six expatriates by 1988. There are likely to be few or no expatriate members of the Executive Council after 1997.

The entry of the local community into the highest levels of the private sector was at first gradual but later rapid. This trend was accelerated by the rapid economic growth of the economy. The multinational companies recruited large numbers of locals, who entered top managerial positions; the old *Hongs* opened their doors to locals; and finally, many indigenous Chinese tycoons made their mark on the economy often replacing, or at least competing with, the old British *Hongs*. (See Basic Law; Emigration; Executive Council; Legislative Council; Royal Hong Kong Police Force.)

LUGARD, SIR FREDERICK (1858–1945). Governor of Hong Kong from 1907 until 1912. His major problem was in controlling the troubles that emanated from the fall of the Ch'ing (Qing) dynasty in China. The revolutionaries had taken control of Kwangtung (Guangdong) province in 1911 and there was agitation for the ending of British rule in the colony. As a consequence, major disturbances broke out with looting, attacks on Europeans, and general violence. Lugard acted promptly by declaring a state of emergency, and giving the police wide powers to deal with the problem. The British garrison was reinforced by two battalions and the situation was rapidly brought under control. In less troubled times he also played a major role in establishing the first university in the colony. The University of Hong Kong was eventually opened in 1912 with the incoming governor, Sir Francis May, becoming its first Chancellor. (See Armed Forces; Ch'ing (Qing) Dynasty; Governors; Universities.)

LUNAR NEW YEAR FESTIVAL. Traditionally the Lunar New Year (the New Moon closest to the Beginning of Spring—February 5th) is the most important festival in the Chinese calendar as it marks the beginning of Spring and the end of Winter. The most important day is New Year's Eve when all the family gather for dinner and symbolic food is eaten, including fish (indicating surplus) and dry oysters (indicating good business). After the reunion dinner there is usually a visit to the flower market to purchase peach and plum trees, which signify good luck. At the Lunar New Year visits are made to temples and *lai see* (lucky money) is given to children and unmarried men and women. The festival lasts for 15 days in total.

-M-

MACDONNELL, SIR RICHARD GRAVES (1814–1879). Governor of Hong Kong from 1866 until 1872 following a twelve-month interval when the colony was administered by the Colonial Secretary. Sir Richard Macdonnell was an active governor who arrived with a brief to investigate problems within the police force and to counter piracy in areas close to Hong Kong. On his arrival, he expanded this brief pursuing major reforms of almost all government departments. Despite widespread opposition, including some members of the Legislative Council, he increased tax revenues both to pay for the new reforms and to regularize public revenue. Returning to his major brief, he took vigorous action against local pirates and successfully reduced police corruption by some necessary dismissals, while also increasing the force's efficiency to combat crime. He also helped establish a long overdue fire service. Gambling was also brought under partial control by a licensing system which had the added benefit of increasing government revenue. Externally he was rather less successful with the Chinese authorities who introduced a blockade upon Hong Kong in 1867 which was to last beyond his departure and only to be finally lifted in 1886. (See Blockade; Governor; Royal Hong Kong Police Force.)

MCKINSEY REPORT. The McKinsey Report, published in 1973 with a full title of "The Machinery of Government; A New Framework for Expanding Services," was a major catalyst in modernizing the colonial civil service to meet the needs of an increasingly complex and growing society. Its main recommendations were for a reduction of centralized control and the reorganization of departments into six major policy areas. (See Civil Service.)

MACLEHOSE, SIR MURRAY (1917–). Sir Murray MacLehose was the territory's longest serving Governor, administering the colony from November 1971 until May 1982. He arrived at a crucial period of economic and social change, and he adopted a far more reformist stance than any other postwar governor. He actively promoted a massive government housing program, introduced compulsory primary education while also raising the school leaving age from 14 to 15 years old, and doubled the size of the civil service. Expenditure in the fields of social and community service were also massively increased. Sustained economic growth throughout his term of office financed these changes without any major opposition.

Externally he was the first governor to pay an official visit to Peking (Beijing), in the improved relationships made possible by the coming to power of Teng Hsiaop'ing (Deng Xiaoping). While in China he raised the question of the future of Hong Kong after 1997, which led to the train of events which culminated in the Joint Declaration of 1984. On leaving Hong Kong, Sir Murray was made a life peer and took his place in the House of Lords becoming an active and respected speaker on debates about the territory. (See Anglo-Chinese Negotiations; House of Lords; Housing.)

MACLENNON ENQUIRY. A public enquiry conducted in 1980–81 to investigate the circumstances surrounding the death of police Inspector John MacLennon. Mr. MacLennon had been the subject of enquiry by the Special Investigations Unit (SIU) of the Royal Hong Kong Police force, who had discovered sufficient evidence to charge him with gross indecency. When the police arrived to arrest him, he was found dead, killed by five shots from a police revolver. The death led to public debate including rumors that he had been murdered because of his threat to name homosexuals in high positions in government if charges were pressed against him. In July 1981 the Commission of Enquiry found that the Inspector had committed suicide, but it also concluded that the police were not only using questionable means against witnesses, but also had been prepared to terminate the contract of a police officer merely on hearsay, and had demonstrated a discriminatory official attitude towards homosexuality. (See Homosexuality; Royal Hong Kong Police Force.)

MAJORITY, AGE OF. The age of majority was reduced from 21 years to 18 years in 1990 for some matters, but not for voting. (See Electorate.)

MANUFACTURING. See Economic System; Trade.

MAO TSE-TUNG (MAO ZEDONG) (1893–1976). Mao Tse-tung (Mao Zedong) was the effective leader of the Chinese Communist Party from 1939 until he died in 1976. He developed a more realistic policy for the party after the *debacle* which had led to the Long March of 1934–1936. His writings on revolutionary warfare and his thinking on the essential part of the Chinese peasant as a revolutionary force projected him to the forefront of the Party. He led the party through its successful war against the Kuomintang (Guomindang), culminating in the establishment of the People's Republic of China in 1949 with himself at the head. However, many of the domestic policies pursued by his government, particularly during the periods of the Great Leap Forward and the Great Proletarian Cultural Revolution, proved to be serious failures. Most judgments of his handling of external relationships are more complimentary, although his theoretical writings on the subject, e.g., in his "Three Worlds Theory," appear simplistic. Mao's critics often suggest that the more significant contribution to Chinese foreign policy was made by Chou En-lai (Zhou Enlai) in this period. Since Mao's death in 1976, his reputation has declined although many of his ideas still command support among many in the party hierarchy.

During the Cultural Revolution in 1967, the existence of Hong Kong as a colonialist and capitalist symbol became an issue for fervent party members in the PRC and in the colony, but Mao himself seems generally to have been prepared to accept the status of the colony. (See China, People's Republic of; Communist Party of

China; Cultural Revolution; Kuomintang (Guomindang); People's Liberation Army.)

MASS MEDIA. The first English-language newspaper published within Hong Kong was the *Friend of China* (1842), although there had been papers, such as the *Chinese Recorder,* published previously for the expatriate communities in Macau and Canton (Guangzhou). Other English-language newspapers which soon became available in the colony included the *China Mail, Hong Kong Daily Press,* the *Hong Kong Sunday Herald,* the *Hong Kong Telegraph,* and the *Overland Friend of China.*

The Chinese press was slower in arrival but was in existence from the mid-19th century. The oldest surviving Hong Kong Chinese newspaper is the *Wah Kiu Yat Pao* of 1895.

The postwar period saw the number of English-medium newspapers decline quite rapidly to four in 1970 and only two in 1989. Of these the *South China Morning Post* (founded 1903) was by far the most popular. On the other hand, the Chinese press expanded massively in the postwar period both in terms of the number of publications and readership. By 1970 there were 66 Chinese newspapers covering a wide political spectrum, although that number was reduced to 39 by 1990. The press in the territory has traditionally been extremely free by Asian standards.

Radio broadcasting, heavily subsidized by the government, began in 1928, and in 1948 the government station was renamed Radio Hong Kong. In 1953, following the British model, the radio service was separated from the Public Relations office, and put under the control of a Director of Broadcasting. Radio broadcasts were publicly funded, but with a high degree of independence from government interference. In 1957 commercial stations were established in the territory. A condition of all licenses was that radio stations carried at least one English channel and at least one Chinese.

The first television service was set up in December 1957. The company produced 28 hours of programs per week, watched by an estimated 63,000 viewers. A second company was franchised in November 1967. By 1970 the estimated number of viewers watching both channels was thought to be in excess of 2 million. The government stipulated that each company had to transmit one channel in the English language and the other in Chinese. By 1990 it was estimated that over 98% of the households in the territory had a television.

MASS TRANSIT RAILWAY. The Mass Transit Railway did much to alleviate travel congestion from its opening in 1 October 1979. It was gradually extended to cover the urban areas on Hong Kong Island, Kowloon, and parts of the New Territories.

MAY, SIR FRANCIS HENRY (1860–1922). Governor of Hong Kong from July 1912 until February 1919. He had already had some experience as acting Governor for six months in 1903 between the governorships of Sir Henry Blake and Sir Matthew Nathan. May was the first governor to come up through the civil service's domestic ranks. Despite being the target of an assassination attempt during his first month in office, he went on to achieve some notable reforms particularly in the education system where he ensured that all schools registered with the Director of Education and conformed to inspection and government regulations. He also dealt severely with a brief period of unrest which broke out in 1912 following the fall of the Ch'ing (Qing) dynasty in China. Near the end of his term of office there were two major disasters in the colony: a fire at the Happy Valley Racecourse in which 600 were killed; and a severe outbreak of meningitis, which killed approximately one thousand people. (See Ch'ing (Qing) Dynasty; Education; Disturbances; First World War; Governor; Li Hong Hung.)

MING DYNASTY (MING) (1368–1644). The Ming dynasty ruled from 1369 until 1644 when it was overthrown by the Ch'ing (Qing) dynasty (1644–1912). During this period the military bases in the region were reorganized and forts and garrisons were built to guard the approaches to the Pearl River to protect the trade route to Canton. In the 15th and 16th centuries Japanese pirates operated in the area which led to the Chinese navy, operating off the coast, to intercept and destroy them. The other danger came from the Portuguese who were anxious to trade. In 1514 the Portuguese forcibly occupied the Tuen Mun forts until they were defeated by the Chinese in 1521.

The region itself was dominated by major *Punti* (Cantonese) families, some of whom had supported the Ming in their successful bid for power. In 1571 the area was set up as a separate county and renamed San-On (Xin-an). It consisted of the Hong Kong area, plus the area just to the north in the Nant'ou (Nantou)–Sham Chun (Shenzhen)–Tapeng (Dapeng) zone. (See Ch'ing (Qing); Forts; Macau entries; *Punti*.)

MUI TSAI (MEI ZI). A traditional custom in many parts of China, including Hong Kong, was the practice of *Mui Tsai (Mei Zi)*. *Mui Tsai (Mei Zi)*, which translates into English as "Little Sister," involved poor families presenting one of the female children into the custody of a richer family. The original idea was that the receivers of the child would feed, clothe and generally look after her. Finally, when the child reached a marriageable age a suitable husband would be found. Unfortunately, in many cases the child became a virtual slave or was even used as a prostitute in a brothel.

As a general rule, the British colonial practice was not to interfere with the customs of a given culture unless they were repugnant to British law. But the issue of *Mui Tsai (Mei Zi)* began to become politically significant in 1917 with a Supreme Court case involving the kidnapping of two "little sisters" aged 10 and 13. In 1921 official government figures put the number of *mui tsai (mei zi)* at 8,653, which, although it was probably a gross underestimate, still represented over 10% of the girls in the colony. Strong pressures for abolition of the practice among the British community in the colony and in Britain were opposed by many Chinese as an unwarranted interference in Chinese customs. Legislation was passed in 1923 which forbade any further employment of new *mui tsai (mei zi)*. There were also attempts to tighten regulations relating to mistreatment of existing *mui tsai (mei zi)*, and an inspectorate was established to enforce the new regulations. This compromise allowed the continuation of the existing system until the children grew up. As expected, the system gradually died out with only a few isolated cases being discovered after the Second World War. In 1969 the Female Domestic Service Ordinance was repealed as obsolete.

MULTI-FIBRE ARRANGEMENTS. The multi-fibre arrangements were an attempt to control the sales of cotton textiles from the newly industrializing economies (NIE) to the developed countries. In the 1950s and 1960s exports from NIE's, such as Hong Kong and South Korea, threatened the more established cotton textile industries of countries, such as the United States and Britain. As a result, a number of bilateral arrangements to control textile exports were concluded under the umbrella of the GATT between the exporting and importing countries. From 1973 Hong Kong entered into a number of such agreements with several developed economies including the European Community and the U.S.A. (See Economic System; Trade.)

MUNICIPAL COUNCILS. See Urban Council and Regional Council.

MUTUAL AID COMMITTEES. The expansion of public housing and the proliferation of high-rise buildings was associated with an increase in crime in certain areas of the territory. As a response, in 1973 the government began to sponsor and encourage the establishment of Mutual Aid Committees. These were concerned with attempts to maintain law and order, principally through the provision of recreational, educational and cultural facilities at strictly local levels. They also provided a means whereby local grievances could be expressed by tenants. However, their influence was insubstantial, and in the 1980s membership fell rapidly. Their most active role became an organizing opposition to rent increases on domestic apartments.

-N-

NANKING (NANJING), TREATY OF. The Treaty of Nanking (Nanjing) was signed on 29 August 1842 on board the HMS *Cornwallis*. Relations between the Chinese and British governments had improved after the signing of the Treaty of Chuanpi (Chuanbi), but deteriorated in February 1841 when negotiations between the two countries broke down. Following the British occupation of Bogue forts and Canton (Guangzhou) in 1840, and an apparent threat to Shanghai and Nanking (Nanjing) in the spring of 1842, the Chinese government signed the Treaty of Nanking (Nanjing) in an attempt to ensure the safety of their cities. The Treaty was seen by the Chinese authorities as a harsh and unfair one imposed by a military victor upon a prostrate country. The Treaty of Nanking (Nanjing) and subsequent concessions extracted from the Chinese in the nineteenth century were referred to as the "Unequal Treaties" the legitimacy of which they never fully accepted.

Some of the treaty's more important provisions were:

1. The ports of Amoy (Xiamen), Canton (Guangzhou), Foochow (Fuzhow), Ningpo (Ningbo) and Shanghai were to be opened for foreign trade and Residents and Consuls were to be appointed in those ports on preferential conditions.
2. Hong Kong Island was to be ceded to the United Kingdom in perpetuity.
3. China was to pay $6 million in compensation for the opium that had been confiscated in Canton (Guangzhou) in exchange for "the lives of British subjects"—the ostensible, though questionable, cause of the outbreak of hostilities in the first place.
4. The *Co-hong* monopoly was to be abolished and foreigners allowed to trade freely. $3 million was to be paid to British merchants by Chinese merchants to settle outstanding debts.
5. The Chinese government had to pay $12 million to the British for the war (which had been largely precipitated by Britain in the first place).

One important omission from this treaty was any mention of the opium trade, which was the cause of the series of open confrontations between the two governments. (See Anglo-Chinese Wars; Chuanpi (Chuanbi), Convention of; Opium Wars; Unequal Treaties.)

NAPIER, LORD (1786–1834). Lord Napier was appointed as British Superintendent of Trade at Canton (Guangzhou) in 1833. His function was to liaise with the Chinese authorities on questions relating to foreign trade (particularly opium). This role had previously been undertaken by the *Co-hong,* a designated group of merchants in Canton (Guangzhou). However, Lord Napier was largely disregarded by the Chinese government as he was not a *"taipan"* or manager. Nor, in the event did he prove very suited to diplomatic relations. He responded to the strengthening of Chinese defence positions on the Pearl River by the dispatch of British troops to Macau and by deploying frigates at the mouth of the river. Such an act was seen by the Chinese authorities as provocative, and led to rapidly deteriorating relations. Lord Napier's military initiative was also not supported by the British community in the area. In consequence, he was forced to comply with the Chinese demand that he remove himself to Macau. Shortly afterwards he died. (See Anglo-Chinese Wars; Opium Wars.)

NARCOTICS. See Drugs.

NATHAN, SIR MATTHEW (1862–1939). Governor of Hong Kong from July 1904 to April 1907. As an engineer, he showed keen interest in the construction of two railways (constructed with the aid of British capital), from Canton (Guangzhou) to Hong Kong and from Canton (Guangzhou) to Hang K'ou (Hangkou).

He had some success in countering the problem of devaluation of the coinage by controlling the supply of coins which were by 1905 far exceeding the needs of the population. In addition, his enquiry into the Sanitary Board in 1907 uncovered the problem of corruption which was widespread in the colonial government.

He left the colony in 1907 to become Governor of Natal. (See Currency; Governor; Kowloon-Canton Railway.)

NEW CHINA NEWS AGENCY *(XINHUA).* The New China News Agency (NCNA) first established in 1948. In the Chinese institutional hierarchy the NCNA is a branch of the Chinese State Council. The Agency's primary functions are to control the media on the mainland, to transmit the current orthodox views of the Chinese government, and to provide information on China to other states.

Its role in Hong Kong has been more complex. The British authorities would not allow any mainland diplomatic representation in Hong Kong, but at the same time the Chinese authorities did not wish to establish a consulate or embassy in the colony because of their insistence that Hong Kong was part of the sovereign state of China. There was, however, a perceived Chinese need for some informal representation in the colony, and this was supplied by the NCNA.

For much of the period 1949–1984 the NCNA adopted a low profile. It had little contact with the colonial government, and its main work was to transmit information back to Peking (Beijing) about the state of public opinion in Hong Kong and any other relevant information. It also attempted to maintain a united and pro-PRC front between the left-wing press and left-wing political organizations in Hong Kong. (See Hsu Chia-t'un (Xu Jiatun).)

NEW TERRITORIES. The area of the territory which came under British control as a result of the Peking (Beijing) Convention in 1898. Before the area was leased to Britain, it was inhabited by four sets of indigenous groups: the *Punti, Hakka, Tanka* and *Hoklo.* The area had been brought under the control of China in 221–224 B.C. by military conquests, but, although there is evidence of increasing Chinese influence, little substantial immigration into the area occurred until the Sung (Song)

(960–1279). To protect trade in the area, some forts were built and a number of walled villages erected. The area now known as the New Territories was part of the Pan-yu county of the Nan-hai prefecture until 331 A.D. In that year it came under the administration of the Bao-an county. The name was altered yet again in A.D. 757 when it became part of Tung Kuan (Dongguan). Finally, in 1573 Tung Kuan (Dongguan) county was divided into Tung Kuan (Dongguan) and San On (Xin-an) counties. This arrangement existed until the British leased the territory from China in 1898.

At the end of the nineteenth century the great powers were actively engaged in competition for Chinese territory, and the British were concerned about the defensibility of Hong Kong. Their main interest in acquiring the New Territories, therefore, was to improve the defence of the colony against possible attack not from China but from the other European powers. The exact border was only fixed some nine months after the signing of the Peking Convention, but British control came into effect on 20 October 1898. Although previous agreements relating to Hong Kong and Kowloon had ceded territory in perpetuity, the Peking (Beijing) Convention put a time limit on British control of 99 years, to run out on 30 June 1997.

On the mainland British jurisdiction was largely confined to the land area bounded to the south by Boundary Street and to the north by the south bank of the Sham Chun (Shenzhen) River. The boundary ran along the Chinese mainland shore to longitude 113° 52″ E, and then ran south across Deep Bay to Lantau, along the shoreline of West Lantau, southward across to the west tip of Tai A Chau in the Soko islands, onwards southwest to latitude 22° 09″ N, then across to a line drawn south from the southernmost point of the east coast of Mirs Bay, then west along the Mirs Bay shoreline to Sha Tau Kok, then along the line of a stream and a small valley and so back to the Sham Chun (Shenzhen) River. Also included in the New Territories were 235 islands, many but not all uninhabited. The most important of these islands were Lantau, Cheung Chau, Ping Chau, Ma Wan, Lamma, and the Po Toi group. The total size of the New Territories was 946.5 square kilometers.

The economy of the New Territories at the time depended primarily upon fishing and agriculture. Its people were highly suspicious of the British occupation and were initially uncooperative. One particularly difficult issue concerned control of the Kowloon Walled City, which the British had originally agreed would remain under Chinese administration.

Gradually the area was brought under British supervision with a system of police and magistrates operating under the general supervision of district officers (indeed until the 1960s district officers were also the magistrates). However, local village, clan and indigenous organizations, such as the Heung Yee Kuk, were allowed to continue following the general British colonial practice of toleration of original systems not repugnant to British law.

The area remained relatively sparsely populated throughout the early part of the twentieth century. Even in the early postwar years there was little of the industrialization or the increases in population seen in the urban areas. The population, which had gone down substantially during the Japanese occupation, began to rise after the war but as late as 1970 it was still less than 500,000.

However, in 1972, the then Governor Sir Murray MacLehose, announced an ambitious housing plan, a basic feature of which was the attempt to alleviate high population density and poor housing in the urban areas by the construction of public housing especially in purposely built New Towns, some of which were to be located in the New Territories. The plan envisaged a huge exodus from the urban areas to the New Towns which would be constructed over the next thirty years. The population increase was to be over 2 million by 1988 rising to over 3.37 million by the late 1990s. Such an increase was to be accompanied by a massive infrastructural program involving a much improved communications system and the creation of an industrial base. Much of this plan has come to fruition, although there has been reluctance from employers to relocate, and a corresponding reluctance among lower income groups to move away from employment opportunities. There has been less reluctance among the expanding middle class to move to the New Towns and commute to more central work places. (See Conventions of Peking (Beijing); District Administration; Heung Yee Kuk; Housing; Joint Declaration; Kowloon Walled City; MacLehose, Sir Murray; Sino-British Negotiations; Unequal Treaties.)

NEWSPAPERS. See Mass Media.

NG CHOY. Ng Choy was the first Chinese barrister in Hong Kong. He was also the first Chinese person appointed to the Legislative Council, replacing H.B. Gibb who was on leave in January 1880. The then Governor, Hennessy, who offered the appointment to Ng Choy, reported back to London in 1880 and asked for reorganization of the Legislative Council which was to contain six official members and five unofficials of whom one was to be Chinese. His appointment was criticized by the Secretary of State for the Colonies who insisted that Ng Choy's appointment would create a precedent making it impossible to avoid appointing a Chinese to one seat in future, even when there was nobody suitable.

NORTHCOTE, SIR GEOFFREY (1881–1948). Governor of Hong Kong from November 1937 to May 1940. He came to office around the time of the outbreak of the Sino-Japanese War, and by 1938 he had to issue emergency regulations partly aimed at maintaining the colony's neutrality in response to the increasing threat of a Japanese invasion. Under these regulations the government acquired powers ranging from controlling food prices to forbidding the repair of Japanese and Chinese ships engaged in the war. These were followed in August 1940 by the Hong Kong Defence Regulations which attempted to prepare the territory more directly for any spilling over into the colony of the wider conflict. Despite the preparations the colony eventually proved ill-prepared to defend itself in the face of the Japanese attack and surrendered on December 25, 1941. (See Emergency Regulations and Powers; Governor; Second World War.)

-O-

OATH OF ALLEGIANCE. Under the Letters Patent and the Royal Instructions it had been incumbent upon the Governor, the Legislative Council, and any other person the Governor might think fit, on assuming office to take the Oath of Allegiance to the reigning monarch in the United Kingdom. However, in 1985 the situation was amended to allow members of the Legislative Council to swear an affirmation or oath to uphold the laws of Hong Kong and serve the Hong Kong people rather than an oath of allegiance to the monarch. This option was not open to the Governor. Under the provisions of the Basic Law there is a requirement that the Chief Executive, principal officials, members of the Executive Council and of the Legislative Council and the judiciary, when assuming office, will swear to support the Basic Law and be loyal to the Special Administrative Region.

OCCUPATION (JAPANESE). The Japanese occupation of Hong Kong lasted from December 25, 1941, when

British forces surrendered, until the end of August 1945. During that period the colony was under direct Japanese military rule. The period was characterized by a major drop in population: from 1,600,000 in 1939 to under 600,000 in 1945. The economic superstructure collapsed, famine was rampant and all allied civilians and prisoners of war were interned under particularly harsh conditions. Although the Japanese surrendered on August 14, it took until August 29 for British forces to arrive in the colony to resume administration. The formal instrument of surrender was signed by the Japanese on 16 September 1945. (See Instrument of Surrender; Population; Second World War.)

OFFICIAL LANGUAGE ISSUE. Throughout the history of Hong Kong as a colony the dominant language of the law, government, and business was English. The vast majority of the population, however, spoke Cantonese, which is a Chinese dialect spoken throughout the southern province of Canton (Guangzhou). The status of Cantonese became a political issue in 1971 when there was a major campaign by students to have Chinese made the official language of government. The authorities responded by allowing speeches in the Legislative Council to be made in Cantonese and this was followed by the Official Languages Ordinance in 1974 which accorded Chinese equal status with English. Despite this, English remained the dominant language in the courts and higher reaches of government. Under the provisions of the Basic Law, it is stated that after the creation of the Special Administrative Region, "in addition to the Chinese Language, English may also be used as an official language by the executive authorities, legislature and judiciary." However, in the case of a dispute in interpretation, the Chinese language will prevail.

OFFICIALS AND OFFICIAL MEMBERS. The term "official members" came from the original Letters Patent and Royal Instructions, which stipulated that persons holding office under the crown in the Legislative Council and the Executive Council would be called "Official Members." In short it was another term for civil servants in the two Councils. Any person sitting in the Councils who was not a civil servant would be referred to as unofficial.

In the Legislative Council the Official Members would represent the government and perform such functions as answering questions on government policy and performance. The figures below trace the changes in the ratio of officials and unofficials.

	Official (inc. *ex officio* and Governor)	Unofficial
1843	4	0
1850	4	2
1884	7	5
1896	8	6
1929	10	8
1947	9	7
1966	13	13
1976	20	22
1980	23	27
1984	19	30
1985	11	46
1989	11	46

The number of officials was further reduced to three in 1991. There will be no officials in the Legislative Council after 1997.

The figures for the Executive Council given below show a less severe shift in the ratio, and this is likely to remain in the near future.

	Official (inc. *ex officio* and Governor)	Unofficial
1843	4	0
1896	7	2
1928	8	3
1946	8	4
1948	7	6
1966	7	8
1978	7	9
1983	7	9
1989	6	9

(See Executive Council; Localization; Legislative Council; Regional Council; Urban Council.)

OMELCO. (Office of the Members of the Executive and Legislative Councils) OMELCO is the office which supports the non-civil service representation in the Executive and Legislative Councils. It was created in October 1986 from its predecessor, the Unofficial Members of the Executive and Legislative Council (UMELCO). OMELCO was set up principally as a support unit for all the unofficial members, but it also developed other functions including:

1. The creation of standing panels to discuss government policy and make recommendations to the administration.
2. Providing means for the redress of grievances for members of the public.
3. Coordinating, where possible, positions on political issues.

ONE COUNTRY, TWO SYSTEMS. A maxim employed by the government of the People's Republic of China after 1978 to describe the positions of both Hong Kong and Macau after the resumption of Chinese sovereignty. It was used to reassure the two territories that they would be allowed a high degree of autonomy. Hence there would be one sovereign state, namely the People's Republic of China, but a different set of political and economic arrangements in Hong Kong and Macau suited to their different needs. The one country-two systems approach was also oriented towards the Taiwan government in the hope of persuading it to accept a return to the People's Republic of China.

OPIUM. See Drugs.

OPIUM WARS. In the two Opium Wars fought between the British and China the British were victorious. These victories led to the establishment of Hong Kong as a British colony in the first case and the acquisition of the Kowloon Peninsula in the second. The first Opium War lasted from 1839 until 1842 and the second from 1858 until 1860. (See Anglo-Chinese Wars.)

-P-

PALMERSTON, HENRY JOHN TEMPLE (1784–1865). Lord Palmerston was the British foreign secretary on three occasions:1830–1834; 1835–1841; and 1846–1851. He was later Prime Minister in 1855–1858 and 1859–1865. As foreign minister he was concerned with the acquisition of Hong Kong and in formulating policy with China in the early years. It was his decision to go to war with China in 1839 and it was he who sent the fleet, without securing parliamentary consent, for that purpose. The failure of the expedition to secure a treaty led to his dismissal of Elliot. He was also Prime Minister when the British acquired Kowloon in 1860. (See Chuanpi (Chuanbi), Convention of; Elliot, Captain Charles; Nanking (Nanjing), Treaty of; Opium War.)

PARLIAMENT, BRITISH. The British Parliament is a bicameral legislative body made up of the House of Commons and the House of Lords. The House of Commons is an elected body whereas the House of Lords is entirely nonelected. Particularly in the twentieth century, the former has increased its power at the expense of the latter.

Any major policies affecting Hong Kong had to seek Parliamentary approval. Despite this, the tendency for Parliament was to allow Hong Kong a large degree of independence in running its everyday business. Rarely was Hong Kong discussed in any depth in Parliament and the government could usually rely on support from the majority of the legislators. (See Constitution; Foreign and Commonwealth Office; Government, British; House of Commons; House of Lords.)

PARSEES (PARSI). A small religio-ethnic minority of some 100,000 worldwide who have been of some significance in the history of Hong Kong. Parsees were followers of Zoroastrianism, which began some two thousand years ago in Persia. Forced out of Persia by the invading Arabs in the 7th century A.D. they took refuge in India. With the arrival of the British, they quickly achieved prominent positions as merchants, agents, and brokers and established a fleet of Parsi clippers which operated in the South China Seas. They were the first Indian settlers in Macau and many moved into Hong Kong with the British arrival in 1841. They established large firms, shipping companies and were great benefactors to the community. Parsi contributions made possible the establishment of the University of Hong Kong and a wide range of medical and social facilities and services.

PARTIES. Hong Kong had no tradition of political parties in the formal sense of the word for much of its history. This was hardly surprising given the fact that there was no means by which parties could compete for power in any of the legislative bodies, either central or local, until well after the Second World War. It has also been argued that the political culture of the colony has not been conducive to the development of political parties. Parties which did exist were for the most part covert and operated under the control of external forces, such as the Nationalist Party for the Republic of China and the Chinese Communist Party under the umbrella of the United Front. It was not until 1990 that the first parties were formed, principally to contest the first direct elections for a limited number of seats in the Legislative Council. The most successful and only clearly defined party was the United Democrats of Hong Kong. In the election of September 1991 they won 12 of the 18 seats being contested, eclipsing all other "groups" including the business coalition and two Peking (Beijing) backed candidates.(See Kuomintang (Guomindang); Lee Chuming, Martin; Legislative Council; United Front.)

PASSPORTS. Only after the First World War did it became necessary to have a passport for the purpose of moving across international borders. In Hong Kong persons holding British passports and resident in the colony were traditionally allowed entry and right of abode in the United Kingdom. However, in 1962 the Commonwealth Immigrants Act was passed by the British Parliament which introduced restrictions on immigration from the Commonwealth (e.g., India, Pakistan) and the Dependent Territories (e.g., Hong Kong). This act was followed by further restrictions in the Immigration Act of 1971.

Ten years later a new British Nationality Act was passed creating three categories of citizenship, with different classifications on passports. They were as follows:

1. British Citizen, with full rights of entry and abode in Britain.

2. British Overseas Citizen, created mainly for members of the new Commonwealth such as India. This category did not allow either right of entry or the right of abode in the United Kingdom.
3. British Dependent Territories Citizen, (BDTC). This was applicable to Hong Kong, and it gave only the right of entry and abode solely in the Dependent Territory itself. It did, however, as with the previous category, provide the right to consular protection while the holder was abroad. In order to qualify for a BDTC, the applicant has to show that she or he was born in Hong Kong or a dependent of a BDTC-holder.

Finally, as a consequence of the Joint Declaration on the future of Hong Kong signed between the British and PRC governments in 1984, another passport was created called the British National (Overseas) Passport. It also excluded the holder from the right of abode in the United Kingdom. Holders of the BDTC could apply for this passport. For those people not eligible for either a BDTC or a BN(O) there were other travel documents, namely the Certificate of Identity (CI) or the Document of Identity (DI). The former was available for any person who had resided in Hong Kong for seven years. It also stated that the holder had the right of abode in Hong Kong. The latter was for those who had resided in Hong Kong for less than seven years. The restriction on this document was that the holder would have to apply for a re-entry visa into the territory before leaving. (See Basic Law; British Dependent Territories Citizen; British National (Overseas); British Nationality Acts; Permanent Resident.)

PEEL, SIR WILLIAM (1875–1947). Sir William Peel was governor of Hong Kong from May 1930–May 1935. He came to the colony during the great depression which saw a huge diminution in world trade and had great difficulty in raising sufficient revenue for the governance of the colony. He also oversaw the transformation of the Sanitary Board to the newly created Urban Council. His relations with the Republic of China were strained and made even more complicated by the rapidly deteriorating relations between China and Japan. He was replaced as Governor by Sir Andrew Caldicott in 1935. (See Sanitary Board; Urban Council.)

PEOPLE'S LIBERATION ARMY. The People's Liberation Army (PLA) which eventually also included all naval and air forces was established, under the wing of the Chinese Communist Party, in August 1927. From the establishment of the PRC in 1949, the PLA had a large number of troops to the north of Hong Kong and could at any time have successfully invaded the colony—especially given the increasingly small size of the British garrison.

With the signing of the Joint Declaration in 1984, it was agreed that the PLA would assume the responsibility for the defence of the future Special Administrative Region. The actual size of any PLA garrison in Hong Kong was a matter of dispute between the British and Chinese negotiators both before the signing of the Joint Declaration and after. This problem was still not resolved some six years after the Joint Declaration was signed. (See Armed Forces; Basic Law; China, People's Republic of; Joint Declaration; Special Administrative Region.)

PEOPLE'S REPUBLIC OF CHINA. See China, People's Republic of.

PERMANENT RESIDENT. A term which became important after the passing of various laws in Britain defining right of abode and right of entry in the period from the early 1960s to the early 1980s. A permanent resident until 1997 was broadly defined as any person who had resided in Hong Kong for seven years and who was "wholly or partly of Chinese race, any person who was defined as a British Dependent Territories Citizen (see relevant entry) and any Commonwealth Citizen who had the right to land before 1 January 1983 because they were either born, naturalized or registered in Hong Kong."

The Basic Law defined a Permanent Resident in a different way. Article 24 of the Basic Law defines permanent residents of the HKSAR as follows:

Permanent residents of the Hong Kong Special Administrative Region shall be:

1. Chinese citizens born in Hong Kong before or after the establishment of the HKSAR;

2. Chinese citizens who have ordinarily resided in Hong Kong for a continuous period of no less than seven years before or after the establishment of the HKSAR;

3. Persons of Chinese nationality born outside Hong Kong of those residents listed in categories (1) and (2);

4. Persons who are not of Chinese nationality but who have ordinarily resided in Hong Kong for a continuous period of no less than seven years and have taken Hong Kong as their place of permanent residence before or after the establishment of the HKSAR;

5. Persons under 21 years of age born in Hong Kong of residents listed in category (4) before or after the establishment of the HKSAR; and

6. Persons other than those residents listed in categories (1–5) who had the right of abode only in Hong Kong before the establishment of the HKSAR.

The above mentioned residents shall have right of abode in the HKSAR and shall be qualified to obtain, in accordance with its law, permanent identity cards which state their right of abode.

(See Basic Law; British Dependent Territories Citizen; British National (Overseas); British Nationality Acts; Illegal Immigration; Special Administrative Region.)

PLAGUE. See Health.

PO LEUNG KUK. A society established in Hong Kong in 1878 whose main function was to end the kidnapping of and trafficking in human beings, particularly women and children for brothels. Its official English name was The Society for the Protection of Women and Girls. It was accorded recognition by the government in 1894. The society was helped by the administration, and in turn the Registrar-General benefitted by having a clear line of communication with influential opinion in the Chinese community. It became active in such fields as restoring females to their families and helping in adoptions and arranging marriages of females. As the incidence of kidnapping and trafficking in Hong Kong was gradually eradicated, the society continued to be influential in providing services to the community. It continues to exist in the early 1990s providing educational opportunities for such groups as disadvantaged children. (See Tung Wah.)

POLICE. See Royal Hong Kong Police.

POLITICAL SYSTEM. Although many of Hong Kong's original colonial political institutions remain, their functions, powers, duties and membership have altered quite radically. When Hong Kong was established as a British colony in 1843, it was under the control of the United Kingdom. Its constitution was based on a number of documents:

1. The Charter, which established Hong Kong as a Crown Colony on 5 April 1843.
2. The Order in Council of 24 October 1860, which annexed Kowloon to Hong Kong.
3. The Order in Council of 20 October 1898, which leased the New Territories for 99 years.

However, the Charter and the two Orders in Council provide little detail on how the colony was to be administered, and the framework of government is spelled out in more detail in the Letters Patent and the Royal Instructions. In those documents provision was made for the appointment of a Governor of Hong Kong, who was the Queen's representative in the colony. The Governor was accorded the authority to make laws for the "peace, order and good government" of Hong Kong. The Governor was also instructed to appoint an Executive Council and a Legislative Council, to appoint civil servants, and to maintain a judicial branch. In formal terms, the Governor was accorded considerable powers for the running of the colony with the restraints upon that power emanating more from London than from within the colony itself. In reality, the Governors of Hong Kong practiced a high degree of restraint for much of the time and usually acted in consultation with the other internal actors, such as the Legislative Council and influential pressure groups. At the same time the government in the United Kingdom gradually granted increased autonomy to the colony. In the postwar era most matters pertaining to Hong Kong were left almost completely in the hands of the colonial government.

Throughout its history the Executive Council was composed of *ex officio* members and members nominated by the Governor. It had no elected members although the membership was eventually expanded to embrace a wider constituency and more locals. The Executive Council was primarily an advisory body. In practice, a Governor rarely acted against its advice. The role of the Executive was to deal with policy at the highest level and propose laws for the consideration of the Legislative Council.

The Legislative Council had the role of passing laws (known as Ordinances in Hong Kong). Again, in formal terms the Governor could refuse to agree to laws passed in the Council, but this has been done only once in 150 years, in 1947. Membership of the Legislative Council expanded over time, with more elected members following the introduction of indirect and direct elections in the period 1985–1991.

The other major institutions developed slightly later. The interwar years saw the development of municipal government, and the widening of local representation through the creation of more powerful District Boards came in the 1970s and 1980s. However, the political system for much of the history of Hong Kong emphasized unitary government in the colony with power concentrated very much in the hands of a central government with only dubious claims to being representative. Indeed, until after the Second World War there was a marked reluctance to widen the base of the institutional structures in place.

This colonial style of government was subjected to a series of shocks in the 1960s with the growing realization that a gulf had grown between the ruling and the ruled. Major demonstrations in the late 1960s led to a greater willingness to allow for a more diverse set of influences on the making and execution of policy. Advisory boards were set up to facilitate communication with the community at large. In addition, a broader representational base became evident in the membership of the Legislative Council in particular and, to a lesser extent, the Executive Council. This was seen most graphically by the reduction in expatriate membership of the councils. The changes came both through the Governor's appointments and through the indirect election of members by functional constituencies and District Boards. However, it was not until 1991 that direct elections based on geographical constituencies were allowed for the Legislative Council and even there the number of seats was limited.

At the informal level pressure groups rather than

political parties have always been significant. Powerful trading and banking interests, composed initially of expatriates, were either formally appointed to the Legislative Council or enjoyed informal access to the government. With the colony's economic growth after the Second World War, these groups were joined by powerful Chinese pressure groups representing business, trade, and banking. To a lesser extent, other pressure groups, such as the social work groups and the educational groups, began to exert some influence in the 1980s especially with the growth of an educated and more affluent Chinese middle class.

Major changes came as a consequence of the Sino-British Joint Declaration. It was agreed in 1984 that after 1997 the British would cease to have any authority over Hong Kong. The colony would become a Special Administrative Region under the sovereignty of the People's Republic of China, and final authority over the territory would therefore lie in Peking (Beijing). The constitution of the territory would be found in the Basic Law which was promulgated in April 1990 and which comes into effect in July 1997. In brief, the Governor would be replaced by the post of Chief Executive who, according to the Basic Law, would be more accountable with a greater separation of powers from the Legislative Council. The Executive Council would continue to perform the role of advising the Chief Executive and there was no specified intention to increase the accountability of its members by electing them. The Legislative Council was to become more democratic in so far as the "official" members were to disappear completely and elections of various types would eventually be introduced for the total membership. The local government institutions would continue to exist with few changes to their responsibilities. At the formal level, pressure groups were to be given an even more important place in the Legislature by the increase in the number of seats allocated to functional constituencies. The Legislative Council was to be completely elected, with 50% directly elected on a geographic basis and 50% from functional constituencies.

The development of political parties in 1990 was an unplanned step towards the orderly competition for the limited number of seats available in the central legislature.

The evolution of the political system, therefore, accelerated in response to the rapidly evolving situation both within the colony itself and in response to the changing demands of the People's Republic of China. Hong Kong began with the simple colonial model which the British imposed upon nearly all its territories. That colonial model, which may be described as one of benevolent paternalism, was to last for over 100 years with only incremental changes.

It was forced into change in the postwar period, however, as the territory's population and economy grew. During this period, the government's preference for a minimal role became subject to question by an ever more sophisticated and demanding Hong Kong population.

Beginning in the late 1960s the government expanded both its role in consulting a wider range of people and its involvement in a wider range of activities. At the same time, the informal actors centered in pressure groups continued to expand their influence both in the institutional framework and in the community at large. Despite this, it was generally recognized that the greater influence still remained in the hands of the central government, retaining a great degree of power for the administration. Externally the question of the exercise of power by the People's Republic of China and whether it would allow the same degree of real autonomy granted *de facto* by the British government was still not resolved. (See Basic Law; Chief Executive; China, People's Republic of;

Constitution; Executive Council; Governor; Joint Declaration; Legislative Council; Letters Patent; Pressure Groups; Royal Instructions.)

POPULATION. Upon the arrival of the British in May 1841 the population of Hong Kong Island was estimated at 7,450. That figure was to swell fairly rapidly to 15,000 by October 1841 and then to nearly 24,000 by 1848. Between 1848 and 1876 the better conditions in the territory, instability in China, and the acquisition of Kowloon in 1860 raised the figure to 122,392. Immediately before the takeover of the New Territories in 1898 the population of Hong Kong Island and Kowloon was estimated to be 254,000. The annexing of the New Territories added a further 100,000 to that total. By 1916 the population was around half a million, increasing to over 840,000 in the early 1930s. With the outbreak of the Sino-Japanese War there was a huge influx of refugees into the colony, which increased the population to an estimated 1.6 million. With the military defeat of the British forces on 25 December 1941 the Japanese, who occupied Hong Kong, forced large numbers to return to the mainland so that by 1945, on the resumption of British administration, the population was thought to be in the region of some 600,000. Once more the instability of China, due to civil war, led to a huge influx of Chinese from across the border so that the population swelled to an estimated 1.8 million by 1947. By 1961 the census showed a population of over 3 million rising to an estimated 5.8 million in 1990.

For much of the period there was a major imbalance between the sexes with males far outnumbering females. This was because large numbers of single Chinese males crossed over into the territory in search of employment. At the same time, the population was fairly young with the influx of these immigrants. The large growth in the population was heavily reduced in 1980 when the government put major restrictions on immigration from the mainland. The high birth rate, which characterized the population through most of its history, also showed a major decline as the standard of living in the territory dramatically improved in the 1970s and 1980s. (See Appendices.)

POTTINGER, SIR HENRY (1789–1856). Sir Henry Pottinger administered Hong Kong from August 1841 until June 1843. He was appointed to replace the dismissed Captain Elliot. He was instrumental in organizing the military expeditions against the Chinese which led to the Treaty of Nanking (Nanjing). Under his administration Hong Kong was declared a colony. (See Charter of 1843; Elliot, Captain Charles; Governors; Letters Patent; Nanking (Nanjing), Treaty of; Royal Instructions.)

PRESSURE GROUPS. From the earliest days of the colony certain pressure groups have had a major influence on the political system. The colony had been set up largely through the insistence of the British traders and merchants. These groups expected to have their expertise respected and their interests protected. They came to be increasingly represented on the Legislative Council by the late nineteenth century and had constant informal access to the civil service and other centers of power. As a general rule, their influence was directed at keeping government expenditure to a minimum, and restricting the political and economic power of the Chinese.

By the late nineteenth century members of the Chinese elite increasingly began to press for representation of their own needs and the needs of the wider Chinese community. The Board of the Tung Wah Hospital and the *Po Leung Kuk* were particularly prominent in promoting Chinese interests in the areas of health and social welfare.

In the twentieth century the trend of expanding the

representation of pressure groups in the legislative body was sustained. However, until the end of the Second World War the old order of the established British elite still dominated policy-making. Small groups of expatriates in the higher levels of the civil service had close working and social links with groups in business and commerce.

Pressure-group activity, represented by labor unions, exerted some influence in the period following the First World War, when strikes were occasionally used to some effect. However, in the post-Second World War period the unions had little impact, partly because of their limited membership—less than 14% of the workforce in 1987. Moreover, attempts to link unions foundered largely over the question of affiliation to political movements outside the colony. The larger Federation of Trade Unions had a marked affiliation to the People's Republic of China, and the smaller Hong Kong and Kowloon Trade Union Council had direct links with the Republic of China. However, the unionization of state employees, in such fields as teaching and the social-work sectors, developed significantly from the late 1970s onwards. Similar trends were seen in the civil service which by 1987 had over 53% of its staff belonging to unions.

In recent times the pressure groups operating in the territory could be categorized as follows:

1. Business groups, e.g., Hong Kong General Chamber of Commerce, American Chamber of Commerce.
2. Professional groups, e.g., Law Society, Institute of Engineers, Professional Teachers Union.
3. Individual trade unions and groupings of unions.
4. Sporting and recreational groups, e.g., the Royal Hong Kong Jockey Club.
5. Religious and charitable groups, e.g., Tung Wah Group of Hospitals, *Po Leung Kuk.*

6. Local and neighborhood groups, e.g., *Kaifongs*.
7. Civic groups, e.g., Rotary, Lions.
8. "Cause" groups, e.g., Friends of the Earth.
9. Political groups, e.g., Hong Kong Observers, Meeting Point.

The importance within the political system of some groups was formally recognized by the government with the setting up of the functional constituencies in 1985. Twelve seats were reserved in the Legislative Council for the following categories:

- Commercial, two seats (Hong Kong Chamber of Commerce, Chinese General Chamber of Commerce);
- Industrial, two seats (Federation of Hong Kong Industries, Chinese Manufactures Association);
- Financial, one seat (Hong Kong Association of Banks);
- Labor, two seats (representatives of all registered employee trade unions);
- Social services, one seat (Hong Kong Council of Social Services);
- Medical, one seat (Hong Kong Medical Association);
- Education, one seat;
- Legal, one seat (Bar Association and Law Society); and,
- Engineers and associated professions, one seat.

The number of functional seats was increased even further in 1988 to 14 and to 21 in 1991. In the Basic Law it was stated that after 1997 in the Special Administrative Region the number of functional constituencies would eventually constitute 50% of the total number of seats on the Legislative Council. (See American Chamber of Commerce; Basic Law; Chamber of Commerce, Chinese

General; Functional Constituencies; General Strike; Hong Kong General Chamber of Commerce; Legislative Council; Localization; Po Leung Kuk; Tung Wah.)

PREVENTION OF BRIBERY ORDINANCE. The Prevention of Bribery Ordinance was passed in Hong Kong in 1970 in an attempt to reduce the incidence of corruption in the territory. It was used as a weapon by the Independent Commission Against Corruption to prosecute large numbers of persons from 1975 onwards. (See Independent Commission Against Corruption.)

PRIVY COUNCIL. The Privy Council was established in England in the eleventh century to advise the monarch when he or she so desired. Its real power declined over the centuries in relation to the growing power of Parliament. Formally, however, it retained its advisory powers, and it was through resolution of the Privy Council that the British formally established their sovereignty over Hong Kong in 1843. Among its functions were to give formal effect to proclamations issued by the Crown. These proclamations, known as Orders in Council, were given the sovereign's assent. An Order in Council was used to acquire Kowloon on 24 October 1860 and the lease on the New Territories on 20 October 1898. It is only the Privy Council and not Parliament that has the formal right to acquire and surrender British territory, although convention demands that Parliamentary approval is always sought in such cases. (See Government, British; House of Commons; House of Lords; Legal System; Order in Council 1843; Parliament, British; Queen.)

PROTECTIONISM. See Economic System.

PUBLIC RECORDS OFFICE. The Public Records Office was established in 1972 to store all official records. It also has a large repository of historical documents and other materials relevant to Hong Kong. Although many prewar records were destroyed during the Japanese occupation (1941–1945), copies of many of them are still available from the United Kingdom.

PUNTI. The name the Cantonese residents of the New Territories gave themselves to distinguish themselves from the *Hakka* ("Strangers"), and now used for all Cantonese speaking residents of Hong Kong. *Punti* stems from the Cantonese *"poon tei"* which means "Local."

-Q-

QIN DYNASTY (221–207 B.C.). See Ch'in Dynasty.

QING DYNASTY (1644–1912). See Ch'ing Dynasty.

QUEEN. Queen Elizabeth II was born in 1926 and became the reigning monarch of the United Kingdom of Great Britain and Northern Ireland in 1952 on the death of her father King George VI. As the reigning British Monarch, she is the head of state and head of the British Commonwealth. Since 1952 it was she who formally appoints all the governors of Hong Kong. Formally, but not in practice, only she had the power to conclude treaties and annex or cede territory, and all government actions in the colony were accountable to the Queen and her ministers. (See Privy Council.)

-R-

RADIO. See Mass Media.

RAILWAYS. See Kowloon-Canton Railway; Mass Transit Railway.

RATIFICATION. The Joint Declaration between the United Kingdom of Great Britain and Northern Ireland and the Government of the People's Republic of China on the future of Hong Kong was ratified by the two governments on 27 May 1985. The document was then lodged in the archives of the United Nations under its treaty series, thus making the agreement valid in international law. (See Joint Declaration; United Nations.)

REACHED BASE POLICY (Touched Base Policy). A system operating in the territory from November 1974 until September 1980 whereby illegal immigrants from the People's Republic of China who could evade the authorities in the New Territories and reach the urban areas of Kowloon and Hong Kong were allowed to remain in the colony as permanent residents. Between 1975 and 1980 over 500,000 of these immigrants arrived in Hong Kong placing a huge strain upon the housing, educational, medical and social services. In response the Hong Kong government, in consultation with the authorities on the mainland, ended the Reached Base Policy. Since 1980 any illegal immigrants from China have been repatriated. However, since 1989 political refugees from the People's Republic of China have been allowed to pass through Hong Kong on their way to Taiwan and the United States of America. (See Illegal Immigration; Snake Heads.)

REFORM ASSOCIATION. The first Reform Association was established in Hong Kong in 1867 in response to the major constitutional reforms taking place in Great Britain, most notably the doubling in the size of the electorate. However, the Hong Kong Reform Association's attempts to make the Legislative Council more accountable died out in 1869 through an almost total lack of support. Another attempt in 1917 by a similar body named the Constitutional Reform Association met the same fate. (See Legislative Council; Pressure Groups.)

REFORM CLUB. A pressure group established in 1952 which pressed for more representational government in Hong Kong along with better social service provision. It was successful in providing the majority of the elected members to the Urban Council. Dominated by expatriates for much of its history, it was to see a reduction in its influence as new Chinese groups established themselves in the 1970s. (See Pressure Groups; Urban Council.)

REFUGEES. See Vietnamese Refugees.

REGIONAL COUNCIL. The Regional Council began operating in 1984 but it was not formally established until 1986. Its role was to provide a municipal service to the New Territories. Its main concerns were with the provision of environmental hygiene, public health, sanitation, liquor licensing, and the provision of cultural and recreation facilities. It was created largely because of the huge increase in the population and the establishment of new towns in the New Territories during the 1970s and early 1980s. The composition of the Regional Council (REGNO) was 12 appointed members, nine indirectly elected from the District Boards and three *ex-officio* members from the traditional representatives of the New Territories, namely the *Heung Yee Kuk*. The Regional Council was allowed to elect one of its members to sit on the central Legislative Council. (See Heung Yee Kuk; Local Government; Urban Council.)

RELIGION. Traditionally the majority of the Chinese in the territory practiced Buddhism, Taoism, and the worship of various traditional Chinese deities. A famous Buddhist monastery was built at Tuen Mun (Castle Peak) in the 5th century A.D. and rebuilt several times in the ensuing 1,500 years. Nearby the granite statue of the Buddhist saint Bei Du (A.D. 420–479) was carved in the 10th century. The 14th-century pagoda at Ping Shan demonstrates the influence of the local belief in geomancy. Other temples in the territory reflect the existence of large numbers of local deities. The most important of these temples is the Tin Hau Temples at Joss House Bay built in the Sung (Song) Dynasty in the 13th century.

With the arrival of the British, the principle of religious freedom was formally established, and other religions quickly established themselves including Christianity, Islam, Hinduism, Sikhism, and Judaism. The Episcopalian (Anglican) St John's Cathedral was opened for services in 1849, a Roman Catholic Cathedral of the Immaculate Conception in 1842 and Bethanie for sick French missionaries in 1875. These, plus the large number of other missionary organizations, such as the American Baptist Mission (1843), attest both to the freedom of religion and to the attempts to proselytize in the colony. No attempts, however, were made by the government to interfere with the religious customs of the local inhabitants and the number of converts to Christianity was never very high. However, it needs to be added that many of the early missions were established in Hong Kong primarily as a base for the spreading of Christianity on the mainland.

The question of Hong Kong's political future after 1997 raised considerable concern among religious organizations fearful that the lack of freedom of religion found in the mainland might be extended to Hong Kong. The Joint Declaration of 1984 went some way to assuaging these fears by stating in Article 3 (5) that freedom of religion was guaranteed, with an addition in the elaboration of the agreements that: "religious organizations and believers may maintain their relations with religious organizations and believers elsewhere, and schools, hospitals, and welfare institutions run by religious organizations." In short, the rules pertaining to the mainland would not apply in the future Special Administrative Region. This freedom of religion was further emphasized in Article 38 of the Basic Law.

REPUBLIC OF CHINA. See China, Republic of.

RIOTS. See Disturbances.

ROBINSON, SIR HERCULES (1824–1897). Governor of Hong Kong from September 1859 until March 1865. Internally he introduced long overdue reforms of the civil service in an attempt to reduce corruption. He also took steps to improve the quality of the administration by reorganizing its structure. He was given the wider task of administering and absorbing into the colony Kowloon and Stonecutters Island which were ceded to Britain in perpetuity by the Chinese in 1860. (See Arrow War; Stonecutters Island.)

ROBINSON, SIR WILLIAM (1836–1912). Governor of Hong Kong from December 1891 until January 1898. He increased the unofficial membership of the Executive Council to two of whom one was to be Chinese. He also put an end to the practice of holding government office and simultaneously having relevant commercial interests. He left the colony on January 1898 six months before the acquisition of the New Territories. (See Executive Council; New Territories.)

ROCK CARVINGS. Rock carvings were discovered at Shek Pik in 1939. They are believed to date from the Bronze Age. Others have been found in many parts of Hong Kong, although none, to date, have been found anywhere outside the territory. Nearly all have been found near to the sea, with the exception of those discovered at

Wong Chuk Hang. The majority are geometric, spiral designs, some with stylized animal faces found in the patterns. (See Map.)

ROYAL ASIATIC SOCIETY. The Royal Asiatic Society was originally founded in London in March 1823. Its aims were to investigate subjects connected with Asia and to encourage the development of science, religion and the arts in that part of the world. It has, in its history, been a rich scholastic source of information on Asia and has done much to improve our knowledge of the region. Branches were established in Bombay and Madras in India in 1838, Ceylon (Sri Lanka) in 1845, Shanghai in 1857, Japan in 1875, Malaya in 1878 and Korea in 1900. The Hong Kong branch was established in 1847 with the Governor, Sir John Davies, as the first president. In 1859 the society collapsed, to be resuscitated on 28 December 1959. Since that time the Hong Kong branch has produced large numbers of papers and articles, many of them of considerable historical interest on matters pertaining to Hong Kong, China, and the Far East.

ROYAL HONG KONG JOCKEY CLUB. See Clubs.

ROYAL HONG KONG POLICE FORCE. The first police in the colony were raised in 1841, but a recognizable force did not come into being until 1845 when it consisted of three officers and 160 rank and file. From the force's very beginning there were problems with corruption. The then Governor Richard Macdonnell (1866–1872) commented that, "I have never met or heard in any colony a body of men so corrupt and worthless *en masse* as the Hong Kong police, or so unreliable in every way or so ineffective in proportion to their numbers."

Determined efforts were made in the 1870s to improve the situation. Senior posts were filled with British officers and an attempt was made to increase the number of Chinese in the lower ranks. By 1874 the balance was 110 Europeans, 177 Indians, and 204 Chinese. This approximate balance remained until the occupation of the colony by Japanese forces in 1941.

After the Second World War there was a major reduction in the recruitment of Indian police with a parallel increase in the number of local Chinese entering the force. At the same time, Europeans were no longer recruited into the junior ranks below that of Inspector. (In the Hong Kong system there were three major divisions in ascending order of authority. The bulk of the force was made up of constables, sergeants, and station sergeants. The second division was Inspector up to Chief Superintendent. The third was Assistant Commissioner up to the Commissioner of Police.)

By 1950, 85% of the rank and file and 75% of the entire force were Chinese. Increasingly attempts were made to localize the officer ranks, although as late as 1988 there were still 264 Overseas (mostly British) officers against 674 locals. The first Chinese Commissioner of Police was appointed in 1988.

It appears that the problem of corruption was substantially reduced in the 1970s and 1980s. In 1973 a major scandal which rocked the force led to the arrest of a senior police officer on charges of corruption and was followed by the establishment of the Independent Commission Against Corruption (ICAC). This organization principally targeted the police in its early operations, and between 1974 and 1979 over 250 police officers were prosecuted by the ICAC on charges of corruption. However, that number gradually decreased so that in 1990 there were only five prosecutions of police officers. (See Godber Affair; Independent Commission Against Corruption; Localization; MacLennon Inquiry.)

ROYAL INSTRUCTIONS. The document known as Royal Instructions were first issued on April 5, 1843 to expand upon and elucidate the Letters Patent. The document is fairly simple. It gives detailed instructions on the Constitution of the Executive and Legislative Council, outlining its powers and functions in relation to the making of laws and ordinances.

The Royal Instructions could be amended when necessary to accommodate changes. Indeed, they were frequently amended in the latter half of the 19th century, and in 1917 they were completely overhauled. All revocations of previous articles are stated in the appropriate way with the date of revocation. In total, there were eight revocations between 1917 and 1985 as well as a number of extensions. The broad areas covered by the Royal Instructions from the 1917 version include the following:

- the provision of oaths or affirmations of allegiance;
- the composition and membership of the Executive Council;
- the rules pertaining to the presiding over the Executive Council by the Governor or his proxy;
- the conditions under which the Governor may or may not consult with the Executive Council, and his powers over it;
- the provision for elections to the Legislative Council and their timing;
- the delineation of the governor's powers relating to the suspension of the Legislative Council;
- the composition of the Legislative Council;
- provision for the suspension of individuals from the Legislative Council;
- the details of the necessary quorum for the Legislative Council and the dates to begin and end each session;
- the provision that the Governor should preside at

meetings whenever possible, and provisions for presidents in his absence;

- the standing rules and orders for proceedings;
- the outline of the procedures for bills to become ordinances and stipulations of reserved bills;
- the requirement that all ordinances be submitted to the British Secretary of State; and,
- provision for the Governor to pardon or reprieve those sentenced to death.

Under the provisions of the Joint Declaration, signed between the governments of the United Kingdom and the People's Republic of China (PRC), Hong Kong will cease to be a colony at the stroke of midnight on 30 June 1997. At that point the Royal Instructions and the Letters Patent will cease to have any authority. (See Basic Law; Constitution; Executive Council; Governor; Joint Declaration; Letters Patent; Oath of Allegiance; Queen.)

ROYAL NAVY. See Armed Forces.

RURAL COMMITTEES. After the end of the Second World War, the Hong Kong government's attempts to improve communication between the village leadership and the central authorities in the New Territories led to the establishment of Rural Committees. The New Territories were divided into 27 districts each having its own Rural Committee with the membership elected or appointed by the villagers themselves. Initially the committees had only the authority that the government-appointed District Officer allowed them. In 1957 the Rural Committees were linked to the *Heung Yee Kuk* with their Chairmen and Vice Chairmen becoming *ex-officio* members of the *Kuk*.

With the rapid urbanization of the New Territories and the concomitant increase in the population, the Rural Committees were reduced in importance as larger organizations, such as the District Boards and Regional Council, grew in significance. The Basic Law of April 1990, which is to come into force with the creation of the Special Administrative Region in 1997, pays little reference to the affairs of the Rural Committees in particular, or the *Heung Yee Kuk* in general, apart from the statement in Article 40 which stated that "the legitimate traditional rights and interests of the indigenous inhabitants of the 'New Territories' shall be protected." (See Basic Law; District Administration Scheme; *Heung Yee Kuk;* New Territories; Regional Council.)

-S-

SALT. Large quantities of salt were produced from salt fields in Hong Kong from at least the seventh and eighth centuries onwards, and even as late as the British arrival in the New Territories there was still a thriving export trade in salt. Because of the imposition of taxes on this commodity by the imperial authorities, salt was smuggled over the border and sold at below the official price. In 1923 Sun Yat-sen's (Sun Yixian) government was eager to take over the revenues from the Chinese Salt Administration which was still under the control of the rival government in the north. When a launch belonging to the Salt Administration took refuge in Hong Kong its internment by the British soured relationships with the Sun Yat-sen (Sun Yixian) government for a time.

During the First World War and again in 1937 proposals were drawn up for the colony to impose its own tax on salt, but on neither occasion was the idea pursued.

SAN ON (XIN-AN). In 1573 the county of Tungkuan (Dongguan) (established in 757 A.D.), of which the Hong Kong area had been a part, was divided, and the southern half renamed San On (Xin-An) county, centered on the city of Nam Tau (Nantou) just to the northwest of Hong

Kong. The Gazetteers, descriptions of the district produced by the local government of this period, provide a valuable historical source of information on Hong Kong.

SANITARY BOARD. See Health.

SECOND WORLD WAR. On 3 September 1939, Britain and France declared war on Germany in response to Hitler's invasion of Poland. Japan, however, declared its neutrality in the conflict. As a consequence, the British colonial administration in Hong Kong, as part of the wider strategy in Asia, took a neutral stance relating to Japan. This proved difficult, given the fact that Japanese forces were occupying territory in China adjacent to the borders of the colony and the understandably pro-Chinese sympathies of the population.

When on 7 December 1941 the Japanese forces attacked Pearl Harbor, the main American naval base in the Pacific, an attack was also launched on Hong Kong. The British forces were inadequately prepared and were rapidly defeated. The Governor announced the surrender of the colony on 25 December. The ensuing years were particularly harsh in the colony with widespread starvation and deprivation. (See Instrument of Surrender; World Wars.)

SHAM CHUN (SHENZHEN). Sham Chun (Shenzhen) is a part of the PRC situated immediately to the north of Hong Kong. It was designated a Special Economic Zone (SEZ) in 1980. The policy of the PRC is to develop a small number of such zones which are free from many of the planning regulations operating elsewhere. Investment in these zones has principally been by joint venture companies linking the Chinese state and foreign companies. A large number of Hong Kong entrepreneurs have set up factories in the SEZs taking advantage of labor costs which are less than half those in Hong Kong, low land costs, and ease of access to outside markets. As a result, there has been a substantial movement of manufacturing establishments out of the territory and into Sham Chun (Shenzhen), and an increasing tendency for those firms which remain to offset their relatively high costs by turning to the production of more sophisticated products. (See Economy: Four Modernizations; Special Economic Zones; Trade.)

SINO-BRITISH JOINT DECLARATION. See Joint Declaration.

SINO-BRITISH NEGOTIATIONS. Under the terms of the Convention of Peking (Beijing) in 1898, the New Territories were leased to Britain with the proviso that they were due to revert to Chinese sovereignty in 1997. No substantive intergovernmental discussions on the issue then took place until 1979 when Sir Murray MacLehose became the first Governor of Hong Kong to pay an official visit to the People's Republic of China. At the time MacLehose was under pressure from business interests in the colony to reduce some of the uncertainties over the future of the New Territories. The question of land leases in the New Territories was particularly problematic given the differences between capitalist Hong Kong and the socialist system in the PRC.

Sir Murray raised the issue with the Chinese authorities but no agreements were reached. Teng Hsiao-p'ing (Deng Xiaoping) simply told the Hong Kong people to put their "hearts at ease," reaffirming an earlier and equally vague statement made by the Chinese authorities at the United Nations in 1972 that the Hong Kong problem would be solved when "conditions are ripe."

In 1982 a British minister, Sir Humphrey Atkins, pressed the Peking (Beijing) authorities to reopen formal negotiations. Subsequently, (on a visit to the People's Republic of China in April 1982) Mr. Edward Heath, a former British Prime Minister, was given further details of Peking's (Beijing's) intentions. Under these proposals Hong Kong would become a Special Economic Zone under Chinese sovereignty, without any British presence but with a high degree of autonomy.

Britain had hoped for some other arrangements which would allow for a continued presence, and the then Prime Minister Mrs. Margaret Thatcher paid a visit to the People's Republic of China in September 1982 to open negotiations aimed at resolving the differences and achieving "stability and prosperity for Hong Kong." Almost immediately, however, relationships were soured when the Prime Minister, Margaret Thatcher, announced in Hong Kong that the original treaties signed in the nineteenth century had been accepted by the two sovereign states and were therefore valid in law. This was in direct contradiction to the Chinese position which had been that what they referred to as "unequal treaties" had been forced upon the Chinese through military defeat and as such were not valid.

Further talks revealed that the positions were too far apart for any substantive progress, and in September 1983 the Chinese, in an attempt to break the deadlock, announced that they would make a unilateral decision in 1984 if mutual agreements could not be concluded. This statement caused panic in Hong Kong with price collapses in both the property market and the stock exchange and a huge run on the Hong Kong dollar.

These events seem to have convinced both the British and the Chinese authorities to adopt more flexible positions. The British, in particular, dropped their preconditions and concentrated on getting as many concessions as possible from the Chinese side. Most importantly they accepted the broad format put forward by Teng Hsiao-p'ing (Deng Xiaoping) concerning the end of British administration and the return of the whole of Hong Kong to Chinese sovereign control.

The deadlock was now broken and agreements were quickly concluded. By April 1984, the British Foreign Secretary was able to visit Peking (Beijing) and settle the outstanding issues. He returned to Hong Kong and announced that British administration would cease in 1997. In September 1984 the talks ended and in the same month the Joint Declaration was released. (See Convention of Peking (Beijing); Joint Declaration; MacLehose, Sir Murray; New Territories; Stability and Prosperity; Teng Hsiao-p'ing (Deng Xiaoping); Thatcher, Margaret.)

SINO-PORTUGUESE JOINT DECLARATION. See Macau entries.

SINO-PORTUGUESE JOINT NEGOTIATIONS. See Macau entries.

SIX DYNASTIES (265–581). During this period the Hong Kong area came under the control of the Ch'in (Qin), Liu Sung, and Chen kingdoms. Considerable trade developed over the years between Canton (Guangzhou) and Indochina. Tuen Mun was made an important customs post to control ships moving in and out of the Pearl Estuary. It is probable that there were exclusion areas around Tuen Mun in which no civilians were allowed to live. There is no evidence of civilian Chinese settlement during this period. It is thought that the first Buddhist monastery was built near Tuen Mun in the mid-fifth century.

SNAKE HEADS. A term used to describe boat owners who smuggled illegal immigrants into Hong Kong before the ending of the Reached (Touched) Base Policy in 1980. Their activities were at their height in the 1960s and 1970s when they relied on fast boats which were difficult to intercept. While their charges were high, the safety of the passengers was a low priority. Moreover, their refusal to guarantee passage to the urban areas meant that their passengers had still to cross the New Territories. Many failed to do this undetected, were arrested and returned to the PRC. (See Illegal Immigrants; Reached Base Policy.)

SOCIETIES ORDINANCE. See Triads.

SOVEREIGNTY. The position of the People's Republic of China regarding Hong Kong was that the treaties signed between the United Kingdom and the Imperial government in the nineteenth century were invalid. They perceived the treaties as "unequal," having been imposed by a powerful state upon a weaker state. Consequently, Britain was seen as never having had any sovereignty over Hong Kong despite having ruled it since 1843. This position was to cause a disruption of the 1982 negotiations regarding the future status of Hong Kong when British claims to sovereignty were disputed by the Chinese authorities. It was not until the British conceded this point that substantive negotiations on the status of Hong Kong in the post-1997 period could continue. Ultimately the Joint Declaration stated that "The government of the People's Republic of China . . . has decided to resume the exercise of sovereignty over Hong Kong." (See Anglo-Chinese Wars; Conventions of Peking (Beijing); Joint Declaration; Nanking (Nanjing), Treaty of; Tientsin (Tianjin), Treaty of; Unequal Treaties.)

SPECIAL ADMINISTRATIVE REGION (SAR). Hong Kong will be termed the Hong Kong Special Administrative Region when it reverts to Chinese control in 1997. The term was first used in the fourth version of the constitution of the People's Republic of China (1982), Article 31. It was to be applied to Hong Kong, Macau, and the Republic of China (Taiwan). The purpose of the SARs is to grant a high degree of autonomy to these regions so that if and when they were reunified with the mainland they could retain different social, political, and economic systems. Macau, under a different set of arrangements is to become a Special Administrative Region in 1999. The Republic of China (Taiwan) did not respond favorably to the idea of being offered SAR status within the PRC. (See Autonomy; Basic Law; Joint Declaration.)

SPECIAL BRANCH. The Special Branch was formed as part of the Hong Kong police force in the 1950s (although a similar organization existed in the interwar period) to monitor any subversive elements in the territory. Its main targets were perceived to be communists residing in the colony but operating under orders from the People's Republic of China. (See Royal Hong Police Force.)

SPECIAL ECONOMIC ZONES (SEZs). Special Economic Zones were created in 1980 in response to the People's Republic of China's new "Four Modernizations" program. Teng Hsiao-p'ing (Deng Xiaoping) announced their creation for the purposes of attracting foreign capital, and introducing new technology and techniques to the mainland. Three were located in Kwangtung (Guangdong) province: Sham Chun (Shenzhen), Chu Hai (Zuhai), and Shantou (Swatow). Others were created at the same time in other provinces on the mainland. Special rules pertained to these SEZs which did not apply in other areas. Most important were the regulations which encouraged outside investment, preferential tax incentives, and provision for the establishment of joint ventures with firms from outside the PRC. (See Economic System; Four Modernizations; Teng Hsiao-p'ing (Deng Xiaoping); Sham Chun (Shenzhen).)

STABILITY AND PROSPERITY. A term first popularized in 1982 by the then Prime Minister Margaret Thatcher and the Chinese leader Teng Hsiao-p'ing (Deng Xiaoping) to express the key conditions needed in Hong Kong in the lead-up to 1997 and beyond. The phrase was included in both the Joint Declaration and in the preamble to the Basic Law, and has become a familiar echo in the territory's political rhetoric. (See Basic Law; Joint Declaration; Teng Hsiao-p'ing (Deng Xiaoping); Thatcher, Margaret.)

STAR FERRY RIOTS. The Star Ferry riots of April 1966 were triggered by the attempts of the Star Ferry Company to increase fares from Hong Kong Island to Kowloon. The riots lasted for three days and led to a public enquiry which recommended that communication between the government and the public needed to be much improved. (See Disturbances.)

STONE AGE. The first evidence of settlement in the Hong Kong area comes from the end of the last Ice Age (18,000–15,000 B.C.). There are at present 12 known sites from the Stone Age and all, except one, are situated on sandbars above the beach. No buildings or structures have been discovered. However, bones of animals and fish have been found along with stone tools and pottery. It is normally assumed that the inhabitants were seafarers rather than permanent residents.

STONECUTTERS ISLAND. Stonecutters Island is a small island situated in Hong Kong Harbor. Along with Kowloon, it was ceded to Britain by China in 1860 under the terms of the Treaty of Tientsin (Tianjin). (See Tientsin (Tianjin), Treaty of.)

STRIKES. See Disturbances.

STUBBS, SIR REGINALD (1876–1947). Governor of Hong Kong from September 1919 until October 1925. He arrived at a difficult period, with the whole of China in a state of political turmoil. In the south of China Sun Yat-sen (Sun Yixian), was providing a focus for rising Chinese nationalism which was to clash with the colonial powers, not the least the colonial government in Hong Kong. In the colony itself many workers identified with the new pride in China and were beginning to press for higher wages, lower prices on staple foodstuffs, and an increase in political influence. Labor relations deteriorated and Stubbs had to deal with general strikes in 1922 and 1925–1926. He was unable to resolve the 1925–1926 strike during his administration. (See Disturbances; General Strike; China, Republic of; Sun Yat-sen (Sun Yixian).)

SUN YAT-SEN, DR. (SUN YIXIAN). (1866–1925). Sun Yat-sen (Sun Yixian) was one of the major figures in the struggle to overthrow the Ch'ing (Qing) dynasty. He was influential in the establishment of the Kuomintang (Guomindang) Party which formed the government in China until overthrown by the Chinese Communist Party in 1949. He was born in Kwangtung (Guangdong) Province just north of Macau, educated in Hawaii, and attended the Hong Kong Medical College from 1897 to 1891. Hong Kong had a major effect upon his thinking and he claimed in 1923 that most of his revolutionary and modern ideas stemmed from observing the economy and administration of the colony. In the 1890s he became involved in revolutionary politics on the mainland and fled from the Chinese authorities to London where his studies led him to crystallize his political ideas. The best known of these were his three "People's Principles," namely Nationalism, People's Rights, and Socialism. These principles, in turn, led to a belief in the need to overthrow the monarchy; to create a republic in China; to remove the colonial powers; to establish an orderly institutional framework with elections and accountable legislative and executive branches in government; and, to ensure greater government control of the economy.

When the Ch'ing (Qing) dynasty collapsed, Sun was declared the provisional president of the first republic. However, he was removed from that position by the warlord Yuan Shih-kai as China descended into a period of warlordism. Dr. Sun fled first to Japan and later to South China, where he reorganized the Kuomintang (Guomindang) Party in 1924.

Dr. Sun died in 1925 and is one of the few figures held in high esteem both in the People's Republic of China and in the Republic of China (Taiwan). (See China, Republic of; Ch'ing (Qing) Dynasty; Chiang Kai-shek (Jiang Jieshi); Kuomintang (Guomindang).)

SUN YIXIAN, DR. See Sun Yat-sen.

SUNG (SONG) DYNASTY (960–1279). The Sung (Song) dynasty, at its height, united China from the Great Wall in the north to Hainan Island in the south. It was to be replaced in 1279 by the Yuan (Yuan) dynasty. The Sung (Song) conquered the Hong Kong area in the mid-tenth century and established a powerful military presence of up to 3,000 men. Centered at Tuen Mun, it was successful in controlling the activities of pirates. With the more settled conditions, trade flourished with Kowloon becoming an important center. The area now attracted settlers to the region with Chinese civilians coming to farm from the eleventh century. The first Chinese gentry families also came and established large estates in the area. One such family, the *Tang,* owned large tracts of land throughout the county. Other major clans established (mainly in the New Territories) during this period were the *Hau* clan and the *Pang* clan.

During the last years of the Sung (Song) period, the

Hong Kong region was in the forefront of Chinese history for the only time prior to the twentieth century. The last two Sung (Song) Emperors fleeing south from the Mongols passed through the area. They stayed at various sites in Hong Kong, including Lantau and Kowloon City. Despite small successes against the Mongol armies in the south, the area fell to the Mongols when an attack was made upon Kowloon by land and sea. The two emperors retreated to Tsuen Wan and then across the Pearl River. In 1279 the Mongol forces finally destroyed the last Emperor and the Sung (Song) dynasty ended.

SUPREME COURT. See Legal system.

-T-

TAIPING REBELLION (1851–1864). The Taiping Rebellion was a peasant uprising in China which threatened the Ch'ing (Qing) dynasty, but was eventually put down by imperial troops aided by the British General Gordon. It caused great instability in the Southern part of China and led to a large increase in the population of Hong Kong as people fled from the troubles on the mainland. (See Ch'ing (Qing) Dynasty.)

TAIWAN. See China, Republic of.

T'ANG (TANG) DYNASTY (618–907). The T'ang (Tang) dynasty revived imperial interest in the Hong Kong area, which had been largely lost during the period of the Sui (Sui), rulers of China from 581–618. The area was actively garrisoned to safeguard and further encourage a growth of trade between Canton to India and Persia. During this period important pearl fisheries were set up in Tai Po in the New Territories; Tuen Mun became an important naval base guarding the approaches to Canton; and the poet Han Yue (819–824) made specific mention of it (the first time any place within the present-day Hong Kong is recorded in any surviving contemporary Chinese source). The Hong Kong area had by this time established a thriving trade in salt. There is no evidence of the region being colonized by civilian Chinese in this period.

TAXI DRIVERS' DISPUTE. The taxi drivers' dispute occurred in 1984. It was caused by Government proposals to increase substantially the annual taxi license fee, to limit the number of taxis, and to impose a surcharge on taxis with diesel engines. A bill was approved by the Executive Council and passed through to the Legislative Council. However, when the taxi drivers heard of the proposals they immediately called a strike. The use of taxis to block main roads quickly paralyzed the road system. On the second day of the strike riots and looting broke out in Kowloon, and, faced with a deteriorating situation, the unofficial members of the Legislative Council came out in opposition to the bill, which was then withdrawn. (See Disturbances; Legislative Council; Unofficial Members.)

TENG HSIAO-P'ING (DENG XIAOPING) (1904–). Teng Hsiao-p'ing (Deng Xiaoping) was born in Szechwan (Sichuan) province in 1904. In his youth he went to study in France with a number of Chinese radicals, including Chou En-lai (Zhou Enlai). He joined the Communist Party in 1925 and spent some time studying in the Soviet Union. He was prominent in the activities of the Chinese Communist Party (CCP) and founded the seventh Red Army. He served in the Red Army's political department from 1932–1934 and edited the newspaper the *Red Star*. During the Long March he gained prominence in the party and became the Secretary of the Central Committee and the Politburo.

In 1950, after the establishing of the People's Republic of China, he became Vice-Chairman in the government. From 1952 to 1954 he was minister of finance and member of the State Planning Commission. In 1954 he became Deputy Premier of the National People's Congress and Deputy Chairman of the Defence Council. When the post of party General Secretary was restored in 1954, Teng (Deng) was elected. From 1956 onwards, he deputized as Acting Premier in the absence of Chou En-lai (Zhou Enlai) and was third in rank in the State Council.

He was to suffer along with many others during the Cultural Revolution, being purged in 1966. Unlike many others, however, he was reinstated in 1973 and again quickly rose in the hierarchy so that by early 1976 he was third in line after Mao and Chou (Zhou). With the death of Chou (Zhou) in 1976, he was expected to take over on the death of Mao, but was again ousted in the abortive attempt by the "Gang of Four" to seize power.

With the removal of the "Gang of Four" he was once more returned to power. He was associated with the liberal wing of the Communist Party and was largely instrumental in bringing in the economic reforms associated with the Four Modernizations. In 1987 Teng (Deng) relinquished all but one of his official positions, namely the Chairmanship of the Party Central Military Commission. He relinquished this post in March 1990. Despite holding no official post, he continued to exercise real political power with the official leaders in the party still remaining wary of his authority.

Tengs's (Deng's) influence on Hong Kong was considerable. It was he who set in train the negotiations which led to the agreements to return the colony to the People's Republic of China in 1997. The "One Country-Two Systems" formula was very much of his making thus providing a formula for the new Special Administrative Region to be established after the handover. He was extremely popular in the colony for his economic liberalizations on the mainland and for his position on Hong Kong. However, his reputation in the territory plunged after the T'ien-an-man (Tiananman) disturbances in 1989. (See China, People's Republic of; Chou En-lai (Zhou Enlai); Communist Party of China; Cultural Revolution; Four Modernizations; Gang of Four; People's Liberation Army; Sino-British Negotiations; Thatcher, Margaret.)

TERRITORY. Until the early 1970s Hong Kong was invariably referred to as a "colony" by the government. The term colony was also to be found on the local currency. However, increasingly sensitive to the pejorative association of the word colony the government began to use the term "territory." This can be illustrated by a comparison of statements in the Government Year Books. In 1982 the Year Book wrote, "Hong Kong is administered by the Hong Kong Government and organized along the lines traditional for a British Colony." In contrast, readers of the 1983 edition learned that, "Hong Kong is administered by the Hong Kong Government, and its administration had developed from the basic pattern applied to all the British governed territories overseas." However, some legal documents are more precise and accurate. In the Letters Patent an amendment to April 1988 Article One states that, "There shall be a Governor and Commander-in-Chief in and over Our Colony of Hong Kong and its Dependencies (hereinafter called the Colony)." (See Colony; Letters Patent).

TEXTILES. See Economy; Trade.

THATCHER, MARGARET HILDA (1925–). Prime Minister of Britain from 1979–1990. She played a major role in the Sino-British negotiations over the future of Hong Kong. She visited Peking (Beijing) in 1982 and on her return to Hong Kong defended the validity of the treaties signed between the British and Chinese in the nineteenth century. This led to a deterioration in Sino-British relations and a major crisis of confidence in the territory.

In 1990 she was also instrumental in pushing through the British House of Commons an Act which allowed for the right of abode in Britain for 50,000 key personnel and their dependents. This Act faced considerable opposition both from the right wing of the Conservative party and from the Labor opposition. She was replaced as leader of the Conservative party in 1990, and resigned from the post of Prime Minister. (See Government, British; House of Commons; Parliament, British; Sino-British Negotiations; Sovereignty; Teng Hsiao-p'ing (Deng Xiaoping).)

THIRTY-YEAR RULE. A rule in Hong Kong which states that government documents not otherwise published cannot be made public for thirty years. This applies, for instance, to the deliberations of the Executive Council whose agenda papers are not available for public scrutiny. Even after thirty years certain parts of any document deemed to be highly sensitive can be removed. Future historians will probably have to wait much longer than thirty years to gain access to either British or Hong Kong sources in order to evaluate the details and progress of the negotiations concerning the future of Hong Kong. Hong Kong, like the United Kingdom but unlike the United States of America, does not have a Freedom of Information Act. (See Executive Council.)

THREE KINGDOMS. (221–265). Little is known of this period with respect to the Hong Kong area, except that it came under the control of the Wu kingdoms who showed little interest in the region.

TIANANMAN. See T'ien-an-man.

TIANJIN, TREATY OF. See Tientsin, Treaty of.

T'IEN-AN-MAN (TIANANMAN). The T'ien-an-man (Tiananman) Square incident was of major significance to Hong Kong as well as the People's Republic of China. During May and June 1989 students and factory workers began gathering at the T'ien-an-man (Tiananman) Square in Peking (Beijing) and calling for reforms to liberalize the political system, combat the level of corruption, and further loosen bureaucratic controls over the economy. The rallying cries were freedom and democracy. The movement gained momentum with support from other major cities in China, and the event gained massive international media coverage. The leadership was divided in their attitude towards these protests, with Chao Tzu–yang (Zhao Ziyang) representing the reformist wing and Li Peng the conservative.

By June the authorities were concerned that the authority of the party and government was being undermined, and on 4 June 1989 the People's Liberation Army (PLA) was used to violently suppress the demonstrations in the Square.

The considerable Hong Kong support for the demonstrations both before and after June 4 was publicly condemned by the Chinese authorities. Their anger was increased by the use of the territory as part of the escape route for fleeing dissidents after the crackdown. Two Hong Kong members of the Basic Law Drafting Committee were expelled and labelled as counter-revolutionaries, and all progress on the Basic Law was postponed. Moreover, when the final draft was released it included provisions for the Special Administrative Region to prohibit any act of treason, secession, sedition, and subversion against the Central People's Republic. (See Basic Law; Lee Chu-ming, Martin.)

TIENTSIN (TIANJIN), TREATY OF. The Treaty of Tientsin (Tianjin) ended the Second Anglo-Chinese Wars (1856–1858) and led to substantial concessions by the imperial Chinese government to the British. (See Arrow Wars.)

TIN HAU FESTIVAL. According to Chinese legend, Tin Hau was the sixth daughter of an official in Fukien (Fujian) province. At the age of 15 Tin Hau was believed to have acquired the ability to ride on clouds. She gained the reputation for saving people in danger, especially those at sea. When she was 28 years old, Tin Hau climbed a hill with her sisters. There she entered a beautiful carriage in the sky, and was carried up to heaven. There are many temples dedicated to this goddess in Hong Kong. They are particularly well-attended on festival dates, especially by fishermen who ask Tin Hau not only to ensure bountiful catches, but also to provide protection from danger at sea. (See Chinese Temples.)

TOUCHED BASE POLICY. See Reached Base Policy.

TRADE. Much of Hong Kong's history has been associated with its importance as a base for trade, arising largely from its position at the mouth of the Pearl River and its proximity to the important trading, manufacturing, and administrative center of Canton (Guangzhou). Naval posts to guard the approaches to Canton (Guangzhou), and to control the trade with Southeast Asia were established as early as the Han (Han) Dynasty (206 B.C.–220 A.D.). By the period 265–581 A.D., Hong Kong was used as a customs post for trade moving between China and Indochina. In the period 618–907 A.D., trade with India and Persia had grown so much that mention is made of the size of the naval base at Tuen

Mun and its pivotal role in protecting the approaches to Canton (Guangzhou).

Trade with China was also generated locally by the flourishing salt farms, incense plantations, and pearl fisheries in the area. Salt and pearls were controlled as imperial monopolies, and were particularly important during the five dynasties period (907–969).

The arrival of the Europeans in the Hong Kong region led initially to considerable friction over trade. The Portuguese in Macau and the ever-increasing pressure by the British to allow greater trade with China culminated in the Anglo-Chinese Wars by which Hong Kong was ultimately acquired by the British.

Hong Kong's usefulness to the British stemmed from its superb deep harbor, its proximity to Canton, and its provision of a base from which to mount military expeditions into China when necessary. These advantages were augmented by a government structure that at the very least provided few obstacles to trade, and that at best provided merchants in the colony with government protection and a stable political system in which to operate.

The colony soon also became an important center for entrepôt activity. As such, it became a clearing house for the import of goods primarily intended for reshipping to China and a center for the export of goods from China. Ocean-going ships using the colony increased from 2,889 ships in 1860 to 23,881 in 1939. Hong Kong itself produced few exports, and the colony remained very much a transit center until the post-Second World War period.

Following the Japanese occupation (1941–1945), when trade virtually ceased in the colony, the increasing instability in the mainland led to dramatic falls in trading activity.

The period following the establishment of the People's

Republic of China in 1949 saw a transformation of the pattern of trade in the colony. Indigenous manufacturing grew up in the territories, especially in textiles, for which there was increasing demand from Western Europe and the United States of America in particular. In the 1950s and 1960s both exports and imports grew constantly, although imports continually exceeded exports. Total trade grew from HK$2,767 million in 1947 to HK$19,230 million in 1967. The main imports during this period were food, raw materials, and fossil fuels. The main exports were increasingly manufactured goods such as textiles, and later plastics, electrical goods and watches.

The largest market for goods from Hong Kong was the U.S., followed by the United Kingdom and the Federal Republic of Germany, rising from over HK$500 million in 1959 to over HK$2500 million in 1967. The most important source of imports to Hong Kong was China, particularly because of the imports of food upon which the colony was highly dependent. China was followed in significance by Japan, the U.S., and the United Kingdom.

The growth of trade continued in the 1970s and 1980s. The United States remained the chief market for the colony's exports with 32% of the total value. Also significant were the People's Republic of China, Germany, the United Kingdom, and Japan. The People's Republic of China was the greatest source of Hong Kong's imports with 35% of the total. Japan, Taiwan, and the United States followed in descending order of importance.

However, the most striking change in the direction of trade came from the huge growth in re-exports from the colony. These grew from a total value in 1980 of HK$30,072 million to over HK$346,405 million by 1989. The main markets for re-exports were the People's Republic of China, which constituted 29.9% of the total, followed by the United States at 20.8%. Overall the key development in the colony's trading pattern in recent years has been the growing importance of the People's Republic of China, and this trend is likely to become even more significant in the years to come.

In the postwar period the colony has remained a free port with no restrictions upon the import and export of goods. It remained a champion of the principle of free trade and was active in promoting free trade and opposing protectionism in bilateral and multilateral meetings. The Special Administrative Region, which will be created in 1997, is to continue this position. It will be allowed to trade freely with other states, remain a free port and be allowed to continue its support of the principles of free trade, both in its own territory and in relation to other states. (See Basic Law; Economic System; GATT; Special Administrative Region.)

TRADE UNIONS. See Pressure Groups.

TREATY OF BOGUE (HUMEN). See Bogue, Treaty of.

TREATY OF NANKING (NANJING). See Nanking, Treaty of.

TREATY OF TIENTSIN (TIANJIN). See Tientsin, Treaty of.

TRENCH, SIR DAVID. (1915–). Governor of Hong Kong from April 1964 until October 1971. He was faced in 1966 with the Star Ferry Riots and in 1967 with the far more serious disturbances arising from the impact of the Cultural Revolution. In the aftermath of the 1966 disturbances, Trench initiated an inquiry, which recommended more contact between the people and government. His administration largely failed to deal with increasing levels of corruption in public life despite increasing pressure in the colony to face the problem.

(See Cultural Revolution; Godber Affair; Star Ferry Riots.)

TRIADS. Triads in relation to Hong Kong are thought to have originated in the nineteenth century in southern China as an opposition group to what was seen as the tyranny of the Ch'ing (Qing) Dynasty. The group named itself San Ho Hui (the Triad Society) or Tien Ti Hui (Society of Heaven and Earth). The symbolism in the term refers to the trinity of Heaven, Earth and People.

With the arrival of the European powers and the decline of authority by the Ch'ing (Qing) dynasty, there was a breakdown in law and order in China. This allowed the Triads to prosper and at the same time move into illegal activities. By the end of the nineteenth century the Triads were heavily involved in such activities as loan sharking (loaning money at exorbitant interest rates), gambling, prostitution, drugs and protection rackets.

As early as 1845 the authorities in Hong Kong recognized that Triads were operating in the territory and passed an ordinance to suppress them. At this point Triads were still widely perceived as being principally concerned with mainland politics rather than criminal activity. By the 1880s, however, the Triad societies had moved into protection, prostitution, gambling, opium smuggling, and blackmail. In 1887 the Societies Ordinance was passed to attempt to control the organizations. Further Society Ordinances were passed in 1911, 1920 and 1952.

From 1949 the newly created People's Republic of China prosecuted the Triads with great success, but in Hong Kong the Triads, now merely a criminal group, remained strongly embedded in society. Three major groups were particularly active in the colony: the 14K group, the *San Yee On* group, and the *Fuk Yee Hing* group.

Until the early 1980s the Royal Hong Kong Police

force had a special unit, the Triad Society Bureau, responsible for dealing with the problem. This was then replaced by the Organized and Serious Crimes Bureau. More recently, attempts have been made to introduce legislation modelled on the American *RICO* Act to combat the Triad organizations.

Despite major attempts to educate youth against the dangers of Triads and despite attempts to suppress them, they remain very active. However, the figures below show that prosecutions for membership of illegal organizations have not risen significantly.

1970	530
1977	1,766
1980	573
1985	682
1990	406

Moreover, these prosecutions have often been of rank and file members. Senior members have usually escaped prosecution, often through the use of apparently respectable front companies as covers for Triad activity. (See Royal Hong Kong Police Force.)

TUNG WAH. The Tung Wah Hospital was founded in 1869 following a scandal which revealed the almost total lack of hospital or medical provision for the Chinese in Hong Kong. The hospital itself was recognized by the Hong Kong government in 1870 and has played an important role in Hong Kong life ever since.

The hospital's establishment can largely be attributed to public shock at the findings of an enquiry into conditions in the Kwong Fuk Che temple. Originally founded as a repository for the ancestral tablets of Chinese who died in Hong Kong away from their family homes in China, the temple also began to provide a place in which people could die without bringing bad luck to the house in which they had normally lived. Unfortunately, conditions in the "death house" were most unsatisfactory with no medical facilities and minimal levels of care. An investigation followed by the publication of a highly critical report prompted several prominent members of the Chinese community to establish a management board for a new hospital. Eventually, in addition to the medical services provided by the hospital, the management board itself became an unofficial but powerful platform for the expression of Chinese interests— particularly during the nineteenth century when Chinese representation on government bodies was minimal.

In 1931 the original hospital amalgamated with other hospitals in the territory to form the Tung Wah Group of Hospitals. The political power of the Tung Wah Group of Hospitals declined in the post-Second World War period partly because of the greater provision of medical and social provision by the government and partly because of the opening up of other major avenues of political influence for the Chinese elite. However, even in the late 1980s the Tung Wah Group of Hospitals still operated five hospitals with a total of 4,000 beds and provided services for the elderly, the young and the physically handicapped. (See Po Leung Kuk.)

TYPHOONS. Severe typhoons, with winds in excess of 118 kilometers an hour, have struck the colony with devastating effect on many occasions. Particularly damaging were those of 1841, 1867, 1874, and 1906, the latter leaving an estimated 10,000 people dead.

-U-

UMELCO. The acronym UMELCO stood for Unofficial Members of the Executive and Legislative Council. This organization was created in 1963 for all those members of the two bodies who were not "official" (i.e., having membership by virtue of being senior government officials). Its role was to monitor and comment upon the activities of the government, and it was later to become a useful channel for redress of public grievances against the government. Its name was changed in October 1986 to the Office of the Members of the Executive and Legislative Council (OMELCO). (See also the Office of the Members of the Executive and Legislative Council, OMELCO).

UNEQUAL TREATIES. The term used by the People's Republic of China to refer to the set of treaties in the nineteenth century which created Hong Kong. According to the Peking (Beijing) authorities, the treaties were imposed by a powerful Britain upon a weak and divided China after military conquest. In the Chinese view, because the treaties were not signed between two equal sovereign powers, they could not be valid in international law. It followed that the Government of the People's Republic of China was not bound to recognize their provisions on such matters as sovereignty over Hong Kong. (See Anglo-Chinese Wars; Conventions of Peking (Beijing); Joint Declaration; Nanking (Nanjing), Treaty of; Sovereignty; Tientsin (Tianjin), Treaty of.)

UNIONS. See Pressure Groups.

UNITED FRONT. A term first used in the context of the Marxist call in 1848 for all groups committed to the overthrow of the ruling governments in Europe to unite. The concept was used by Communists in China in 1923 when they entered their brief alliance with the Nationalists. In 1949 it was adopted by the People's Republic of China in its claim to represent all peoples organizations and socialist working people. The Chinese Communist Party Constitution refers to all those "compatriots" abroad who were working towards the unification of the "motherland"—which included Taiwan (The Republic of China), Macau, and Hong Kong.

Subsequently the significance of the United Front concept has been difficult to gauge. Some members of left-wing trade unions and some of candidates for District Board elections have probably seen their activities in these terms. At the grass roots level membership probably expanded during the 1980s, and there has probably been a direct, although never admitted, connection with the work of the New China News Agency. (See Communist Party of China.)

UNITED KINGDOM OF GREAT BRITAIN AND NORTHERN IRELAND. The full and correct title given to the sovereign power which rules Hong Kong until 1997. Until Ireland (later to become Eire in 1937) was given Dominion status in 1921 the title was the United Kingdom of Great Britain and Ireland. Six counties remained under the control of the British Crown and were known as Northern Ireland or Ulster. Great Britain is made up of three units namely England, Scotland, and Wales. The full title is rarely used, so other terms such as the United Kingdom, Great Britain, and Britain are more commonly employed. Some refer to the state as England, which is even less accurate as it ignores Scotland, Wales, and Northern Ireland.

UNITED NATIONS. The United Nations Organization was established on 24 October 1945. Its original membership grew rapidly with the creation of new sovereign states as a result of the decolonization process of the postwar period. In 1988 there were 159 members, all of them members of the General Assembly. The smaller Security Council has five permanent members including the United Kingdom and the People's Republic of China, and ten rotating members. A Secretariat administers

United Nations activities, and finance is provided by the member states. Other associated organs include the Trusteeship Council, the International Court of Justice, and the Economic and Social Council.

Hong Kong is not a sovereign state and therefore cannot be a member of the United Nations. Its interests have been formally represented by the United Kingdom, and after 1997 this responsibility will pass to the People's Republic of China. (See Basic Law; Joint Declaration.)

UNITED NATIONS HIGH COMMISSION FOR REFUGEES (UNHCR). The United Nations High Commission for Refugees (UNHCR) was created in 1951 taking over from its predecessor, the International Refugee Organization. It became particularly active in Hong Kong following the influx of Vietnamese refugees after 1978. The UNHCR was relatively successful in settling the refugees in other countries in the early 1980s, but found it difficult to resettle the increased numbers arriving in later years. (See Vietnamese Refugees.)

UNIVERSITIES. The oldest university in Hong Kong is the University of Hong Kong established in 1911. In 1963 it was joined by the Chinese University of Hong Kong and in 1990 by the Hong Kong University of Science and Technology. (See Education.)

UNOFFICIAL MEMBERS. Unofficial Members was the term applied to those members of the Executive Council, Legislative Council, the Urban Council, Regional Council, and District Boards who were not civil servants. In each Council, the Unofficial Members elect a Senior Member, who wields considerable influence as the spokesperson of the whole body of Unofficial Members. The Governor appointed these persons in the Executive and Legislative Council under the terms of the Letters Patent, thus giving the term a legal status. District Board,

Urban Council, and Regional Council unofficial members were legitimized by ordinances of the Legislative Council, which gave the Governor the power to make appointments. Although the term was officially dropped in 1985, it is still used in common parlance in Hong Kong. (See OMELCO.)

URBAN COUNCIL. The Urban Council (URBCO) was established in 1936 to replace the Sanitary Board which had operated since 1883. Its functions are to provide services such as street cleaning, refuse collection, environmental hygiene, public libraries, and various recreational and cultural activities. Since 1973 it has enjoyed considerable financial autonomy.

The Urban Council was one of the first bodies to have an elected membership, although this was originally on a restricted franchise. In 1983 those restrictions were lifted so that the potential electorate was in excess of 3.4 million. Initially it was largely made up of government officials, but by the 1980s this practice had been abandoned. By 1983 there was a total of 30 members with 50% elected and 50% appointed by the government from key sections of society. From 1988 one member of the Urban Council, elected by his or her fellow members, has had a seat on the Legislative Council. (See Local Government; Regional Council; Sanitary Board.)

-V-

VICTORIA. Victoria is still the official title for the capital of Hong Kong. It was first used on 29 June 1843, when the Governor, Sir Henry Pottinger, was given British approval to change the title from Queenstown. The name is now rarely used and the area covered by Victoria is normally referred to as Central.

VIETNAM, DEMOCRATIC REPUBLIC OF. Since the end of the Vietnamese War, the Democratic Republic of Vietnam has not been afforded official diplomatic representation in Hong Kong. There was, however, a Vietnamese Trade Delegation in the colony which looked after the country's interests. The difficulties of this task have arisen from the frequently hostile relations between Vietnam and the PRC, the poor relationships between Vietnam and western states, and Hong Kong's irritation at numbers of Vietnamese refugees who have left the country since its reunification to seek refuge in Hong Kong. (See Vietnamese Refugees.)

VIETNAMESE REFUGEES. Before June 1989 all arrivals from Vietnam were referred to as Vietnamese refugees. However, the introduction of a new screening system at this time led to the term "Vietnamese boat people" being applied to all arrivals unless they met the requirements of refugee status set out in the new policy.

The first refugees who arrived in 1975 were quickly resettled in Hong Kong or other countries. However, later arrivals proved more difficult. In December 1978, the ship "Huey Fong" brought in 3,300 refugees, followed by another 2,600 in February 1979. The root of the problem was the British Government's policy which made Hong Kong a "Port of First Asylum." Under this policy the Hong Kong Government was obliged to offer shelter and food to those refugees for whom Hong Kong was their first landing place. While most other Southeast Asian countries ensured that refugees never landed, Hong Kong adopted a more humane system. The result was that between 1975 and 1981, a total of 105,155 refugees were provided with shelter in Hong Kong of whom 14,000 were offered permanent residence. By the end of 1980, there were 24,000 Vietnamese refugees in camps in Hong Kong.

In face of the growing reluctance of other countries to resettle the refugees and the increasing public resentment towards refugees in Hong Kong, in 1982 the government introduced a "closed camp" policy which aimed to discourage new arrivals by confining refugees to basically equipped camps and making it clear it did not intend to resettle them. In response, the refugee intake dropped to only 2,230 in 1984. However, the figures began to rise gradually in 1986/87 and increased sharply in 1988, largely because of an agricultural crisis in Vietnam.

The Hong Kong Government's next initiative was a new "screening policy" announced in June 1988. This scheme involved the use of internationally-accepted criteria to distinguish "genuine refugees" from "economic migrants." This scheme which was endorsed in the Geneva Conference in June 1989 was applicable to all those who arrived after midnight 15 June 1988. However, the intended purpose of reducing the number of refugees staying in Hong Kong has not been realized. By the end of October 1989, only 264 refugees had been returned. Discussion between the British, Hong Kong, and Vietnamese governments continued, and in September 1990 an agreement was reached to repatriate those who were not genuine refugees and who were "not opposed to going back." The scheme was to be administered by the United Nations High Commission on Refugees. On 12 December 1989, 51 boat people were sent back to Vietnam against their will and to a chorus of international criticism. Labor Members of Parliament in Britain criticized the deportation as "tyrannical" and "shameful," while a spokesperson for the U.S. President stated that "the repatriation is unacceptable until conditions improve in Vietnam."

While there was sympathy in Hong Kong for those ethnic Chinese refugees who were discriminated against by the Vietnamese Government, especially after the

Sino-Vietnamese War in 1979, this did not generally extend to those ethnic Vietnamese who were seen as economic migrants. Also significant was the changing of policy in the territory towards illegal immigrants from China who from 1980 were forcibly returned to China. Policy was seen as being unequal and discriminatory against Chinese people. Even more significant was the large and mounting cost of supporting the refugees.

These mass attitudes were reflected in the tough stance taken by the Legislative Council's *ad hoc* committee established to monitor the situation. The committee urged the relaxation of the First Asylum Policy, argued for refusal to increase accommodation for new arrivals, and attempted to secure greater contributions to the cost of the policy from the United Nations High Commission for Refugees.

In the early 1990s existing camps were almost full; no satisfactory solution had been found to repatriate or resettle substantial numbers of refugees; and large numbers of new arrivals continued to reach the territory. (See Illegal Immigrants; United Nations.)

VILLAGE REPRESENTATIVES. Although the use of village representatives was never actively pursued by the British in Hong Kong and Kowloon, the New Territories, with its predominantly rural population provided a more suitable context. There the village enjoyed a high degree of autonomy from state supervision, even before the signing of the Treaty of Peking (Beijing) in 1898 leased the area to the United Kingdom. The basic administrative unit remained intact, with each district subdivided into a number of *tung* (valleys) and *heung-yeuk* (villages). The villages formed part of a hierarchy with village leaders making up an administrative council. Larger villages even had a system of law and order with individuals appointed and paid to keep the peace by the village leaders.

After 1898, the villagers were highly suspicious of the new colonial government, one typical example arising in March 1899, when the colonial police chief met with considerable opposition to the establishment of police stations and government offices. This was seen as an unwarranted intrusion into the autonomy of the villages, who had not experienced similar interference from the Chinese authorities in the period prior to the British arrival. Two meetings were initiated by leaders of the *Tang* clan, and it was agreed to resist the colonial government. The main confrontation between the colonial government and the villagers in the New Territories took place at Tai Po in March 1899 when government contractors attempted to erect temporary headquarters for the British administration on a hill near the market. They were hindered by the villagers who believed that the *fung shui* was being disturbed. A short (nine-day) war was quickly ended by the surrender of the Chinese villagers.

Gradually the control of central government was increased. The clan feuds were brought to an end, the political power of the gentry vanished, and, most important of all, the influence of the village councils was generally reduced. However, the villages still retained some control over their own affairs, and continued to exert some influence over the policies of the central government.

The urbanization of the New Territories began in the 1970s with the government decision to undertake substantial public housing projects away from existing urban areas. However, this urbanization, was not fully mirrored in the power of the relevant political institutions. Although the percentage of the New Territories population living in rural communities had dropped to around 12.6% in 1986, an elaborate set of institutions preserved their representation on the relevant local government bodies. In the late 1980s there remained over 900 village representatives who were elected or appointed from the 509 villages in the New Territories. These representatives were grouped into 27 Rural Committees, each of which elected an executive committee. The Chair and Vice-Chair of each executive committee, in turn, sat on the full council of the *Heung Yee Kuk,* which continued to form part of the local government system in the New Territories. The Regional Council established in 1986 maintained a formal link with the *Heung Yee Kuk* through the ex-officio membership of the chair and the two vice-chairs on the council. Moreover, three of its appointed members were chosen from the members of the *Heung Yee Kuk* to ensure a strong relationship with the traditional inhabitants of the New Territories. (See Heung Yee Kuk; New Territories; Regional Council.)

VISAS. A document which visitors to Hong Kong had to obtain from the Immigration Department before they were allowed to enter the territory. Although visas were generally easy to obtain, citizens of Soviet Bloc countries were not given visas in the territory until the early 1990s. The visa could be extended if the applicant had employment in the territory or desired a longer stay. Holders of full British Passports were entitled to stay up to twelve months and were free to seek work in the territory. This privilege will end in 1997.

To facilitate the visits of Taiwanese—many of whom got around the absence of direct communications links between Taiwan and the PRC by using Hong Kong as a convenient means of entering the PRC—a new type of entry permit for multiple visits was introduced on 1 June, 1990. (See Taiwan.)

VOTING; VOTING BEHAVIOR. The use of a universal franchise in the territory took place for the first time in the 1981 Urban Council Elections. Prior to that time, the Urban Council was elected on a limited franchise. Voters had to belong to one of 23 categories such as taxpayers, journalists, holders of the School Certificate Examination or other diplomas or degrees, business people, or members of professional organizations. This system recognized only 440,0000 people as potentially eligible voters, and out of these only 35,000 registered their right to the vote, and approximately one-third of this smaller number actually voted in the 1979 Urban Council election.

The right to vote at all institutional levels was gradually extended to people over the age of 21, who had lived for seven years in Hong Kong and voluntarily registered on to the electoral register. The only exclusions were lunatics, prisoners who had not yet served their sentence, members of the armed forces, and those convicted in the previous ten years of corrupt or illegal practices.

Under the provisions of the Basic Law eligibility to vote is restricted to those who will be permanent residents of the future Special Administrative Region. The voting age of 21 years and the existing set of excluded persons will remain.

The District Board Elections, held every three years since 1982, met with a poor response from the electorate. Only 37% and 30.3% of the registered voters turned out to vote in the District Board Elections in 1985 and 1988 respectively, although turnout in the New Territories (38% in 1988) has generally been slightly higher than that in the urban areas (26% in 1988). This probably indicates the greater cohesiveness of the Rural Committees since the pattern in the new towns was closer to the urban figures. This low turnout rate for the District Board elections may be partly explained by the political culture of Hong Kong people which emphasizes the perceived deviousness of politicians, but it probably also reflects the limited functions and powers wielded by the District Boards.

Elections to the Legislative Council were not established until 1985. However, the initial electoral system (based on functional constituencies and indirectly-elected members) for the 24 seats was very limited in scope. Although the functional constituencies were to elect 12 members in the Legislative Council, their membership covered only a small fraction of the adult population and was drawn overwhelmingly from the professional classes. For the indirectly-elected members, the public were not involved except for having originally voted for the District Board members, who then elected 10 members to the Legislative Council from among themselves.

The following table shows the membership of the Legislative Council since 1965:

	Civil Servants	Business and Finance	Professional	Others
1965	13	10	2	1
1971	13	9	3	1
1975	15	9	6	0
1982	23	11	13	3
1985	11	23	21	2
1988	11	23	20	3

(See Electorate; Familism; Legislative Council; Local Government; Regional Council; Urban Council.)

-W-

WAGES. Traditionally wages in the colony have been largely set by market forces. For most of the nineteenth century they were kept low by the continual influx of cheap labor from the mainland. In the twentieth century, and particularly after the First World War, trade unions attempted to use collective bargaining to increase wage levels. However, they met with little success, and although the

Government passed a Minimum Wage Ordinance in 1932, it was never acted upon.

After the Second World War the huge influx of refugees, in tandem with a very low membership of trade unions, helped keep wages relatively low. Nevertheless, wage levels did gradually improve in real terms. Using an index of wage levels adjusted for inflation and starting in 1950 with 100 as a base, the figure had risen to 140 by 1963 and 203 by 1967. The ending of the Reached Base Policy in 1980 reduced the supply of cheap labor, and wage levels began to rise at greater speed. In 1989 the overall average daily rate for workers was estimated at HK$167. There was, however, a significant difference between the daily wages of men and women with men receiving an average of HK$201 and women HK$144.

Partly as a consequence of the rising wage levels in the territory there was, particularly in the late 1980s and early 1990s, a large movement out of the territory and into the Special Economic Zones of the PRC of those manufacturing firms which relied on cheap labor. (See Economy; Population; Reached Base Policy; Sham Chun (Shenzhen); Special Economic Zone; Trade.)

WALLED CITY. See Kowloon Walled City.

WATER SUPPLIES. Water supplies have always been a problem for Hong Kong. Although the total level of rainfall is high, much of it normally falls in the months of May to September. The problems this causes were more manageable when the population was low, but the increase in population soon led to an increasing use of water from untreated wells and streams. Not surprisingly this, in turn, led to regular outbreaks of cholera, dysentery, and typhoid during the nineteenth century. The situation was not resolved by the construction of reservoirs first at Pokfulam and later at Tai Tam Tuk and in the newly acquired New Territories.

After the First World War the still rising population and the occurrence of periodic droughts made necessary the occasional importing of water by boat from Foochow (Fuzhou), Shanghai, and Japan. From 1945 the situation deteriorated further. Not only did the population continue to expand, but also much of the industrial expansion taking place was in sectors, such as textiles, that used considerable amounts of water. Clearly the construction of reservoirs in an already small land area could provide only a partial solution, and so in 1960 successful negotiations took place to purchase water from the People's Republic. The supplies, which reached Hong Kong by pipeline, proved to be adequate to meet a steadily increasing demand. For example, the demand for water increased from 387 million cubic meters in 1977 to 800 million cubic meters in 1988. The scale of the contribution of the PRC supplies is exemplified by the fact that in 1990 Hong Kong imported over 500 million cubic meters from the mainland with the remainder being supplied domestically. Under an agreement signed in 1989, the PRC will further increase supplies to 660 million cubic meters by 1994–1995.

WEI HAI WEI (WEIHAIWEI). Wei Hai Wei is situated in north China at the entrance to the inner Yellow Sea, and was leased to Britain in 1898 at the same time as the New Territories. Some observers in Hong Kong have argued that it offers an instructive analogy for the Hong Kong situation. Although it prospered under British administration, when it was returned to China in 1930 its significance declined.

WHITE PAPER. A "White Paper" is the term given to a publication produced by the government of Hong Kong outlining major government proposals in administrative or legislative matters. The most important White Paper in recent years was the one which set out the territory's political future after 1997, entitled "A Draft Agreement between the Government of the United Kingdom of Great Britain and Northern Ireland and the Government of the People's Republic of China" (26 September 1984).

During the Governorship of Sir Murray MacLehose (1971–1982), publications known as "Green Papers" were also introduced. Their purpose was to introduce government proposals at an early stage in order to provide time for public consultation. Although the discussion arising from Green Papers sometimes led to the modification of the government's proposals, they have been used only occasionally.

WILSON, SIR DAVID (1934–   ). Sir David Wilson became the Governor of Hong Kong in April 1987, following the death of Sir Edward Youde. He had previously held office in the British Foreign and Commonwealth Office (FCO), had been political advisor to the Governor Sir Murray MacLehose, and had taken part in the negotiations over the future of Hong Kong as Under-Secretary for Far Eastern Affairs in the FCO. Major developments during his term of office were: the prolonged negotiations over questions relating to the changeover of power; the great stock market crash of 1987; major changes in the territory's representative institutions; the repercussions of the suppression of demonstrations in the People's Republic of China in June 1989; and the publishing of the Basic Law in 1990. (See Basic Law; Foreign and Commonwealth Office; T'ien-an-man (Tiananman).)

WINTER FESTIVAL. A traditional festival celebrated in Hong Kong on December 22, the winter solstice, the shortest day according to the solar calendar.

WORK FORCE. For much of Hong Kong's history the dominant issue relating to the work force has been the balance between a steadily increasing demand for labor and the immigration of workers from the mainland. Throughout the nineteenth century and well into the twentieth, the work force expanded continually to meet the demand from the colony for mostly semiskilled or unskilled labor.

By 1931, the work force was estimated to be nearly 471,000 a figure which increased massively with the major influxes of 1937–1941 and 1945–1949.

By the 1961 census the work force was estimated to be over 1.2 million out of a total population of over 3.1 million. This was to increase to 1.454 million out of a total population of 3.7 million in 1966. The vast majority of the work force in the 1960s were to be found in the manufacturing sector (475,000 in 1961), followed by the community services (123,020), and by commerce (131,279). Of those, the overwhelming majority were unskilled or semiskilled labor, with only a fairly small professional or managerial pool to draw upon.

Between 1977 and 1990 Hong Kong's total population increased from 4.63 million to 5.86 million, and the percentage of those available for work also grew from 41% to 49% of the total population. In 1990 64% of the work force were male and 36% female.

However, these figures conceal some significant changes. In particular, with the ending of the Reached Base Policy in 1980, Hong Kong entered a period of shortage of labor. Emigration from the territory increased during the 1980s, and was concentrated in the areas of Hong Kong's greatest shortage, namely the managerial and professional classes. Wages, responding to market forces where demand for labor exceeded supply, went up rapidly in the period 1980–1990. The response by many firms in the manufacturing sector has been to relocate in the Special Economic Zones of the PRC. (See Economy; Population; Reached Base Policy; Special Economic Zones.)

WORLD WARS. The First World War had little direct impact upon the colony. There was no compulsory military service for the Chinese population and it was not introduced for Europeans until 1916. Hong Kong was largely used as a recruiting station for Chinese, who volunteered to work on the western front as noncombatant labor.

In the Second World War Hong Kong fell to Japanese military forces after a short campaign lasting from 8 December to 25 December 1941. During the occupation, shortages of food and work led to a major exodus of the population, which fell from 1.6 million to 0.6 million. The Japanese surrendered their forces in August 1945, and the British resumed their administration of the colony. The population declines of the Japanese occupation were quickly reversed with the total reaching 1.8 million by 1947. (See Second World War.)

-X-

XIANGGANG. (Hong Kong). Xianggang is the Pinyin for Hong Kong. It means literally "incense port."

XINHUA. See New China News Agency/NCNA.

XU JIATUN. See Hsu Chia-t'un.

-Y-

YEH MING-CH'EN (Yeh Mingchen). Yeh Ming-ch'en (Yeh Mingchen) was the Imperial Commissioner of China who dealt with the request from Governor of Hong Kong Sir John Bowring for revisions of the Treaty of Nanking (Nanjing), which was first signed in 1842.

The underlying goals of British proposals were as follows:

(1) To gain entry to Canton (Guangzhou);
(2) To obtain the abolition of the Tea Commission;
(3) To establish regular meetings with Chinese officials;
(4) To lease land for British merchants in Henan; and,
(5) To obtain redress for British people attacked by the Chinese

Bowring tried several times to meet Yeh to discuss the proposed revisions, but when they met on 22 May 1854 outside Canton (Guangzhou) Yeh effectively rejected the proposals. Relations between Britain (Hong Kong) and the Chinese authorities deteriorated further ultimately culminating in the outbreak of the Arrow War (see Arrow War).

Yeh was captured in Canton (Guangzhou) by British forces in January 1858, and was sent to exile in Calcutta where he later died. (See Anglo-Chinese Wars; Arrow Wars; Bowring, Sir John.)

YOUDE, SIR EDWARD (1924–1986). Governor of Hong Kong from 1982 to 1986. He died in office in Peking (Beijing) in December 1986. His involvement in the Sino-British negotiations over the future of Hong Kong was as a member of the British delegation and not as a representative of Hong Kong, which would have been unacceptable to the Chinese. His efforts as Governor were almost wholly concerned with bringing about a negotiated settlement for the future of the territory. He was known as a hard negotiator who did much to safeguard, as far as possible, the interests of the territory. An indication of the high regard in which he was held was reflected by the grief shown by many sectors of the community at his funeral. (See Governor; Joint Declaration; Sino-British Negotiations.)

YOUNG, SIR MARK (1886–1947). Governor of Hong Kong from September 1982 to May 1947. When the Japanese invasion in Hong Kong began in December 1941, he refused to surrender; but, then following serious bombing in many parts of Hong Kong—and on the advice of General Maltby, he ordered the surrender. He was taken prisoner by the Japanese and suffered cruel treatment that caused him to become ill in captivity.

Nonetheless, he resumed his governorship on 30 April 1946, and oversaw the restoration of the civil government. (See Instrument of Surrender; Second World War; Young Plan.)

YOUNG PLAN. The Young Plan was drawn up by the then Governor Sir Mark Young in August 1946 at a time when the Hong Kong government was attempting to reestablish its legitimacy following the Japanese occupation. Refugees had crowded into the colony following the Japanese surrender, and at the same time criticisms were being raised over the completely nonrepresentative nature of the colonial government. The main features of the Plan were:

(1) The Municipal Council would consist of 48 members of which one-third would be elected by non-Chinese voters and the remaining two-thirds would be chosen by Chinese and non-Chinese institutions equally. This Council would have limited functions and its responsibilities would be confined to the urban areas.

(2) The Legislative Council would be composed of seven official and eight unofficial members. The Governor would be *ex officio* with a casting vote. The proposed Municipal Council would nominate

two unofficial members to sit on the Legislative Council.

Although the Plan met with a degree of public approval, the new Governor, Sir Alexander Grantham, faced considerable opposition to it from unofficial members of the Legislative Council. Initially the proposals were watered down, and the Plan was quietly abandoned in 1952. It was not until 1980 that any major institutional reforms, based on electoral criteria, were seriously considered again. (See Legislative Council; Young, Sir Mark; Regional Council; Second World War; Urban Council.)

YUAN (YUAN) DYNASTY (1260–1368). Unfortunately little is known of Hong Kong during this period. There is evidence of a reduction of imperial presence and a significant increase in settlement in the area by the remnants of the Sung (Song) court. The area probably fell under the control of a local warlord in this period. It is believed that coastal trade declined which would have had a detrimental effect upon the Hong Kong area.

-Z-

ZHAO ZIYANG. See Chao Tzu-yang.

ZHOU ENLAI. See Chou En-lai.

ZHOU NAN. See Chou Nan.

BIBLIOGRAPHY

INTRODUCTORY ESSAY

For a territory of less than 400 square miles and a current population of less than six million, of whom only a small percentage are fluent English speakers, Hong Kong is well covered by academic work written in English. Perhaps not surprisingly, however, the emphasis in much of the earlier English language literature reflects the colonial situation. Certainly much of the material written on early Hong Kong emphasizes the history of the British administration and its problems, rather than the lives and concerns of the indigenous population. More recently, some of these emphases have shifted slightly, especially with the emergence of larger numbers of Chinese academics and centers for research on Hong Kong and the wider region in which it is set.

The notes which follow identify a small number of works from most of the categories in the main bibliography. In most cases the works have been selected partly for their more general approach, and partly with a view to their probable accessibility within good library systems.

For accounts of Hong Kong's distinctive character and how this derives partly from its historical development two reliable and very readable introductions are Morris, J. *Hong Kong: epilogue to an empire*. Rev. ed. Harmondsworth, England: Penguin, (1990) and Wilson, R. *Hong Kong! Hong Kong!* London: Unwin Hyman Limited (1990).

More systematic are two annual publications produced locally. Firstly, the Hong Kong Government's own review of the year, *Hong Kong* (date changeable) provides a statement from the government's view of the colony's economy, constitution, education system, etc. It also contains helpful appendices, including the latest sets of government statistics on key aspects of government activity, the economy, and social trends. To complement this, the Chinese

University Press produces an annual version of "The other Hong Kong report." (See, for example, Sung, Y. W. and Lee, M. K. *The other Hong Kong report 1991*. Hong Kong: Chinese University Press, (1991).) These volumes contain a series of essays which provide more critical perspectives on the topics covered by the official government publication.

As a major tourist center, and having a substantial but mobile expatriate community, Hong Kong also generates a reasonable market for books which make extensive use of large photographs and which are often bought as souvenirs of a stay in the territory. Perhaps the best of these to give a flavor of the territory today are Roberts, L. *Over Hong Kong,* which has an introduction by Spurr, R., Hong Kong: South China Morning Post, (1989); and the "Insight Guide" to the territory, by Lockhart, S. and Eu, G. (eds.) *Destination: Hong Kong.* Hong Kong: A.P.A., (1989). There are also some good quality books of this genre which emphasize the colony's historical development. Good examples are Fishbeck, F. *Building Hong Kong: a history of the city through its architecture.* Hong Kong: Formasia, (1989) and Wiltshire, T. *Great cities of the world: old Hong Kong.* Hong Kong: Formasia, (1987).

Two books which remain well illustrated but provide a more thorough account of the colony's history are Birch, A. *Hong Kong: the colony that never was.* Hong Kong: Odyssey Press, (1991) and Cameron, N. *An illustrated history of Hong Kong.* Hong Kong: Oxford University Press, (1991). The standard general introduction to the history of the territory is Endacott, G. B. *A history of Hong Kong.* Hong Kong: Oxford University Press, (1973).

The territory's relative unimportance prior to the establishment of the colony is reflected in a relative dearth of literature. While the Government's *Report of the Hong Kong Archaeological Survey* (5 vols.). Hong Kong: Hong Kong Government Printer, (1985) provides a meticulous account of the archeological finds in the region, a useful overview can be found in Meacham's short book, Meacham, W. *Archaeology in Hong Kong.* Hong Kong: Heinemann, (1980).

The political setting for the early years of the colony is admirably covered in Fairbanks, J. K. *Trade and diplomacy on the China coast: the opening of the treaty ports 1842–1854* (2 vols.). Cambridge, Massachusetts: Harvard University Press, (1964). An interesting contemporary source is the work by Eitel, first published in 1895, which emphasizes most of the major political developments of the nineteenth century—Eitel, E. J., *Europe in China,* introduction by Lethbridge, H. J., Hong Kong: Oxford University Press, (1983). Some interesting aspects of social conditions in the colony's early years and their relationship to an evolving political system can be found in Sinn, E. *Power and charity: the early history of the Tung Wah hospital, Hong Kong.* Hong Kong: Oxford University Press, (1989). Some excellent essays on the period which also raise issues of continuing significance are to be found in Lethbridge, H. J. *Hong Kong: stability and change.* Hong Kong: Oxford University Press, (1978).

The events surrounding Britain's acquisition of the New Territories are well covered in Wesley-Smith, P. *Unequal treaty 1898–1997: China, Great Britain and Hong Kong's New Territories.* (Rev. ed.), Hong Kong: Oxford University Press, (1984). An authoritative work on major political issues of a slightly later period is Miners, N. *Hong Kong under imperial rule, 1912–1941.* Hong Kong: Oxford University Press, (1987). Interesting reading about the social mores of the Western and Chinese elites of the period is provided in Gillingham, P. *At the Peak: Hong Kong between the wars.* Hong Kong: Macmillan, (1983).

An interesting illustrated account of the 1941–45 period is Lindsay, O. *At the going down of the sun: Hong Kong and Southeast Asia 1941–45.* London: Hamish Hamilton, (1981). But the most comprehensive treatment of the period remains Endacott, G. B., edited and with additional material by Birch, A., *Hong Kong eclipse.* Hong Kong: Oxford University Press, (1978).

Some interesting aspects of Hong Kong in the 1950s and 1960s are covered in Jarvie, I. C. with Agassi, J. *Hong Kong: a society in transition.* London: Routledge & Kegan Paul, (1969). However, the literature on the postwar period is dominated by the implications of the change in sovereignty due in 1997. Analysis of the agreement and its implications has varied from the polemical to the systematic. A good example of a reasoned critique of the emerging political situation is Shawcross, W. *Kowtow!* London: Chatto and Windus, (1989). A useful collection of papers on the agreement for politics, the law, the economy and society is Jao, Y. C., Leung, C. K., Wesley-Smith, P., and Wong S. L. (eds.) *Hong Kong and 1997: strategies for the future.* Hong Kong: Centre of Asian Studies, University of Hong Kong, (1985). Although the contributions are somewhat uneven in quality and differing in their underlying assumptions, the collection reveals much about modern Hong Kong as well as its possible future. It also contains the full text of the Joint Declaration.

The literature on politics and administration in modern Hong Kong is relatively well developed. An essential overview is Miners, N. *The government and politics of Hong Kong,* (5th ed.), Hong Kong: Oxford University Press, (1991). A more overtly analytical approach is to be found in Scott, I. *Political change and the crisis of legitimacy in Hong Kong.* London: Hurst; Hong Kong: Oxford University Press; Honolulu, Hawaii: University of Hawaii Press, (1989). Also of great interest is Davies, S. and Roberts, E. V. *Political dictionary for Hong Kong.* Hong Kong: Macmillan, (1990). This not only provides a description of major features of politics, economics, and society in Hong Kong, but also examines the meanings of key political concepts within the Hong Kong context.

Two recent comprehensive academic guides to the Hong Kong economy which can be recommended are Ho, H. C. Y. and Chau, L. C. (eds.) *The economic system of Hong Kong.* Hong Kong: Asian Research Service, (1988), and Peebles, G. *Hong Kong's economy: an introductory macroeconomic analysis.* Hong Kong: Oxford University Press, 1988. A more brief but well argued and clearly presented introduction is Davies, K. *Hong Kong to 1994: a question of confidence.* London: The Economist Intelligence Unit, (1990).

Some key issues in society are covered in two readers: Kwan, A. Y. H. and Chan, D. K. K. (eds.) *Hong Kong society: a reader.* (2d ed.), Hong Kong: Writers' & Publishers' Cooperative, 1989.; and Leung, B.K.P. (ed.) *Social issues in Hong Kong.* Hong Kong: Oxford University Press, (1990). A well argued treatment of social attitudes is Lau, S. K. and Kuan, H. C. *The ethos of the Hong Kong Chinese.* Hong Kong: Chinese University Press, (1988). Finally, an interesting account of social policy which covers social conditions, social attitudes, and policy responses is Jones, C. *Promoting prosperity: the Hong Kong way of social policy.* Hong Kong: Chinese University Press, (1990).

The literature on crime in Hong Kong is generally very specialized, and readers can best be referred to Komala, M., Tang, P. P. L. and Cheung, S. *A bibliography of criminological literature in Hong Kong.* Hong Kong: Centre for Hong Kong Studies, Chinese University of Hong Kong, (1989).

Burkhardt, V. R. *Chinese creeds and customs,* (3 vols.), Hong Kong:

South China Morning Post, (1953), (1955), (1958) is the standard work on traditional Chinese religion in the territory, while Smith, C. T. *Chinese Christians: elites, middlemen and the Church in Hong Kong,* Hong Kong: Oxford University Press, (1985) provides some interesting insights onto the influence of Christianity in Chinese society.

The title of Wesley-Smith, P. *An introduction to the Hong Kong legal system.* Hong Kong: Oxford University Press, (1987) is appropriate. Some essays which set legal issues in wider political and economic frameworks can be found in Wacks, R. (ed.). *The future of the law in Hong Kong.* Hong Kong: Oxford University Press, (1989).

Histories of key figures and companies are relatively common, and can provide significant comments on wider social contexts. Interesting examples are: Choa, G. H. *The life and times of Sir Hai Ho Kai: a prominent figure in nineteenth century Hong Kong.* Hong Kong: The Chinese University Press, (1981); Keswick, M. (ed.) *The thistle and the jade: a celebration of Jardine, Matheson and Co.* London: Octopus, (1982); and King, F. H. H., King, C. E., and King, D. J. S. *The history of the Hongkong and Shanghai Banking Corporation,* (4 vols.), Cambridge, England: Cambridge University Press, (1987), (1988). Endacott, G.B. *A biographical sketch book of early Hong Kong* Singapore: Eastern Universities Press, (1962) is more eclectic in ranging over a number of individuals, but is well researched and written.

The two daily English language newspapers, *The South China Morning Post* and the *Hong Kong Standard,* are of high standard especially given their limited potential readership. The weekly *Far Eastern Economic Review* is well informed and well written. It covers a wider area than Hong Kong, takes an appropriately wide-ranging view of what is "economic," and contains regular series of statistics on the economic performance of countries throughout the region.

Of the available bibliographies, Scott, I. *Hong Kong (Volume 115 of The World Bibliography Series)* Oxford: Clio Press, (1990), emphasizes the modern period and contains helpful paragraphs outlining the content, approach, and quality of the sources cited.

Finally, the Hong Kong Government produces large quantities of generally accurate and frequently helpful statistics on many aspects of the economy and society. Unfortunately, however, many of the pre-Second World War government records were wantonly destroyed by the Japanese during the occupation of the colony between 1941 and 1945.

1. General

Baker, H. R. D. *Hong Kong images: people and animals.* Rev. ed. Hong Kong: Hong Kong University Press, 1990.

Balke, G. *Hong Kong voices.* Introduction by Lawrence, A. Hong Kong: Longman, 1989.

Boyden S., Miller, S., Newcombe, K. and O'Neill, B. *The ecology of a city and its people: the case of Hong Kong.* Canberra: Australian National University Press, 1981.

Buruma, I. and Wetzell, Z. B. *Great cities of the world: Hong Kong.* Hong Kong: Formasia, 1989.

Chiu, T. N. and So, C. L. (eds.) *A geography of Hong Kong.* 2d ed. Hong Kong: Oxford University Press, 1986.

Chung, W.N. *Contemporary architecture in Hong Kong.* Hong Kong: Joint Publishing (H.K.) Co. Ltd., 1989

Coates, A. *Prelude to Hong Kong.* London: Routledge, 1966

Davies, D. A. C. *Another Hong Kong: an explorer's guide.* Hong Kong: Emphasis, 1989.

Fishbeck, F. *Building Hong Kong: a history of the city through its architecture.* Hong Kong: Formasia, 1989

Hong Kong 1991: a review of 1990. Hong Kong: Government Printer, 1991.

"Hongkong" in *Asia 1990. Yearbook.* Hong Kong: Review Publishing, 1990, p. 122–31.

Kirkup, J. *Hong Kong and Macau.* London: Dent, 1970

Lockhart, S. and Eu, G. (eds.) *Destination: Hong Kong.* Hong Kong: A.P.A., 1989.

Morris, J. *Hong Kong: epilogue to an empire.* Rev. ed. Harmondsworth, England: Penguin, 1990.

Nan, C. W. *Contemporary architecture in Hong Kong.* Hong Kong: Joint Publishing, 1989.

Parkin, E. *Hong Kong heritage: a personal view.* Hong Kong: Oxford University Press, 1979.

Patrikeeff, F. *Mouldering pearl: Hong Kong at the crossroads.* London: Hodder & Stoughton, 1990.

Roberts, L. *Over Hong Kong.* Introduction by Spurr, R. Hong Kong: South China Morning Post, 1989.

Rodwell, S. *Historic Hong Kong: A visitor's guide.* Hong Kong: Odyssey, 1991.

Sinn, E. Y. Y. *Between East and West: aspects of social and political development in Hong Kong.* Hong Kong: Centre of Asian Studies, University of Hong Kong, 1990.

Sung, Y. W. and Lee, M. K. *The other Hong Kong report 1991.* Hong Kong: Chinese University Press, 1991.

Tsim, T. L. and Luk, B. H. K. (eds.) *The other Hong Kong report 1989.* Hong Kong: Chinese University Press, 1989.

Walker, A. and Rowlinson, S. M. *The building of Hong Kong: constructing Hong Kong through the ages.* Hong Kong: Hong Kong University Press, 1990.

Wiltshire, T. *Great cities of the world: old Hong Kong.* Hong Kong: Formasia, 1987.

———. *Hong Kong: the last prize of empire.* Hong Kong: Formasia, 1991.

Wong, R. Y. C. and Cheng, J. Y. S. *The other Hong Kong report 1990.* Hong Kong: Chinese University Press, 1990.

Yee, A. H., foreword by Cheng, J. Y. S. *A people misruled: Hong Kong and the Chinese stepping stone syndrome.* Hong Kong: UEA Press, 1989.

2. History

2.1 General History

Birch, A. *Hong Kong: the colony that never was.* Hong Kong: Odyssey Press, 1991.

Cameron, N. *Hong Kong: the cultured pearl.* Hong Kong: Oxford University Press, 1978.

———. *An illustrated history of Hong Kong.* Hong Kong: Oxford University Press, 1991.

Chan, L. K. C. *China, Britain and Hong Kong, 1895–1945.* Hong Kong: Chinese University Press, 1990.

Endacott, G. B. *A history of Hong Kong.* Hong Kong: Oxford University Press, 1973.

———. *Government and people in Hong Kong 1841–1962: a constitutional history.* Hong Kong: Hong Kong University Press, 1964.

Fok, K. C. *Lectures on Hong Kong history: Hong Kong's role in modern Chinese history.* Hong Kong: Commercial Press, 1990.

Lane, K. *Sovereignty and the status quo: The historical roots of China's Hong Kong policy.* Boulder, CO.: Westview Press, 1990.

Rafferty, K. *City on the rocks: Hong Kong's uncertain future.* London: Viking, 1989.

Sawyer, G. R. *Hong Kong 1862–1919.* Hong Kong: Hong Kong University Press, 1975.

Smith, C. T. "The emergence of a Chinese elite in Hong Kong" *Journal of the Hong Kong Branch of the Royal Asiatic Society,* 1971, Vol. 11, pp.74–115.

Sweeting, A. *Education in Hong Kong pre 1841 to 1941: materials for a history of education in Hong Kong.* Hong Kong: Hong Kong University Press, 1990.

————. *Education in Hong Kong pre-1841 to 1941: fact and opinion.* Hong Kong: Hong Kong University Press, 1990.

2.2 Pre-Colonial Period

Balfour, S. F. "Hong Kong before the British." *Journal of the Hong Kong Branch of the Royal Asiatic Society,* Vol. 10 (1970), pp. 134–79.

Bard, S. *Solomon Bard's in search of the past: a guide to the antiquities of Hong Kong.* Hong Kong: Urban Council 1988.

Beeching, J. *The Chinese opium wars.* London: Hutchinson, 1975.

Chang, H. P. *Commissioner Liu and the Opium War.* Harvard: Harvard University Press, 1964.

Coates, A. *Macao and the British 1637–1842: prelude to Hong Kong.* Hong Kong: Oxford University Press, 1988.

Collis, M. *Foreign mud: being an account of the opium imbroglio at Canton in the 1830's and the Anglo-Chinese war that followed.* London: Faber & Faber, 1946.

Fay, P. W. *The opium war 1840–1842: barbarians in the celestial empire in the early part of the nineteenth century and the war by which they forced her gates ajar.* Chapel Hill, NC: University of North Carolina Press, 1975.

Lo, H. L. (et. al.) *Hong Kong and its external communications before 1842: the history of Hong Kong prior to British arrival.* Hong Kong: Institute of Chinese Culture, 1963.

Meacham, W. *Archaeology in Hong Kong.* Hong Kong: Heinemann, 1980.

————. *The archaeology of Hong Kong.* "Archaeology," vol. 33, no. 4 (July/August 1980), pp. 16–23.

Ng, P. Y. L. prepared for press and with additional material by Baker, H. D. R. *New Peace county: a Chinese gazetteer of the Hong Kong region.* Hong Kong: Hong Kong University Press, 1983.

Report of the Hong Kong Archaeological Survey. 5 Vols. Hong Kong: Hong Kong Government Printer, 1985.

So, C. L. "Landforms and archaeology." *Journal of the Hong Kong Archaeological Society,* Vol. 1 (1968), pp.24–28.

Waley, A. *The opium war through Chinese eyes.* Stanford, CA: Stanford University of Press, 1958.

2.3 Colonial Period (1841–1898)

*British parliamentary papers. China 24: correspondence, annual reports, returns, conventions and other papers relating to the affairs of Hong Kong 1882–99.*Shannon, Republic of Ireland: Irish University Press, 1971.

————. *China 24: correspondence, dispatches, reports, ordinances and other papers relating to the affairs of Hong Kong 1846–60.* Shannon, Republic of Ireland: Irish University Press, 1971.

————. *China 25: correspondence, dispatches, reports, returns, memorials and other papers respecting the affairs of Hong Kong 1862–81.* Shannon, Republic of Ireland: Irish University Press, 1971.

Crisswell, C. N. *The taipans: Hong Kong's merchant princes.* Hong Kong: Oxford University Press, 1981.

Eitel, E. J. *Europe in China.* Introduction by Lethbridge, H. J. Hong Kong: Oxford University Press, 1983.

Endacott, G. B. *A biographical sketch-book of early Hong Kong.* Singapore: Eastern Universities Press, 1962.

————. *An eastern entrepot: a collection of documents illustrating the history of Hong Kong.* London: HMSO, 1964.

Fairbanks, J. K. *Trade and diplomacy on the China coast: the opening of the treaty ports 1842–1854.* 2 Vols. Cambridge, MA: Harvard University Press, 1964.

Hayes, J. *The Hong Kong region 1850–1911: institutions and leadership in town and countryside.* Hamden, CT: Archon Books, 1972.

Lethbridge, H. J. *Hong Kong:stability and change.* Hong Kong: Oxford University Press, 1978.

Pope-Hennessy, J. *Verandah: episodes in the Crown Colonies, 1867–1889,* London: Allen and Unwin, 1964.

Sayer, G. R. *Hong Kong 1862–1919: years of discretion.* Edited with additional notes by Evans, D. M. E. Hong Kong: Hong Kong University Press, 1975.

————. *Hong Kong 1811–1862: birth, adolescence and coming of age.* With a new introduction and additional notes by Evans, D. M. E. Hong Kong: Hong Kong University Press, 1980.

Sinn, E. *Power and charity: the early history of the Tung Wah hospital, Hong Kong.* Hong Kong: Oxford University Press, 1989.

Smith, C. T. *Chinese Christians: elites, middlemen and the Church in Hong Kong*. Hong Kong: Oxford University Press, 1985.

————. "The emergence of a Chinese elite in Hong Kong" *Journal of the Hong Kong Branch of the Royal Asiatic Society*, 1971.

Warner, J. *Fragrant harbour: early photographs of Hong Kong*. Hong Kong: John Warner Publications, 1976.

————. *Hong Kong 100 years ago*. Translation by Wong, L. Hong Kong: Urban Council, 1970.

————. *Hong Kong illustrated: views and news 1840–1890*. Hong Kong: John Warner Publications, 1981.

Wong, J. Y. *Anglo-Chinese Relations 1839–1860*, Oxford: Oxford University Press, 1983.

Young, L. K. *British policy in China 1859–1902*. Hong Kong: Oxford University Press, 1970.

2.4 1898–1941

Gillingham, P. *At the Peak: Hong Kong between the wars*. Hong Kong: Macmillan, 1983.

Groves, R. G. "Militia, market and lineage: Chinese resistance to the occupation of Hong Kong's New Territories in 1899." *Journal of the Hong Kong Branch of the Royal Asiatic Society*, vol. 9 (1969), pp. 31–64.

Leeming, F. "The earlier industrialization of Hong Kong." *Modern Asian Studies*, Vol. 9, no. 3 (1975), pp. 337–342.

Mills, L. A. "Hong Kong" in *British rule in Eastern Asia*. Oxford: Oxford University Press, 1942, pp. 373–513.

Miners, N. *Hong Kong under imperial rule, 1912–1941*. Hong Kong: Oxford University Press, 1987.

Perham, M. *Lugard: the years of authority*. London: Collins, 1960. See especially pp. 283–374.

Wesley-Smith, P. *Unequal treaty 1898–1997: China, Great Britain and Hong Kong's New Territories*. Rev. ed. Hong Kong: Oxford University Press, 1984.

2.5 Japanese Occupation (1941–1945)

Birch, A. and Cole, M. *Captive years: the occupation of Hong Kong 1941–45*. Hong Kong: Heinemann, 1982.

Chan, L. K. C. "The Hong Kong question during the Pacific War." *Journal of Imperial and Commonwealth History*, Vol. 2 (1973–74), pp. 56–77.

Endacott, G. B. *Hong Kong eclipse*. Edited and with additional material by Birch, A. Hong Kong: Oxford University Press, 1978.

Lindsay, O. *At the going down of the sun: Hong Kong and Southeast Asia 1941–45*. London: Hamish Hamilton, 1981.

Luff, J. foreword by Maltby, C. M. *The hidden years*. Hong Kong: South China Morning Post, 1967.

2.6 1945–1997

Beijing Review, *The Hongkong solution*. Beijing Review Foreign Affairs Series, no. 6, 1985.

Bonavia, D. *Hong Kong 1997: the final settlement*. Hong Kong: South China Morning Post, 1985.

Burns, J. P. "The process of assimilation of Hong Kong (1997) and the implications for Taiwan." *American Enterprise Institute Foreign Policy and Defence Review,* Vol. 6, no. 3 (1986), pp. 19–26.

Cheng, J. Y. S. (ed.) *Hong Kong in search of a future.* Hong Kong: Oxford University Press, 1984.

Ching, F. *Hong Kong and China: for better or for worse.* New York: China Council of the Asia Society and Foreign Policy Association, 1985.

Chiu, H. "The 1984 Sino-British agreement on Hong Kong and its implications on China's unification." *Issues and Studies,* Vol. 21, no. 4 (1985), pp. 13–22.

Chiu, H. D., Jao, Y. C. and Wu, Y. L. *The future of Hong Kong: towards 1997 and beyond.* New York: Quorum, 1987.

Clark, D. "Taking the Basic Law seriously." *Asian Journal of Public Administration,* Vol.12, no.2 (December 1990), pp. 256–70.

Cooper, J. *Colony in conflict: the Hong Kong disturbances: May 1967–January 1968.* Hong Kong: Swindon Book Company, 1970.

Davis, M. C. *Constitutional confrontation in Hong Kong: issues and implications of the Basic Law.* London: Macmillan, 1989.

Domes, J. and Shaw, Y. M. (eds.) *Hong Kong: a Chinese and international concern.* London: Westview, 1988.

Duncanson, D. " 'Hong Kong, China'—repossession and penetration." *World Today,* Vol. 42 (1986), pp. 104–7.

Hicks, G. *Hong Kong countdown.* Hong Kong: Writers and Publishers Cooperative, 1989.

Hong Kong Government. *An agreement between the government of the United Kingdom of Great Britain and Northern Ireland and the government of the People's Republic of China on the future of Hong Kong.* Hong Kong: Government Printer, 1984.

Hopkins, K. (ed.) *Hong Kong: the industrial colony*. Hong Kong: Oxford University Press, 1971.

Hughes, R. *Borrowed place, borrowed time: Hong Kong and its many faces*. London: Andre Deutsch, 1976. (2d ed.).

Jao, Y. C., Leung, C. K., Wesley-Smith, P. and Wong S. L. (eds.) *Hong Kong and 1997: strategies for the future*. Hong Kong: Centre of Asian Studies, University of Hong Kong, 1985.

Jarvie, I. C. with Agassi, J. *Hong Kong: a society in transition*. London: Routledge & Kegan Paul, 1969.

Lau, S. K. *Basic Law and the new political order of Hong Kong*. Hong Kong: Institute of Social Studies, Chinese University of Hong Kong, 1988.

————. "Social change, bureaucratic rule and emergent political issues in Hong Kong." *World Politics* Vol.35 no.4 (1983), pp.544–62.

Lau, S. K. and Kuan, H. C. "Hong Kong after the Sino-British agreement: the limits to change." *Pacific Affairs,* Vol. 59, no. 2 (Summer 1986), pp. 214–36.

Lo, S. H. "The politics of decolonization in Hong Kong." *Issues and Studies,* Vol.25 no. 5, (May 1989), pp.73–101.

McGurn, W. (ed.) *Basic Law, basic questions: the debate continues*. Hong Kong: Review Publishing, 1988.

Morris, P. "The effect on the school curriculum of Hong Kong's return to Chinese sovereignty in 1997." *Journal of Curriculum Studies,* Vol. 20, no. 6 (1988), pp. 509–20.

Mushkat, M. "Environmental change and policy response in Hong Kong." *Journal of East and West Studies,* Vol. 27, no. 1 (Spring-Summer, 1988), pp. 55–70.

Mushkat, M. and Roberts, E. V. "Environmental adaptation in Hong Kong public enterprises." *Asian Profile,* Vol. 14, no. 2. (April 1986), pp. 119–128.

————. "Perceptions of the political environment and top management orientations in Hong Kong public enterprises." *Asia Pacific Journal of Management,* Vol. 4, no. 1, (September 1986), pp. 55–56.

Mushkat, R. "The transition from British to Chinese rule in Hong Kong: a discussion of salient international legal issues." *Denver Journal of International Law and Policy,* Vol. 14, no. 23, (Winter-Spring 1986).

Pye, L. W. "The international position of Hong Kong." *China Quarterly,* no. 95 (September 1983), pp. 456–68.

Rafferty, K. *City on the rocks: Hong Kong's uncertain future.* London: Viking, 1989.

Shawcross, W. *Kowtow!* London: Chatto and Windus, 1989.

Tsang, S. Y. T. *Democracy shelved: Great Britain, China and attempts at constitutional reform in Hong Kong, 1945–1952.* Foreword by MacDougall, D. M. Hong Kong: Oxford University Press, 1988.

Wesley-Smith, P. "The Hong Kong Act 1985." *Public Law,* (Spring 1986), pp.122–36.

Wesley-Smith, P. and Chen, A. (eds.) *The Basic Law and Hong Kong's future.* Singapore: Butterworths, 1988.

3. Politics and Administration

Bristow, R. *Land-use planning in Hong Kong: history, policies and procedures.* Hong Kong: Oxford University Press, 1984.

Cheek-Milby, K. and Mushkat, M. (eds.) *Hong Kong: the challenge of transformation.* Hong Kong: Centre of Asian Studies, University of Hong Kong, 1989.

Cheng, J. Y. S. *Hong Kong in transition.* Hong Kong: Oxford University Press, 1986.

Cheng, J. Y. S. "The democracy movement in Hong Kong." *International Affairs,* Vol. 65, no. 3 (Summer 1989), pp. 443–62.

———. "The post-1997 Government in Hong Kong." *Asian Survey,* Vol. 27, no.7 (August 1989), pp. 86–103.

Davies, S. and Roberts, E. V. *Political dictionary for Hong Kong.* Hong Kong: Macmillan, 1990.

Harris, P. B. *Hong Kong: a study in bureaucracy and politics.* Hong Kong: Macmillan, 1988.

———. *Public administration and public affairs in Hong Kong.* Hong Kong: Heinemann, 1983.

Hills, P. "Environmental protection in a laissez-faire economy." *Built Environment,* Vol. 11, no. 4 (1985), pp. 268–81.

——— (ed.) *Environmental planning, management and technology in Hong Kong.* Hong Kong: Centre of Urban Studies and Urban Planning, University of Hong Kong, 1988.

Ho, A. P. Y. "The organizational and political resources of environmental pressure groups in Hong Kong." *Asian Journal of Public Administration,* Vol.12, no.1 (June 1990) pp.101–18.

Hong Kong Government, *Pollution in Hong Kong: a time to act.* Hong Kong: Government Printer, 1989.

Lau, S. K. *Decolonization without independence: the unfinished political reforms of the Hong Kong government.* Hong Kong: Institute of Social Studies, Chinese University of Hong Kong, 1987.

244 / Bibliography, Hong Kong

———. *Institutions without leaders: Hong Kong Chinese views of political leadership.* Hong Kong: Centre for Hong Kong Studies, Chinese University of Hong Kong, 1990.

Lau, S. K. and Kuan, H. C. *Chinese bureaucrats in a modern colony: the case of Hong Kong.* Hong Kong: Centre for Hong Kong Studies, Institute of Social Studies, Chinese University Press, 1986.

———. "The 1985 district board elections in Hong Kong: the limits of political mobilization in a dependent polity." *Journal of Commonwealth and Comparative Politics,* Vol. 25, no. 1 (March 1987), pp. 82–102.

Leung, J. Y. H. "Functional representation in Hong Kong: institutionalization and legitimation of the business and professional elites." *Asian Journal of Public Administration,* Vol.12, no.2 (December 1990) pp.143–75.

Lo, C. S. S. *Public budgeting in Hong Kong: an incremental decision making approach.* Hong Kong: Writer's and Publisher's Cooperative, 1990.

Miners, N. *The government and politics of Hong Kong.* 5th ed. Hong Kong: Oxford University Press, 1991.

Perry, J. L. and Tang, S. Y. "Applying research on administrative reform to Hong Kong's 1997 transition." *Asian Journal of Public Administration,* Vol. 9, no. 2 (December 1987), pp. 113–29.

Scott, I. "Administration in a small capitalist state: the Hong Kong experience." *Public Administration and Development,* Vol. 9, no. 2 (April–May 1989), pp. 185–99.

———. "Policy implementation in Hong Kong." *Southeast Asian Journal of Social Science,* Vol. 15, no. 2 (1987), pp. 1–19.

———. "Policy-making in a turbulent environment: the case of Hong Kong." *International Review of Administrative Sciences,* Vol. 52, no. 4 (December 1986), pp. 447–69.

————. *Political change and the crisis of legitimacy in Hong Kong.* London: Hurst; Hong Kong: Oxford University Press; Honolulu, Hawaii: University of Hawaii Press, 1989.

Scott, I. and Burns, J. P. (eds.) *The Hong Kong civil service and its future.* Hong Kong: Oxford University Press, 1988.

Walden J. *Excellency, your gap is growing.* Hong Kong: All Noble Co., 1987.

White, R. M. "Hong Kong, nationality and the British Empire." *Hong Kong Law Journal,* Vol. 9, no. 1 (1989), p. 10–42.

————. "Nationality aspects of the Hong Kong settlement." *Journal of International Law,* Vol. 20, no. 1 (Winter, 1988), p. 225–51.

Yee, H. S. and Wong, Y. C. "Hong Kong: the politics of the Daya Bay nuclear plant debate." *International Affairs,* Vol. 63, no. 4 (Autumn 1987), pp. 617–30.

4. The Economy

American Chamber of Commerce. *Doing business in today's Hong Kong: a review of what makes Hong Kong work.* Hong Kong: Oxford University Press, 1988.

Arn, J. A. F. "Economic development, class formation and trade unionism" in *Planning and development of coastal open cities. Part two: Hong Kong.* Edited by Choi, Y. P. L. (et al.). Hong Kong: Centre of Urban Studies and Urban Planning, University of Hong Kong, 1986, pp. 46–63.

Bowring, P. and Cottrell, R. *The Carrian file.* Hong Kong: Far Eastern Economic Review, 1984.

Chambers, G. *Supertrader: the story of trade development in Hong Kong.* Hong Kong: Hong Kong Trade Development Council, 1989.

Chen, E. K. Y. "Foreign trade and economic growth in Hong Kong: experience and prospects" in *Trade and structural change in Pacific Asia*. Edited by Bradford, C. and Branson, W. Chicago: University of Chicago Press, 1987, pp. 333–78.

Chiu, P. Y. W. *Banking, trade and finance*. Hong Kong: Enterprise Publishing, 1987.

—————. *The economy of Hong Kong*. 2d ed. Hong Kong: Enterprise Publishing, 1989.

Cooper, E. "Karl Marx's other island: the evolution of peripheral capitalism in Hong Kong." *Bulletin of Concerned Asian Scholars*, Vol. 14, no. 1 (January-March 1982), pp. 25–31.

Davies, K. *Hong Kong to 1994: a question of confidence*. London: The Economist Intelligence Unit, 1990.

Deyo, F. (ed.) *The political economy of new Asian industrialization*. Ithaca, NY: Cornell University Press, 1987.

Economist Intelligence Unit. *China, Japan and the Asian NICs,* London: The Economist Intelligence Unit, 1988.

England, J. *Industrial relations and law in Hong Kong*. 2d ed. Hong Kong: Oxford University Press, 1989.

Freris, A.F. *The Financial markets of Hong Kong*. London: Routledge, 1991.

Ghose, T. K. *The banking system of Hong Kong*. Singapore: Butterworths, 1987.

Government Information Services, Hong Kong Government. *Hong Kong: the facts: agriculture*. Hong Kong, 1989.

Hartland-Thunberg, P. *China, Hong Kong, Taiwan and the world trading system*. New York: St. Martin's Press, 1990.

Ho, H. C. Y. and Chau, L. C. (eds.) *The economic system of Hong Kong.* Hong Kong: Asian Research Service, 1988.

Hsia, R. and Chau, L. *Industrialization, employment and income distribution: a case study of Hong Kong.* London: Croom Helm, 1978.

Industry Department, Hong Kong Government. *Hong Kong's manufacturing industries 1990.* Hong Kong: Government Printer, 1991.

Jacobs, P. "Hong Kong and the modernization of China." *Journal of International Affairs.* Vol. 39, no. 2 (Winter 1986), pp. 65–75.

Jao, Y. C. (ed.) *Hong Kong's banking system in transition: problems, prospects and policies.* Hong Kong: Chinese Banks Association, 1988.

––––––. (et al.) *Labour movement in a changing society: the experience of Hong Kong.* Hong Kong: Centre of Asian Studies, University of Hong Kong, 1988.

––––––. "Hong Kong's future as a free market economy." *Issues and Studies,* Vol. 22, no. 6 (June 1986), pp. 111–43.

Ledic, M. "Hong Kong and China: economic interdependence." *Pacific Review,* Vol. 2, no. 2 (1989), pp. 141–50.

Lethbridge, D. G. (ed.) *The business environment in Hong Kong.* 2d ed. Hong Kong: Oxford University Press, 1984.

Lin, T. B. and Mok, V. "Trade, foreign investment and development in Hong Kong" in *Foreign trade and investment: economic development in the newly industrializing Asian Countries.* Edited by Galenson, W., Madison, WI: University of Wisconsin Press, 1985, pp. 219–56.

Liu, W. H. "Hong Kong dimensions in post-Mao economic strategy." *Issues and Studies,* Vol. 22, no. 10 (October 1986), pp. 89–120.

Mushkat, M. *The economic future of Hong Kong.* Boulder, CO: London: Lynne Reiner, 1990.

Ng, S. H. "Electronics technicians in an industrialising economy: some glimpses of the 'New Middle Class'." *Sociological Review,* Vol. 34, no. 3 (August 1986), pp. 611–40.

Ng, S. H. and Sit, V. F. S. *Labour relations and labour conditions in Hong Kong.* London: Macmillan, 1989.

Peebles, G. *Hong Kong's economy: an introductory macroeconomic analysis.* Hong Kong: Oxford University Press, 1988.

Rabushka, A. *The new China: comparative economic development in mainland China, Taiwan and Hong Kong.* Boulder, CO: Westview, 1987.

Sit, V. F. S. and Wong, S. L. *Small and medium industries in an export-oriented economy: the case of Hong Kong.* Hong Kong: Centre of Asian Studies, 1989.

————. *Small and medium industries in an export-oriented economy.* Hong Kong: Centre of Asian Studies, University of Hong Kong, 1989.

So, A. Y. "The economic success of Hong Kong: insights from a world-system perspective." *Sociological Perspective,* Vol. 29, no. 2 (1986), pp. 241–58.

Sung, Y. W. "The Hong Kong development model: neoclassical economics in a Chinese society" in *Economic development in Chinese societies: models and experience.* Edited by Yao, Y. C., Mok, V. and Ho, L. S.. Hong Kong: Hong Kong University Press, 1989., pp. 155–76.

Turner H. A. (et al.) *The last colony—but whose?: a study of labour movement, labour market and labour relations in Hong Kong.* Cambridge, England: Cambridge University Press, 1980.

Woronoff, J. *Capitalist Paradise.* Hong Kong: Heinemann, 1980.

Wu, Y. L. and Jao, Y. C. "The economic consequences of 1997." *Journal of International Law,* Vol. 20, no. 1 (Winter 1988), pp. 17–41.

Youngson, A. J. *Hong Kong: economic growth and policy.* Hong Kong: Oxford University Press, 1982.

5. Society

Aijmer, G. "Expansion and extension in Hakka society." *Journal of the Hong Kong Branch of the Royal Asiatic Society,* Vol. 7, (1967), pp. 42–79.

Baker, H. D. R. "Life in the cities: the emergence of Hong Kong man." *China Quarterly,* no. 95 (September 1983), pp. 469–79.

Bibliography on gender studies in Hong Kong. Hong Kong: Centre for Hong Kong Studies, Chinese University of Hong Kong, 1989.

Bond, M. H. "Intergroup relations in Hong Kong" in *Ethnic Conflict.* Edited by Boucher, J. et al., Beverly Hills: Sage Publications, 1987.

Bond, M. H. and Lee, P. W. H. *Face-saving in Chinese culture: a discussion and experimental study of Hong Kong students.* Hong Kong: Social Research Centre, Chinese University of Hong Kong, 1978.

Bracey, D. H. "Economy, household structure and the Hakka women." *Journal of Asian Affairs,* Vol. 4, no. 2 (1979), pp. 5–28.

Bristow, R. *Hong Kong's new towns: a selective review.* Hong Kong: Oxford University Press, 1989.

Burns, J. P. "Immigration from China and the future of Hong Kong." *Asian Survey,* Vol. 27, no. 6 (June 1987), pp. 661–82.

Census and Statistics Department. *Hong Kong 1986 by-census: main report.* 2 Vols. Hong Kong: Government Printer, 1988.

Chen, A. H. Y. "The development of immigration law and policy: the Hong Kong experience." *McGill Law Journal,* Vol. 33, no. 4 (1988), pp. 630–75.

Cheng, K. M. "Traditional values and western ideas: Hong Kong's dilemmas in education." *Asian Journal of Public Administration,* Vol. 8, no. 2 (December 1986), pp. 195–213.

Cheung, F. M. and Pun, S. H. *A source book on women's studies in Hong Kong, 1975–1985.* Hong Kong: Institute of Social Studies, Chinese University of Hong Kong, 1987.

Cushman, J. and Wang, G. W. (eds.) *Changing identities of the Southeast Asian Chinese since World War Two.* Hong Kong: Hong Kong University Press, 1988.

Family Planning Association, *Report on the survey of family planning: Knowledge, attitudes, practice.* Hong Kong: Family Planning Association, 1987.

Fan, S. C. and Lee, S. L. "The ageing population of Hong Kong." *Journal of the South Seas Society,* Vol. 42, nos. 1 & 2 (1987), pp. 103–13.

Faure, D., Hayes, J. and Birch, A. (eds.) *From village to city: studies in the traditional roots of Hong Kong society.* Hong Kong: Centre of Asian Studies, University of Hong Kong, 1984.

Gaw, K. *Superior servants: the legendary Cantonese amahs of the Far East.* Singapore: Oxford University Press, 1988.

Ho, S. C. "Women's labor force participation in Hong Kong 1971–1981." *Journal of Marriage and the Family,* Vol. 46, no. 4 (November 1984), pp. 947–53.

Hong Kong Council of Social Service. *Social Research Index 1989.* Hong Kong: Hong Kong Council of Social Service, 1989.

Hong Kong Government. *Long term housing strategy: a policy statement.* Hong Kong: Government Printer, 1987.

Jaschok, M. *Concubines and bondservants: a social history.* Hong Kong: Oxford University Press, 1988.

Jones, C. *Promoting prosperity: the Hong Kong way of social policy.* Hong Kong: Chinese University Press, 1990.

Kelly, B. and London, M. *The four little dragons.* New York: Simon and Schuster, 1989.

Keung, J. K. "Government intervention and housing policy in Hong Kong." *Third World Planning Review,* Vol. 7, no. 1 (February 1985), pp. 23–44.

King, A. Y. C. and Lee, R. P. L. (eds.) *Social life and development in Hong Kong.* Hong Kong: Chinese University Press, 1981.

Kwan, A. Y. H. and Chan, D. K. K. (eds.) *Hong Kong society: a reader.* 2d ed. Hong Kong: Writers' & Publishers' Cooperative, 1989.

Lau, S. K. *Society and politics in Hong Kong.* Hong Kong: Chinese University Press, 1982.

Lau, S. K. and Kuan, H. C. *The ethos of the Hong Kong Chinese.* Hong Kong: Chinese University Press, 1988.

Lau, S. K. et al. *Indicators of social development, Hong Kong 1988.* Hong Kong: Hong Kong Institute of Asia Pacific Studies, 1991.

Leeming, F. *Street studies in Hong Kong: localities in a Chinese city.* Hong Kong: Oxford University Press, 1977.

Leung, B. K. P. (ed.) *Social issues in Hong Kong.* Hong Kong: Oxford University Press, 1990.

Leung C. K., Cushman, J. W. and Wang, G. (eds.) *Hong Kong: dilemmas of growth.* Canberra: Research School of Pacific Studies, Australian National University; Hong Kong: Centre of Asian Studies, University of Hong Kong, 1980.

Mushkat, R. "Refuge in Hong Kong." *International Journal of Refugee Law,* Vol. 1, no. 4 (1989), pp. 449–80.

Ng, R. S. Y. and Ingram, S. C. *Chinese culture in Hong Kong.* Hong Kong: Asia 2000 Ltd., 1989.

Osgood, C. *The Chinese: a study of a Hong Kong community.* 3 Vols. Tucson, Arizona: University of Arizona Press, 1975.

Pan, L. *Sons of the Yellow Emperor: The Story of the Overseas Chinese.* London: Secker and Warburg, 1990.

Phillips, D. R. "Traditional and modern health services in new planned communities: the Hong Kong experience" in *City planning: problems and prospects.* Edited by Yadav, C. S.. New Delhi: Concept Publishing, 1987., pp. 171–88.

———. *The epidemiological transition in Hong Kong: changes in health and disease since the nineteenth century.* Hong Kong: Centre of Asian Studies, University of Hong Kong, 1988.

Salaff, J. W. *Working daughters of Hong Kong: filial piety or power in the family?* Cambridge, England: Cambridge University Press, 1981.

Skeldon, R. "Hong Kong and its hinterland: a case of international rural-to-urban migration." *Asian Geographer,* Vol. 5, no. 1 (1986), pp. 1–24.

Tisdall, C. *In times of great chaos.* Hong Kong: Helping Hand, 1989.

Tung, H. S. C. "The position of women in the labour market in Hong Kong" *Labour and Society,* Vol. 10 no. 3 (September 1985) pp. 333–44.

Ward, B. E. *Through other eyes: essays in understanding 'conscious models'—mostly in Hong Kong.* Hong Kong: Chinese University Press, 1985.

Watson, J. L. "Rural society: Hong Kong's New Territories." *China Quarterly,* no. 95 (September 1983), pp. 480–90.

————, ed. "Transaction in people: the Chinese market in slaves servants and heirs" in *Asian and African Systems of Slavery.* Oxford: Basil Blackwell, 1980., pp.223–50.

Wong, S. L. *Emigrant entrepreneurs: Shanghai industrialists in Hong Kong.* Hong Kong: Oxford University Press, 1988.

————. "Modernization and Chinese culture in Hong Kong." *China Quarterly,* no. 106 (June 1986), pp. 306–25.

6. Crime

Census and Statistics Department. *Crime and its victims in Hong Kong 1986: a report on the crime victimization survey.* Hong Kong: Government Printer, 1988.

Clark D. J. "A community relations approach to corruption: the case of Hong Kong." *Corruption and Reform,* Vol. 2 no. 2, (1987), pp. 235–57.

————. "Ten years after: corruption and anti-corruption in Hong Kong." *Asian Journal of Public Administration,* Vol.8, no.1 (June 1986), pp. 113–32.

Crisswell, C. and Watson, M. *The Royal Hong Kong Police (1841–1945).* Hong Kong: Macmillan, 1982.

Lethbridge, H. J. *Hard graft in Hong Kong: scandal, corruption, and the ICAC.* Hong Kong: Oxford University Press, 1985.

————. "Prostitution in Hong Kong: a legal and moral dilemma." *Hong Kong Law Journal,* Vol. 8, no. 2 (1978), pp. 149–73.

————. "Rape, reform and feminism in Hong Kong." *Hong Kong Law Journal,* Vol. 10, no. 3 (1980), pp. 260–91.

Morgan, W. P. *Triad societies in Hong Kong.* Hong Kong: Government Press, 1960.

O'Callaghan, S. *The triads: the mafia of the Far East.* London: W. H. Allen, 1978.

Pullinger, J. and Armitage, C. *Crack in the wall: life and death in Kowloon Walled City.* London: Hodder & Stoughton, 1989.

Sinclair, K. *Asia's finest: an illustrated account of the Royal Hong Kong Police.* Hong Kong: Unicorn, 1983.

7. Religion

Berkowitz, M. I. *The tenacity of Chinese folk tradition: two studies of Hong Kong Chinese.* Singapore: Institute of Southeast Asian Studies, 1975.

Burkhardt, V. R. *Chinese creeds and customs.* 3 Vols. Hong Kong: South China Morning Post, 1953, 1955, 1958.

Endacott, G. B. and She, D. E. *The diocese of Victoria, Hong Kong: a hundred years of church history 1849–1949.* Hong Kong: Kelly & Walsh, 1949.

King, D. *St John's cathedral: a short history and guide.* Hong Kong: St. John's Cathedral, 1987.

Potter, J. M. "Wind, water, bones and souls: the religious world of the Cantonese peasant." *Journal of Oriental Studies,* Vol. 8 (1970), pp. 139–53.

Savidge, J. *This is Hong Kong: temples.* Hong Kong: Government Information Services, 1977.

Smith, C. T. *Chinese Christians: elites, middlemen and the Church in Hong Kong.* Hong Kong: Oxford University Press, 1985.

8. Law

Clark, D. J. *Hong Kong administrative law: a source book.* Hong Kong: Butterworths, 1989.

Wacks, R. (ed.) *The law in Hong Kong 1969–1989.* Hong Kong: Oxford University Press, 1989.

————. *The future of the law in Hong Kong.* Hong Kong: Oxford University Press, 1989.

Wesley-Smith, P. *An introduction to the Hong Kong legal system.* Hong Kong: Oxford University Press, 1987.

————. *Constitutional and administrative law in Hong Kong.* 2 Vols. Hong Kong: China & Hong Kong Law Studies, 1987, 1988.

9. Biographies and Company Histories

Cameron, N. *Power: the story of China Light.* Hong Kong: Oxford University Press, 1982.

Choa, G. H. *The life and times of Sir Hai Ho Kai: a prominent figure in nineteenth century Hong Kong.* Hong Kong: The Chinese University Press, 1981.

Coates, A. *Quick tidings of Hong Kong.* Hong Kong: Oxford University Press, 1990.

————. *A mountain of light: the story of the Hongkong Electric Company.* London: Heinemann, 1977.

————. *Whampoa ships on the shore.* Hong Kong: South China Morning Post, 1980.

Collis, M. *Wayfoong: the Hongkong and Shanghai Banking Corporation.* London: Faber and Faber, 1965.

Drage, C. *Taikoo.* London: Constable, 1970.

Endacott, G. B. *A biographical sketch book of early Hong Kong.* Singapore: Eastern Universities Press, 1962.

Hutcheon, R. *First Sea Lord: the life and times of Sir Y.K. Pao.* Hong Kong: Chinese University Press, 1990.

————. *Wharf: the first hundred years.* Hong Kong: Wharf (Holdings), 1986.

Keswick, M. (ed.) *The thistle and the jade: a celebration of Jardine, Matheson and Co.* London: Octopus, 1982.

King, F. H. H., King, C. E. and King, D. J. S. *The history of the Hongkong and Shanghai Banking Corporation.* 4 Vols. Cambridge, England: Cambridge University Press, 1987, 1988.

Phillipps, R. J. *Kowloon-Canton Railway (British Section); a history.* Hong Kong: Urban Council, 1990.

Who's Who in Hong Kong. 4th ed. Hong Kong: Who's Who in Hong Kong; Asianet Information Services, 1988.

10. Newspapers and Periodicals

Arts of Asia. Hong Kong: Arts of Asia Publications. 1971–. Bimonthly.

Asian Geographer. Hong Kong: Hong Kong Geographical Association, 1982–. Biannually.

Asian Journal of Public Administration. Hong Kong: Department of Political Science, University of Hong Kong, 1983–. Biannually.

Asian Profile. Hong Kong: Asian Research Service. 1973–. Six times a year.

Asian Wall Street Journal. Hong Kong, 1976–. Daily.

Asiaweek. Hong Kong, 1975–. Weekly.

Far Eastern Economic Review. Hong Kong, 1946–. Weekly.

Hong Kong Current Law. Hong Kong: Sweet & Maxwell, Hong Kong Current Law Services. 1986–. Eleven times a year.

Hong Kong Law Journal. Hong Kong: Hong Kong Law Journal. 1971–. Three times per year.

Hong Kong Standard. Hong Kong, 1949–. Daily.

International Herald Tribune. Hong Kong. Daily.

Journal of Oriental Studies. Hong Kong: Centre of Asian Studies, University of Hong Kong. 1954–. Biannually.

Journal of the Hong Kong Branch of the Royal Asiatic Society. Hong Kong: Hong Kong Branch of the Royal Asiatic Society. 1960–. Annual.

South China Morning Post. Hong Kong, 1903–. Daily.

11. Bibliographies

Bibliography on gender studies in Hong Kong. Hong Kong: Centre for Hong Kong Studies, Chinese University of Hong Kong, 1989.

Birch, A., Jao, Y. C. and Sinn, E. Y. Y. *Research materials for Hong Kong studies*. Hong Kong: Centre of Asian Studies, 1984.

Cheung, F. M. and Pun, S. H. *A source book on women's studies in Hong Kong, 1975–1985*. Hong Kong: Institute of Social Studies, Chinese University of Hong Kong, 1987.

Ho, D. Y. F., Spinks, J. A. and Yeung, C. S. H. *Chinese patterns of behavior: a sourcebook of psychological and psychiatric studies*. New York: Praeger, 1989.

Komala, M., Tang, P. P. L. and Cheung, S. *A bibliography of criminological literature in Hong Kong*. Hong Kong: Centre for Hong Kong Studies, Chinese University of Hong Kong, 1989.

Scott, I. *Hong Kong (Volume 115 of The World Bibliography Series)*. Oxford: Clio Press, 1990.

12. Statistics

Asia 1990. Yearbook. Hong Kong: Review Publishing, 1990., pp. 122–31.

Census and Statistics Department. 2 Vols. *Hong Kong 1986 by-census: main report*. Hong Kong: Government Printer, 1988.

————. *Hong Kong social and economic trends 1978–1988*. Hong Kong: Government Printer, 1990.

————. *Hong Kong social and economic trends 1979–1989*. Hong Kong: Government Printer, 1991.

————. *Social data collected by the general household survey*. 5 Vols. Hong Kong: Government Printer, 1983–89.

————. *Hong Kong trade statistics: exports and re-exports, imports*. 2 Vols. Hong Kong: Government Printer, 1990.

————. *Hong Kong annual digest of statistics.* Hong Kong: Government Printer, 1991.

Economic Services Branch, Government Secretariat. *Half-yearly economic report 1991.* Hong Kong: Government Printer, 1991.

Hong Kong 1991: a review of 1990. Hong Kong: Government Printer, 1991.

APPENDICES

APPENDIX 1: A BRIEF OUTLINE HISTORY OF HONG KONG

1. Prehistory. (Dates are approximate)

Palaeolithic Era. (?–10,000 B.C.).

Mesolithic Era. (9000–7000 B.C.).

Neolithic Era. (7000–3000 B.C.).
　　Lantau and Lamma Island sites.

Bronze Age. (circa 2500 B.C.).
　　Tung Wan site at Shek Pik and others.

2. Chinese Dynasties.

Ch'in (Qin). (221–207 B.C.).

　　Military conquest of the Hong Kong region.
　　Coins from period excavated.
　　Salt farms established probably under Imperial control.

Han (Han) (206 B.C.–220 A.D.).

　　Hong Kong region under control of the Nan Yueh kingdom
　　from c.208–111 B.C. Military conquest of the Hong Kong
　　region.
　　Coins excavated dated c. 220 A.D.
　　Brick-built tomb discovered—probably early to middle Han.
　　Naval base probably established in Tuen Mun.

Three Kingdoms (221–265).

> Hong Kong region within the Wu kingdom.
> Little Imperial interest in the region.

Six Dynasties (265–581).

> Hong Kong region within Chin, Liu Sung, and Chen kingdoms.
> Buddhist monastery established in mid-5th century at Tuen Mun.
> Substantial trade between China and Indochina. Tuen Mun a customs post before ships move up to major trading center in Canton (Guangzhou).

Sui (Sui) (581–618).

> Little Imperial interest in Hong Kong region.

T'ang (Tang) (618–907).

> Important pearl fishery established at Tai Po.
> Trade through Canton (Guangzhou) expanded especially with India and Persia.
> Tuen Mun important naval base guarding approaches to Canton (Guangzhou) with outforts.
> Han Yue writes poetry which refers to Tuen Mun (819–824).

Five Dynasties (907–960).

> Hong Kong region under Nan Han Kingdom.
> Chinese Imperial presence.
> Naval walled fort built at Tuen Mun—visited by Nan Han Emperor.
> Nan Han emperors establish Imperial pearl monopoly at Tai Po in 907.
> Four salt commissions established.
> Monastery at Tuen Mun rebuilt and further monastery established at Tang Leung Chau.
> Salt farms and naval station established at Kowloon.
> Network of naval and customs forts established throughout the Hong Kong region.

Sung (Song) (960–1279).

Garrison in Hong Kong believed to have three thousand troops.
First "Gentry" settlers from China into the Hong Kong region.
First Tin Hau temple established.
First evidence of growing Chinese settlement at end of 11th century.
Last two Sung (Song) emperors fleeing from the Mongols stay in Kowloon and at a Lantau Imperial Estate in 1279.

Yuan (Yuan) (1260–1368).

Reduction of Imperial presence.
Significant expansion of settlement by remnants of Sung (Song) court.
Little surviving evidence of this period in relation to Hong Kong.

Ming (Ming) (1368–1644).

Hong Kong region increasingly ravaged by pirates and bandits.
Area set up as different county in 1571 with senior official sent to restore order and reestablish military garrisons.
Forts set up to guard coasts with naval fleet to patrol off shore.
Portuguese occupy Tuen Mun forts between 1514 and 1521.
Region dominated by *Punti* families.
Incense trade reaches peak in Hong Kong region.
First ancestral halls built in the area.

Ch'ing (Qing) (1644–1912).

1661.   Hong Kong region ravaged by pro-Ming factions. New Imperial dynasty introduces "scorched earth policy." No civilians within 50 *li* (12 miles) of coast and houses pulled down.

1669.   Imperial order rescinds coastal evacuation policy. *Hakka* farmers move in from 1669 to repopulate area.

1729.   Imperial court introduces first prohibitions on opium.

1736–95.   Trade with Europeans restricted to Canton (Guangzhou).

1834.   British Lord Napier sent to China as Chief Superintendent of Trade to assist in the development of diplomatic ties. Unsuccessful in mission, but establishes desire by Britain to occupy Hong Kong.

1839.   First Opium War (not formally declared until 1840).

3. Colonial Period.

1841.   *January.* Captain Charles Elliot and Sir Gordon Bremer proclaim British sovereignty over Hong Kong.

1841.   *January.* Convention of Chuanpi (Chuanbi) cedes Hong Kong to Great Britain. Convention disavowed by both governments.

1841–42.   Renewed hostilities lead to military victories by British

1842.   *August.* Treaty of Nanking (Nanjing).

1843.   *June.* Treaty of Nanking (Nanjing) ratified by both governments and Hong Kong formally declared a colony.

             October. Supplementary Treaty of the Bogue.

1844.   Colonial Police force established.
             Executive and Legislative Councils begin to function.
             Use of opium accepted by Chinese government.

1846.   Ordinance establishes that the laws of England are to be enforced in the colony.

1852.   Outbreak of T'ai P'ing (Taiping) Rebellion results in large influx of refugees into Hong Kong.

1854.   Outbreak of Crimean War and strengthening of defenses in the colony.

1856.   Second Opium War (Arrow War) breaks out.

1860.   Treaty of Tientsin (Tienjin) signed between British, French and Chinese governments.
          Kowloon ceded to Britain in perpetuity.

1862.   Boatmen strike as protest against registration.

1863.   *Coolie* (Chinese laborers) strike in protest at ordinance for regulation of vehicles.

1864.   Torrential rains lead to collapse of several buildings.
          Hongkong and Shanghai Bank established.

1869.   Suez canal opened for navigation from Europe to the Far East.

1870.   China's proposal to set up consulate in Hong Kong rejected by the British government.

1874.   Hongkong and Shanghai Bank provides $600,000 loan to Chinese government.

1884.   Sino-French Wars begin. Britain increases defence expenditure on colony.

1894.   Sino-Japanese War begins.
          Great bubonic plague (black death) breaks out in colony.

1898.   New Territories leased to Britain for 99 years.
          Walled City still claimed by China.

1910.   All opium houses closed after international opium conference held in Shanghai.

1912.   Attempted assassination of the Governor of Hong Kong, Sir Francis Henry May.

1914–18.   Period of First World War. Colony supplies large numbers of laborers for the western front, but is otherwise largely unaffected by hostilities.

1919.   Riots over the price of rice.

1920.   Strike of dockyard mechanics.

1925.   General strike as protest against May 30 massacre in Shanghai.

1935.   In line with China, Hong Kong changes monetary system. Silver coins replaced by newly issued $1 dollar notes and nickel based coins.

1938.   Emergency regulations enacted following landing of Japanese army in Bias Bay, Canton (Guangzhou).
             Large numbers of Chinese refugees enter Hong Kong.

1939.   Bombs dropped by Japan on Sham Chun (Shenzhen).
             Refugees continue to arrive in Hong Kong.
             Negotiations between the British and Japanese to reopen Hong Kong—Canton (Guangzhou) navigation route.
             Britain declares war on Germany.

1940.   Food rationing introduced in Hong Kong.

1941.   Japanese assets in Hong Kong frozen.
             Japan attacks Hong Kong (December 8) and British surrender (December 25).

1945.   Japanese surrender to Allies. Vice-Admiral Harcourt leads British battleships into the harbor and Hong Kong reverts to status of British colony.

1949.   Communist government established on mainland. Large influx of refugees from China. Nationalist Chinese banished to Taiwan.

1950.   Hong Kong government ignores protests of the People's Republic of China concerning the restrictions placed upon Chinese immigration.
Korean war breaks out and British military garrison strengthened.

1952.   Riots in Kowloon.

1958.   Pro-nationalist celebrations in Hong Kong lead to riots. Martial law declared.

1963.   A report in the official *People's Daily* makes it clear that the People's Republic of China would settle the Hong Kong problem when the "time was ripe" and until that date there would be no changes.

1966.   Riots triggered by the raising of fares on the Star Ferry.

1967.   Cultural revolution in mainland spills over into Hong Kong. Major demonstrations and riots. British troops used in support of civilian authorities.

1972.   The PRC clarifies its position on Hong Kong and Macau to the United Nations Special Committee on Colonialism stating that, "the Chinese government has consistently held that they (. . . the questions of Hong Kong and Macau) should be settled in an appropriate way when conditions are ripe."

1973.   Major falls in stock market.

1974.   Large number of Vietnamese refugees begin to arrive in Hong Kong.

1979.   Governor of Hong Kong, Sir Murray MacLehose, visits Peking (Beijing) and meets the Vice Premier Teng Hsiao-p'ing (Deng Xiaoping), who informs the Governor that investors can, "put their hearts at ease" over the future of Hong Kong.

First Party Secretary of Kwangtung (Guangdong) declares that Hong Kong and Macau are special regions of China.

1980.   *July.* British Government publishes a White Paper on the proposed British Nationality Bill. Under its provisions 2.6 million Hong Kong Chinese would no longer be designated as British Citizens but would be "Citizens of the British Dependent Territory of Hong Kong."

October. Following consultations with the PRC, the government places major controls on the increasing numbers of illegal immigrants entering the territory by abandoning the "Reach Base" policy and requiring all residents to carry an identity card.

1981.   Major changes announced in the organization of district Administration. Partial use is to be made of direct elections at local government level.

1982.   *April.* Teng Hsiao-p'ing (Deng Xiaoping) in a meeting with the former British Prime Minister Edward Heath in Peking (Beijing) states that there would be provision for Hong Kong people to rule Hong Kong after 1997 and constitutional provisions would be made to allow for the creation of a Special Administrative Region.

September. British Prime Minister Thatcher arrives in Peking (Beijing) to discuss the possible future arrangements for Hong Kong after the expiration of the lease for the New Territories due to run out in June 1997. Teng (Deng) and the British Prime Minister then release a joint communique which states that, "The two leaders of the two countries held far reaching talks in a friendly atmosphere on the future of Hong Kong. Both leaders made clear their respective positions on the subject. They agreed to enter talks through diplomatic channels with the common aim of maintaining the stability and prosperity of Hong Kong." On her return to Hong Kong Mrs. Thatcher states that the nineteenth-century treaties between China and Britain relating to Hong Kong could be altered but not abrogated. This position is rejected by the Chinese authorities. Differences over the sovereignty of Hong Kong emerge.

December. Chinese government promulgates a new Constitution one article of which provides for the establishment of a Special Administrative Region for Hong Kong.

1983.

June. The Chinese Premier makes it clear in a speech to the National People's Congress that China will recover sovereignty over Hong Kong.

July. In the second phase of talks on the future of Hong Kong the Chinese authorities concede for the first time that, the Governor of Hong Kong, would be allowed to take part in the negotiations.

August. The talks become bogged down with evidence of a wide rift in the respective positions. For the first time a Chinese official gives 1 July 1997 as a clear date for the resumption of Chinese sovereignty.

September. A further round of talks makes little progress. Both sides are stuck on the question of sovereignty and Mrs. Thatcher, the British Prime Minister, reports that, "Great financial and political uncertainty existed concerning Hong Kong's future." This leads to a collapse in the value of the Hong Kong dollar.

October. The Chinese reiterate that the original treaties were invalid and confirm a deadline for an agreement as September 1984. Failure to meet this would result in a unilateral declaration of its position. A major run on the Hong Kong dollar leads to the pegging of the local currency to the United States dollar.

November. Britain concedes on the question of sovereignty, and the talks begin to take on a substantive form. From this point on the talks, held in complete confidence, were described as, "useful and constructive."

1984.   *January.* Outbreak of the most violent riots since 1967 in Mongkok during a taxi drivers dispute with the government.

July. Legislation published setting the introduction of indirect elections to the Legislative Council for 1985.

December 19. The Sino-British Joint Declaration is signed by British Prime Minister Thatcher and the Prime Minister of the People's Republic of China Mr. Chao Tzu-yang (Zhao Ziyang).

1985.   *July.* First meeting of the Joint Liaison Group and of the Drafting Committee of the Basic Law which sets the timetable for public consultation on the first draft for early 1988.

September. First (indirect) elections to the Legislative Council.

1986.   *April 1.* Hong Kong joins the General Agreement on Tariffs and Trade.

December. Sir Edward Youde, the Governor of Hong Kong, dies while on a visit to Peking (Beijing). Sir David Akers-Jones becomes Acting Governor.

1987.   *April.* Sir David Wilson becomes new Governor.

          October. Major collapses on local stock market.

1988.   *February 10.* Publication of White Paper on the development of representative Government which for the first time anticipates direct elections to the Legislative Council (scheduled for 1991).

          April. Publication for public consultation of the first draft version of the proposed Basic Law.

          June. Sir Geoffrey Howe, the British Foreign Secretary, arrives in Hong Kong and reasserts Britain's commitment to the observance of the Joint Declaration.

          June. The government announces a screening policy for Vietnamese immigrants which will attempt to distinguish between political refugees and economic migrants.

          October. Appointment of the first Chinese Chief Justice.

          November. The Governor visits Peking (Beijing) to meet Premier Li Peng and other senior Chinese officials.

1989.   *May.* The government announces it will allow the importation of 3,000 skilled foreign workers to meet labor shortages in certain sectors of the economy.

          May 18. First of the series of mass rallies in support of the democratic movement in China.

          June 4. Over 1 million Hong Kong people gather to protest against the violent suppression of the Beijing demonstrations.

June 13. The Governor argues for mandatory repatriation of the Vietnamese boat people as the only solution to the problem. The government's policy of screening the Vietnamese with the intention of repatriating nonrefugees is endorsed by the United Nations High Commission for Refugees.

October. The Governor delivers his annual policy speech in which he announces a massive port and airport development scheme costing HK$127 billion. This project is to become a focus for the PRC's attempts to become involved in policy making in issues which straddle 1997.

October. Publication of the second draft of the Basic Law for public consultation.

December. The British government announces that 50,000 heads of household in Hong Kong and their dependents will be granted full British National passports with right of abode in the United Kingdom. Chinese authorities declare that they will not accept the validity of these passports.

1990.   *March.* Publication of draft Bill of Rights to come into force in the territory before 1997.

April. Publication of the final version of the Basic Law.

September. Agreement is reached between the Vietnamese, British and Hong Kong governments, under which those boat people who were not recognized as genuine refugees would be repatriated to Vietnam by the United Nations High Commissions for Refugees.

December. The three-month application period commences for British Citizenship under the British Nationality Act. At first the scheme meets with a poor response from the public, although the numbers applying increase slowly.

APPENDIX 2. TABLES

2.1 Table 1: Population by Ethnic Background

Hong Kong-born Chinese.(1990): 59.3%

Chinese born on mainland. (1990): 38.7%

Other: 2.0%

Country of Origin of Other (1986 by census) 5,000 and above.

Filipino: 39,100

Indian: 15,800

American: 14,700

British (excluding armed forces): 14,100

Malaysian: 10,200

Thai: 10,100

Canadian: 9,100

Australian: 8,800

Japanese. 8,500

Pakistani: 7,700

Portuguese: 7,600

Singaporean: 5,300.

Sources: Hong Kong Government, *Hong Kong* (Years 1988, 1991). Hong Kong: Government Printer (1988, 1991).

2.2 Table 2: Population of Hong Kong

1841	7,450
1848	21,000
1861	122,000
1897	254,000
1898	354,000
1931	500,000
1941 (November)	circa 1,600,000
1944	circa 600,000
1947	1,800,000
1951	2,070,000
1961	3,209,500
1971	3,848,179
1980	5,147,900
1990	5,859,100

Sources: Various but in particular for postwar figures. Hong Kong Statistics Department, *Hong Kong Statistics 1947–1967*. Hong Kong: Government Printer (1969). Hong Kong Government, *Hong Kong* (Years 1971, 1981, 1991). Hong Kong:Government Printer (1971, 1981, 1991).

2.3 Table 3: Vital Statistics

	1951	1971	1980	1990
Crude Birth rate	34.0	19.0	16.9	11.8
(Per 1,000 population)				
Crude Death rate	10.2	5.0	5.0	5.0
(Per 1,000 population)				
Infant Mortality	36.9	18.4	11.8	5.9
(per 1,000 live births)	(1962)			
Life Expectancy at birth				
(Years)				
Male	—	—	—	74.6
Female	—	—	—	80.3

Sources: Various but in particular for postwar figures. Hong Kong Statistics Department, *Hong Kong Statistics 1947–1967*. Hong Kong:Government Printer, (1969). Hong Kong Government, *Hong Kong* (Years 1971, 1981, 1991). Hong Kong: Government Printer (1971, 1981, 1991).

2.4 Table 4: Trade (Postwar)

(Millions of Hong Kong Dollars)

	Imports	Exports	Re-exports
1951	4,870	4,433*	—
1961	5,970	2,939	991
1971	20,256	13,750	3,414
1980	111,651	68,171	30,072
1990	642,530	225,875	413,999

* The figures on re-exports were not included in the figures as they were not regarded as significant by the Statistics Department at this time.

Sources: Various but in particular for postwar figures. Hong Kong Statistics Department, *Hong Kong Statistics 1947–1967*. Hong Kong:Government Printer, (1969). Hong Kong Government, *Hong Kong* (Years 1971, 1981, 1991). Hong Kong:Government Printer (1971, 1981, 1991).

2.5 Table 5: Principal Sources of Import and Export (Postwar)

(Millions of Hong Kong Dollars)

1951

Imports (to Hong Kong)		Exports (from Hong Kong)	
PRC	863	PRC	1,604
UK	619	Sing*	714
Sing*	394	Indonesia	245
Japan	392	Macau	228
USA	373	UK	215
Germany	214	Japan	193
India	159	Pakistan	188
Thailand	156	USA	163
Pakistan	144	Taiwan	139

1961

Imports (to Hong Kong)		Exports (from Hong Kong)		Re-exports (from Hong Kong)	
PRC	1,028	USA	679	Sing*	185
Japan	846	UK	589	Japan	123
UK	757	Sing*	267	PRC	91
USA	729	Indonesia	173	Macau	56
Thailand	256	Japan	107	Taiwan	53
Germany	186	Germany	105	Indonesia	52
Switzerland	157	PRC	07	Cambodia	41

* Sing includes Singapore, Malaya, Sabah and Sarawak.

1971

Imports (to Hong Kong)		Exports (from Hong Kong)		Re-exports (from Hong Kong)	
Japan	4,926	USA	5,708	Japan	644
PRC	3,330	UK	1,946	Singapore	397
USA	2,535	Germany	1,128	Indonesia	312
UK	1,593	Japan	484	USA	303
Taiwan	991	Canada	484	Taiwan	200
Germany	732	Australia	402	Macau	123

1980

Imports (to Hong Kong)		Exports (from Hong Kong)		Re-exports (from Hong Kong)	
Japan	25,644	USA	22,591	PRC	4,642
PRC	21,948	Germany	7,384	USA	3,085
USA	13,210	UK	6,791	Indonesia	2,761
Taiwan	7,691	Japan	2,329	Singapore	2,510
Singapore	7,384	Australia	1,941	Taiwan	2,229
UK	5,456	Singapore	1,791	Japan	2,201

1990

Imports (to Hong Kong)		Exports (from Hong Kong)		Re-exports (from Hong Kong)	
PRC	236,134	USA	66,370	PRC	110,908
Japan	103,362	PRC	47,470	USA	87,752
Taiwan	58,084	Germany	17,991	Japan	24,376
USA	51,788	UK	13,496	Germany	23,406
Korea*	28,155	Japan	12,079	Taiwan	21,248
Singapore	26,122	Singapore	7,796	Korea*	13,011

* Korea refers to the Republic of Korea (South Korea).

Sources: Various but in particular for postwar figures. Hong Kong Statistics Department, *Hong Kong Statistics 1947–1967*. Hong Kong: Government Printer, (1969). Hong Kong Government, *Hong Kong* (Years 1971, 1981, 1991). Hong Kong: Government Printer (1971, 1981, 1991).

MACAU

Introduction

Macau lies at the most southwesterly tip of the Pearl River estuary in southern China. It is about 45 miles west of Hong Kong and 90 miles to the southwest of Canton (Guangzhou). It consists of a peninsula of 2.1 square miles together with the two islands of Taipa (1.4 square miles) and Coloane (2.6 square miles). The peninsula is separated from the Chinese mainland by a narrow sandy isthmus. A Barrier Gate serves as the customs post and "borderline" between Macau and China. Official statistics in 1988 gave Macau a population of 443,500, most of whom are Chinese. Since most of them are concentrated on the tiny peninsula, the population density there is among the highest in the world.

Early Chinese historical records show Macau as being largely deserted before the South Sung (Song) dynasty. However, in 1276 the South Sung (Song) were defeated by the forces of what became known as the Yuan dynasty, and the royal family in exile, together with their loyal followers in 2,000 junks, headed south. In the vicinity of Taipa and Coloane Islands they encountered a typhoon and were soon compelled to go ashore. Although the Yuan troops followed, they were met with strong resistance from the South Sung (Song) supporters who finally prevailed and became the first inhabitants of Macau.

The first commercial interest in the area was shown by the *Hoklo* boat people who found the harbor of Macau a useful center for coastal trade in the southern provinces. However, Macau was not a major settlement before the arrival of the Portuguese in 1557. During the 15th century, Portugal began her sea expeditions in search of new trade routes to the East. The next 400 years of Macau history were epitomized by the Western penetration of the area and the East-West interactions which ensued. Macau not only became a hub of international trade and a base for regional missions, but also a shelter for less salubrious activities, such as trade in opium and in coolie labor.

The scene was set when Vasco da Gama completed his voyage to Goa, via the Cape of Good Hope in 1498. Building upon this pioneering discovery of a new trade route, the Portuguese subsequently captured Malacca which became a stepping-stone for further trade expansion into China and Japan. In 1513, Jorge Alvares, a Portuguese captain, arrived at the Bay of Tuen Mun and traded unofficially with the local Chinese. However, it was not until 1517 that the first Portuguese envoy, Tome Pires, arrived to try to establish an "enduring" official Sino-Portuguese trading relationship. Although he was granted an audience with the Emperor, the death of the Emperor led to the failure of the mission.

At this time, the profitable trade between China and Japan had further lured the Portuguese to seek a coastal stronghold near Chekiang (Zhejiang) and Fukien (Fujian). However, their market in Liampo was destroyed by the Chinese official, Ch'u Yuan (Chu Yuan), who wished to ban all "evil" foreign trade. Under these circumstances, the Portuguese had to leave Liampo and search for a new base in the south. In 1535, they reached Lampacao and were allowed to moor in Macau, then called Haochingol. On the pretext of drying out soaked cargo they set up trading depots ashore in 1553. Four years later in 1557, the Portuguese, through paying tribute, succeeded in settling in Macau. Hence, many consider 1557 to be the foundation year of Macau as a Portuguese settlement. In 1582, a lease was finally signed between the two countries, and the Portuguese agreed to pay an annual ground rent of 500 taels of silver in exchange for the Macau leasehold.

Macau, under the Portuguese, became the first and most important trading post between the Orient and the Occident.

It monopolized the sea routes between Europe and China. Concurrently, it developed as a bastion of Christianity and became known as "the city of the Name of God." In August, 1568, the first bishop of Macau, Dom Melchior Carneiro, visited Macau, and in 1575, Macau was decreed by the Pope as the first Asian diocese. By 1621, Macau had a population of about 20,000 with most of them engaged in crafts related to trade such as shipbuilding, cannon forging, and ammunition production.

Between the 16th century and the first half of the 17th century, three lucrative trade routes began to emerge; firstly, Macau–Malacca–Goa–Lisbon; secondly, Canton (Guangzhou)–Macau–Nagasaki; and, finally, Macau–Manila–Mexico. Large quantities of silk, brocade, cotton, textiles, gold, minerals, potteries, and herbal medicines were exchanged for silver, spices, and ivory, of which silver constituted the largest share. From the trading ventures initiated from Macau, 900,000 *taels* (at 1.33 ounce per *tael*) of silver were shipped from Goa between 1585 and 1591, and about 14,890,000 *taels* were shipped in the Nagasaki trade between 1585 and 1630.

Because of the high returns of this trade, other seapowers such as the Spanish, the Dutch, and the British contested Portuguese monopoly in between 1580 and 1808. Following the Union of Crowns between Portugal and Spain in 1580, the Spanish shared the profit obtained from the South Sea trade around the Philippines, but they did not challenge Portuguese hegemony in Macau. This contrasted sharply with the attitude of the Dutch at the beginning of the 17th century. However, Dutch naval onslaughts and challenges between 1622 and 1627 proved unsuccessful and they eventually turned their attention to Taiwan.

British activity in the area began in 1635 when Captain John Weddel forced China to open trade along the Pearl River. However, it was not until 1808 that the British attempted a more direct challenge. On the pretext of protecting Macau from French attack, the British occupied the

Portuguese enclave. At this point the Chinese authorities joined the Portuguese in the attempt to resist British penetration. The joint pressure of China and Portugal proved effective, and the British withdrew voluntarily.

This Sino-Portuguese "cooperation" was something of an exception to their general relationship. There were constant tensions over jurisdictional and administrative issues over the period of Portuguese occupation, and Portugal only gradually evolved as the *de facto* ruler of the territory with China exerting economic and symbolic pressures in the form of levying ground rent, setting up a customs office, sending officials to visit the territory, and expressing her claim to sovereignty.

Initially the Portuguese paid ground rent to the Chinese authorities, recognizing the fact that land was leased and not owned by the Portuguese. The internal affairs of the Portuguese community in Macau were administered by an elected Senate and the Captain-Major of the Japan Voyage. For their part, the Chinese set up a China Office in Macau to deal with Chinese subjects and with the Portuguese trading relationship.

At the beginning of the 17th century, Dutch onslaughts necessitated the erection of fortifications and the building of a city wall by the Portuguese. This was met with resistance from the Chinese who feared that this was a means to occupy the territory permanently. In 1623 the first Governor of Macau, Dom Francisco de Mascarenhas, was appointed. The presence of a governor constituted symbolic threat to Chinese sovereignty, but did not lead to open conflict at the time. Indeed it was only two centuries later that events took a more violent turn. In 1846, the Portuguese appointed Joao Maria Ferreira do Amaral as the Governor of Macau, and in an attempt to emulate British successes in Hong Kong, Amaral was instructed to establish Macau as a truly Portuguese territory and to preempt Chinese influence. His expansionist policies included taxing Chinese subjects in Macau; expanding the territory beyond the Barrier Gate (i.e., the border); demolishing the Chinese customs office and expelling the officers. Such actions invited Chinese retaliation and, finally, Amaral was assassinated.

In 1862, Portugal sent Isidoro Francisco Guimaraes to sign the Treaty of Tientsin (Tianjin). With the mediation of the French ambassador, the Chinese intended to maintain Macau as a tributary territory under Chinese overlordship; but the Portuguese demanded that talks on the assassination of the Governor be held first. After lengthy negotiation, an agreement was reached, but it was never ratified—largely because the Chinese discovered that the French translation of the treaty was different from their version in that it suggested that Macau would be severed from China.

In 1887, a Draft Agreement of the Luso-Chinese Treatise was concluded. This was ratified as the Luso-Chinese Treatise of Friendship and Trade in 1888. It recognized that "Portugal will forever administer Macau" but the question of border delimitation was postponed for further negotiations.

The failure to delimit the border led to continuing but low key disputes on the issue of Macau's sovereignty for decades to come, and an end to the *impasse* came only with dramatic changes in Portuguese domestic politics. Following a military *coup d'etat* in 1974, which toppled the monarchy in Lisbon, the new Portuguese Constitution of 1976 stated that Macau would be governed by an Organic Statute which was promulgated by the Portuguese Parliament. Under this statute, a Legislative Assembly was established giving the city some avenues for citizen representation and participation. In 1979, China and Portugal entered into formal diplomatic relations and jointly accepted "Macau as a Chinese territory under Portuguese administration" with her future status to be solved through negotiation at the appropriate time. In 1987, the Sino-Portuguese Joint Declaration was finally signed. China will resume the exercise of sovereignty of Macau on December 20, 1999 when Macau will become a Special Administrative Region under the formula of "One Country-Two Systems." To clarify the details of this relationship a

Basic Law Drafting Committee was set up in 1989, and the Basic Law will be promulgated by Peking (Beijing) in 1992.

Associated with these diplomatic changes, in recent years Macau's economy has also diversified considerably and moved away from its traditional role as a Portuguese trading center. At present, manufacturing and tourism are the mainstays of Macau's economy. Manufacturing industries such as garments, plastics and electronics account for about 40% of total GDP, whereas tourism accounts for about 25%. The opening up of trade with China in the 1980s enabled Macau to benefit from her unique location and connections with the nearby Chuhai (Zhuhai) Special Economic Zone. It is possible that Macau is in a position to reassert her historic role as an entrepôt for trade, this time under clear-cut Chinese sovereignty.

THE DICTIONARY

AGRICULTURE. Although there were few signs of agriculture in the pre-twentieth century maps and sketches of Macau, by 1918 some reclaimed land and low-lying land on Taipa Island was being used for growing rice. But it was between the mid-1940s and the late 1960s that Macau's agriculture began to develop. A drought in the Shantau (Swatow) area in 1946 caused many starving peasants to move to Macau and to begin vegetable gardening and paddy farming. In addition, when in 1952, the "Barrier Gate Incident" led to Chinese restrictions on food imports, the Macau government encouraged residents to take up vegetable growing. By the 1960s, the colony could satisfy about half its demands. However, the rapid industrialization and urbanization of the 1970s diminished the importance of agriculture in Macau, and since the late 1970s, China has exported large quantities of fresh vegetables and other foodstuffs to Macau.

At present, only 3 percent of Macau's land area is used for farming. Horticulture is the most important sector and is mostly located in Coloane. There is also a small livestock industry devoted to cattle, pigs, chickens, and ducks. Fishing is also important with some of the catch being exported to Hong Kong.

ALVARES, JORGE. Alvares was the first Portuguese to set foot on southern China. In 1513 while employed as the treasurer of the Malacca trading post, Alvares was sent by the Captain-General of Malacca to the Pearl River area with orders to explore the possibility of trading with China. In the same year, he arrived at the Bay of Tun

Men (now called Tuen Mun in Hong Kong), and stayed near Neilingding Island.

Although Alvares succeeded in establishing informal relationships with the local Chinese, he was unable to formalize any enduring Sino-Portuguese trading relationship by contacting top-ranking Chinese officials or concluding a commercial treaty. These tasks later fell to Tome Pires and Simao Peres de Andrade. In July 1521, Alvares died and was buried. (See Pires, Tome.)

AOMEN (MACAU). The Chinese/Pinyin name for Macau.

ARCHITECTURE. Macau, with more than 400 years of Chinese and Portuguese influences, exhibits unique architectural features bequeathed from both the *Cidade Crista* (Christian City) and the *Cidade Chinesa* (Chinese City).

Several churches and fortresses were erected by the Portuguese in the *Cidade Crista* from the 16th to the 18th centuries. The greatest of Macau's churches was built in 1602 adjoining the Jesuit College of Sao Paulo. Between 1617–1626, the first fortress, Sao Paulo do Monte, was built by Mascarenhas in a predominantly European baroque style.

The *Cidade Chinesa* was located outside the *Cidade Crista* and called *Wangxia* by the Chinese. The common architectural structures in the *Cidade Chinesa* were single two-story buildings and temples. The former consisted of a commercial area on the ground floor and a living space on the first floor. The roof usually overhung the ground area with decorated wooden eaves. Also typical are the blue bricks and timber windows.

Temple designs were influenced by the Chinese architectural traditions of *fung shui*. Ideally, temples should face the sea or a broad valley and back onto a hill, which is regarded as the home for potentially dangerous dragons. Architecturally, the roof is usually of green- or yellow-rounded tiles. Stone lions often guard the door.

Despite the existence of two distinct cities for centuries, pure Portuguese-style buildings have not existed in Macau. Rather Portuguese architecture has been subject to Chinese influences such as those seen in roofing materials and designs and the Eastern motifs carved on some Portuguese facades.

ART. The arts have provided useful literary and visual records of Macau in the 16th-to-18th centuries. Written works, such as William C. Hunter's *Bits of Old China* (1911), are the literary counterparts of the visual records left by painters. Paintings by the Jesuits are of particular importance. The most well-known depictions of pre-1840 Macau are a pair of watercolors showing the Porto Interior and the Praia Grande, in the collection of the Luis de Camoes Museum of Macau. Other important works were influenced by George Chinnery (1774–1852). His impact was greatest on Lamqua (Guan Qiaochang), who produced paintings on Macau that bear Chinnery's style, and on Auguste Porget (1808–1877), who specialized in portraying the life of the common people of Macau. Some of his most famous sketches were published as lithographs in his book *La Chine et Les Chinois,* published in Paris in 1842.

ASSEMBLEIA LEGISLATIVA (Legislative Assembly.) The *Assembleia Legislativa* makes laws on matters of exclusive interest to Macau rather than Portugal. It also approves the annual budget, supervises the executive, and proposes amendments to the Organization Statute. Decisions of the Assembly are normally made by majority vote, a two-thirds majority being required only in special cases.

Before 1974, the *Assembleia Legislativa* had only an appointed membership. In 1975, the Armed Forces Movement in Portugal promised some directly-elected seats in Macau, and in 1976, the Organization Statute initiated the first *Assembleia Legislativa* containing elected members. Of its 17 members, five were appointed, six indirectly-elected and six directly-elected. The term of office was three years.

The second Assembly, which was scheduled to close in June 1984, was dissolved on February 23, 1984 because of the power struggle between the Governor, Vasco de Almeida e Costa, and the Macanese legislators. Four days later, Governor Costa introduced new electoral reforms which paved the way for the widening of registration and the reallocation of more of the indirectly-elected seats to the Macau Chinese. The main beneficiaries of these changes were the pro-Peking (Beijing) businesspeople. (See Organization Statute.)

-B-

BASIC LAW OF MACAU. After the signing of the Sino-Portuguese Joint Declaration in 1987, the Chinese Premier, Li Peng, proposed to the National People's Congress in 1988 that a Macau Basic Law Drafting Committee (BLDC) be set up. The BLDC had a number of representatives from Macau (19 out of 48), most of whom were pro-Peking (Beijing) capitalists, such as Dr. Ma Man-kee (Ma Wanqi), Stanley Ho, and Victor Wu. The timetable for drafting the Basic Law was set out at its first meeting in October 1988. It was planned that the first draft would be ready for canvassing of public opinion by the second half of 1991. The revised draft would be submitted to the Standing Committee of the National People's Congress in Peking (Beijing) for promulgation by the second quarter of 1992, and a formal draft Basic Law would be ready for final approval by the beginning of 1993.

In April 1989, the 19 Macau representatives on the BLDC approved a list of 88 members of the Basic Law

Consultative Committee. The list included deputies, trade unionists, bankers, traders, business executives, and senior civil servants from Macau.

Up to 1991, the Basic Law Drafting Committee had worked quickly without any of the public dramas displayed in its Hong Kong counterpart. This may be partly because a substantial proportion of residents of Macau already have the right of abode in Portugal, and partly because the *Assembleia Legislativa* (Legislative Assembly) has since 1976 contained a directly-elected element. (See Dual Nationality; "Macau People Ruling Macau"; Macau Special Administrative region; Sino-Portuguese Joint Declaration.)

BRITISH OCCUPATION. Before the founding of Hong Kong in 1842, the British frequently used Macau as a place for residence when they were waiting for the next opportunities to trade in Canton (Guangzhou). However, following the invasion of Portugal by Britain's enemy France in 1801, the British colonial authorities became concerned that a treaty between Portugal and France would threaten their interests in Macau. Accordingly, Lord Wellesley, the British Governor of India, occupied the territory in 1802 on the pretext of protecting Macau against the French. This particular action was quickly abandoned when China threatened to intervene, but in 1808, Lord Rear-Admiral Drury directed a second attack on Macau. Although the Portuguese were compelled to accept British occupation, the Chinese authorities in Kwangtung (Guangdong) threatened to expel the British by force. Once again the British, fearing serious interruption to trade, withdrew voluntarily.

-C-

CAMARA MUNICIPAL DAS ILHAS. One of the municipal councils in Macau, established in 1962 with jurisdiction over the municipal duties of the Taipa and Coloane Islands. The new Electoral Law in July 1988 expanded the size of the *Camara Municipal das Ilhas*. Previously it had no elected members, but it now has 11 councilors of which eight are elected. Its decisions on budgets and loans are subject to the Governor's approval. (See Coloane Island; *Conselho Consultivo; Leal Senado*.)

CAPTAIN-GENERAL. The term refers to a military governor role in the early years of the Portuguese colonial administration. The first Captain-General to be appointed in Macau was Dom Francisco Mascarenhas, who in 1623 was appointed as governor of the territory with this rank. Originally such an appointment had been sought by the Portuguese in Macau who had been concerned that the previous arrangement whereby the territory was only overseen by a Captain-Major had left the colony potentially weak in the face of Dutch attacks.

However, when Mascarenhas began to use the full range of his powers, the reaction among Senate members, Jesuits and the local Portuguese population as a whole was generally unfavorable. These powers included: the right to appoint most government officials (with the exception of legal personnel); command of the local garrison; the right to appoint, after consultation with the *Senado da Camera* (the Senate), all military commanders; and the right to arrest, and if necessary deport "any citizens who have shown themselves riotous, mutinous, or disturbers of the peace." (See Captain-Major; Mascarenhas; Senate.)

CAPTAIN-MAJOR. Like Captain-General, Captain-Major was a Portuguese military and naval title. In the context of 16th-century Macau, the relevant post was the Captain-Major of the Japan Voyage. At this time the trade from Malacca to Nagasaki was very lucrative, and a

Captain-Major was appointed by the Portuguese Crown or the Viceroy of India to organize this trade trip as a royal monopoly. In effect, the person concerned was the *ex officio* chief of all Portuguese ships and settlements between Malacca and Japan. He could also share the profit from the ventures. Since the ships involved needed to moor in Macau before the next trading season, the Captain-Major effectively became the interim governor in Macau for that particular period. The post of the Captain-Major was replaced in 1623 with the appointment of the first Captain-General and Governor. (See Captain-General; Portuguese Trade Routes; Senate.)

CATHOLIC CHURCH. From the early 16th century, missionaries came with traders to the Far East, arriving usually on board the annual carrack from Goa and Malacca. Macau soon became a strong Christian community with a flourishing religious life. On 23 January 1576, the Diocese of Macau was formally founded, and more churches were subsequently built in the 16th and 17th centuries. Religious orders such as the Jesuits, Franciscans, Augustinians, and Dominicans also founded branches in Macau.

At the creation of the Diocese of Macau, the Vatican also announced its intention of creating more than 600 dioceses in Asia. Macau thus became the bridgehead of Christianity, and has sometimes, rather extravagantly, been known as "the Rome of the Far East." Evidence of this missionary activity shows that from 1578 to 1740 a total of 463 Jesuits left Lisbon for Macau.

However, the development of the Catholic Church in Macau was not trouble-free. In the early 18th century the Vatican ruled against the Jesuit practice of allowing Chinese converts to continue their customs of "ancestor worship." The split over this controversy which followed damaged the missionary effort in China, and the Augustinian fathers were expelled from Macau in 1712. In 1767, under a decree of the Marquis of Pombal in Portugal, the Jesuits were also expelled, only to return in the 19th century.

The Church's role in education and science has been considerable, with the major initiatives often coming from the Seminary of Sao Paulo in Macau. As early as 1588, a printing press was established to make publishing of scientific and religious works possible.

In more modern times many religious orders and congregations have been responsible for building schools, orphanages, old people's homes, and refugee centers in Macau. There are five parishes: the Cathedral; Sao Laurenco; Santo Antonio; Sao Lazaro; and Our Lady of Fatima. The island of Taipa is covered by the parish of Our Lady of Mount Carmel and Coloane is covered by the mission of St. Francis Xavier. (See Jesuits; Madre de Deus School; Sao Paulo Church; Seminary of Sao Paulo.)

CENTRO DEMOCRATICO DE MACAO. Following the introduction of direct elections under the terms of the 1976 Organization Statute (Organic Statute), a group of Portuguese and Macanese formed the *Centro Democratico de Macao* (CDM) to nominate candidates for elections. This group has been most critical of corruption and bureaucratism in the Macau Government. Its weekly radio program, "Democracy on the March," was banned by the Governor Nobre de Carvalho with the support of the Macanese organization, Association for the Defence of the Interests of Macao (ADIM.)

CHINESE AND MACANESE DIALECTS. Although Cantonese and Fukienese (Fujianese) dialects were widely used in Macau, today standard Cantonese is more common, and has become the medium of teaching in schools. These changes reflect the influence of immigration from Canton (Guangzhou) and the integration of Macau into the regional economy. About 70 percent of the people are Chinese and most of them speak Cantonese.

The Macanese dialect is influenced by other languages and dialects from Goa, Malacca and Canton (Guangzhou). The resultant Creole thus became differentiated from today's Portuguese. Although this dialect was once very important as the commercial language along the China coast, its usage seems likely to die out along with its predominantly older generation speakers.

CHINESE DEPENDENT TERRITORY UNDER PORTUGUESE ADMINISTRATION. Following the Portuguese *coup d'etat* of 25th April 1974, the post-revolutionary government of Portugal initiated its decolonization program through the 1976 Organization Statute (Organic Statute). Macau changed from a Portuguese colony into a "territory under Portuguese administration." Apart from abiding by the legal system of Portugal and the principles of the Organization Statute, Macau has enjoyed administrative, economic, financial and legislative autonomy.

CH'U, YUAN (CHU YUAN). Ch'u Yuan (Chu Yuan) was appointed as the Governor of Fukien (Fujian) and Chekiang (Zhejiang) in 1547, and was instructed by the royal edict to prohibit the illicit seatrade with foreign countries, especially Portugal. By this time, Portuguese middlemen in Macau were already making high profits from trade between China and Japan, and the livelihood of the coastal population had been improved by increasing trade. In 1548, Chu attacked the Portuguese ships in Liampo and destroyed the trading center. However, the ban on all foreign seatrade was unwelcome to many Chinese coastal traders who saw opportunities to trade with the Southeast Asia countries. Their influence led to Chu's dismissal, and, following his subsequent humiliation by fellow ministers, Chu committed suicide in 1549.

Trade quickly began to flourish again in the Fukien (Fujian)-Chekiang (Zhejiang) region, but the destruction of Liampo as a trading post had essentially forced the Portuguese to shift their operations south, and to concentrate on the use of Macau. (See Liampo.)

CITY OF THE NAME OF GOD. When the Portuguese established Europe's first settlement on the Chinese coast in 1557, they expected it to be a bastion of Christianity as well as a trading post, and accordingly they called it "City of the Name of God, Macau." The first settlers included priests, and some of the first buildings were churches dedicated to "Mother of God" and named after popular saints. (See Catholic Church.)

CIVIL SERVICE INTEGRATION SCHEME. As part of Macau's decolonization process, the Portuguese authorities introduced a scheme to integrate Macau civil servants into the Portuguese civil service after 1999. Under this scheme, one-quarter of the civil servants could be given the option to work in Portugal when Macau reverts to Chinese rule. The civil servants would not be asked to make their choices until 1993–1994. The Macau Government estimated the number involved to be between 1,500 and 2,500.

COLOANE ISLAND (LUHUAN). Macau's territory covers the peninsula, together with the islands of Taipa and Coloane. Sovereignty over this territory was confirmed by treaty with China in 1887.

Coloane Island is linked to Taipa by a causeway and to the peninsula by a bridge. Recently there has been extensive industrial, tourism, and residential development on the island. Coloane is administered under the jurisdiction of the *Camara Municipal de Ilhas* established in 1962.

COMISSAO DE DEFESA DO PARTIMONIO AR-QUITECTONICO PAISAJISTICO E CULTURAL (Committee for the Preservation of Macau's Heritage). The *Comissao de Defesa do Partimonio Arquitectonico Paisajistico e Cultural* was founded in 1976 and strengthened in 1984. It has close links with the *Instituto Cultural de Macau* (Cultural Institute of Macau) and supports the Government in its preservation policy. Its choice for preservation is not confined to major monuments, but also extends to groups of houses and structures which contribute to the urban heritage.

CONSELHO CONSULTIVO (Consultative Council). Under the terms of the 1976 Organization Statute (Organic Statute), the *Conselho Consultivo* (Consultative Council) advises the Governor on all matters relating to the territory. The Council consists of the Governor as the President, five elected members, three ex officio members and two appointed members. Two out of the five elected members are returned from the *Leal Senado* and the *Camara Municipal das Ilhas* (i.e., the municipal councils); one by groups representing moral, cultural, and welfare interests; and two by economic associations. The ex officio members are the Secretary for Public Administration, the Attorney General, and the Director of the Financial Department. The two other councilors are community leaders appointed by the Governor. The members of the *Conselho Consultivo* cannot simultaneously be deputies of the *Assembleia Legislative* (Legislative Assembly). The meetings of the Council are held in secret. (See Organization Statute.)

COOLIES TRADE. In the 17th century, the infamous "coolies trade" involved laborers being lured from China to Macau where they were sold and shipped overseas as "coolies." At the height of the trade in the 1670s there were said to be more than 300 "Labour Recruitment Houses" in Macau.

-D-

DUAL NATIONALITY. After the signing of the Sino-Portuguese Joint Declaration on 13 April 1987, the Portuguese Government promised full citizenship rights for the ethnic Chinese residents of Macau and their descendants after 1999. This policy contradicted a statement made by Chinese Foreign Minister Wu Xueqian to the National People's Congress on 2 April in which he said that Chinese citizens in Macau who held Portuguese travel documents would not be able to pass their nationality to the next generation after 1999. On 18 April 1987 the Portuguese Government reiterated that under Portuguese law, nationality is transmitted by bloodline and not by place of birth. Children born to Portuguese citizens can acquire Portuguese nationality by Portuguese law, and the Joint Declaration would not represent a change in Portuguese policy. However, the Chinese Government continues to regard Portuguese passports held by Macau Chinese only as travel documents. To Peking (Beijing), all ethnic Chinese in Macau are Chinese nationals and thus they cannot hold dual nationality if they live in Macau after 1999.

DUTCH INVASIONS. In the 17th century, the Dutch rose as a third colonial power in Asia after Spain and Portugal. Over a period of years the Dutch managed to challenge the Portuguese position of trading preeminence in the Indies. It was also clear that they wished to take over the lucrative Japanese trade, then in the hands of the Portuguese. Alarmed by Dutch ambitions, the Viceroy of Goa sought to strengthen the Portuguese military position, but the Spanish (and Portuguese) King, Philip

III (1598–1621), ignored these requests for reinforcement. In the first decade of the 17th century, the Dutch launched a number of small-scale attacks on Macau; which were repulsed by the Macau Portuguese. An uneasy peace came in 1609, when the Netherlands and Spain signed the Truce of Antwerp, which was intended to last for twelve years. However, this did not restrain the Dutch from challenging the Portuguese trade monopoly, nor deter the Portuguese from strengthening the fortifications of Macau.

Finally in 1622, a 13 ship-strong Dutch fleet, with about 800 soldiers, joined two Dutch and two English ships already moored near Macau. With many of the able-bodied population absent on trading missions, there were less than one thousand people in the enclave, and probably less than one-tenth of these were capable of bearing arms. However, under the leadership of Captain-Major Lopo Sarmento de Carvelho, the Macau Portuguese succeeded in protecting the enclave.

In the summer of 1627, a further attack by four Dutch ships was again defeated.

-E-

ELECTORAL UNION. The Electoral Union was formed in 1984 from a powerful alliance of pro-Peking (Beijing) business interests plus the Macanese elites. The group is headed by barrister and former *Assembleia Legislativa* Chairman, Carlos d' Assumpcao, who intended to boycott the 1984 election. However, after his visit to Peking (Beijing), there was speculation that he was urged to cooperate with the pro-Peking (Beijing) Chinese leaders in Macau. Subsequently, he formed the Electoral Union which was supported by Dr. Ma Man-kee (Ma Wanqi). The group won four directly-elected seats in 1984. In 1988, the Union won the majority of directly-elected and indirectly-elected seats in the *Assembleia Legislativa.* (See *Assembleia Legislativa;* Flower of Friendship and Development of Macau; Ma Man-kee (Ma Wanqi).)

-F-

FIDALGO. The term is derived from the Portuguese *"filho d'algo"* meaning someone of aristocratic background (literally "sons of somebody"). At the end of the 14th century and the beginning of the 15th century, the *Fidalgo* class became increasingly involved in the Portuguese exploration and colonization. Vessels would be commissioned by one of the great nobles and captained by a *fidalgo* of his household. This system allowed the monarch to control the expansion of imperial power while the *fidalgo* could retain their status and privileges. Later, the term *"fidalgo"* was also used to refer to the Captain-Majors, Captain-Generals, merchants, missionaries, and Crown administrators at the time. (See Captain-General; Captain-Major; Portuguese Trade Routes.)

FLOWER OF FRIENDSHIP AND DEVELOPMENT OF MACAU. Prior to 1980, the Chinese population in Macau were not active in elections of the *Assembleia Legislativa.* Only 4,000 registered electors cast their vote. Subsequently, young Chinese liberals established a political group called the Flower of Friendship and Development of Macau to contest the 1984 election. Three of its candidates obtained a total of 3,500 votes and one of them, Alexandre Ho (He), was elected to the assembly. In 1988, He, together with two other liberals, won three seats in the *Assembleia Legislativa.* The remaining seats were won by the Electoral Union, which represents pro-Peking (Beijing) business interests. Such an electoral success by the liberals marked a protest against what some viewed as interference in the electoral process by Governor Carlos Melancia. (See Electoral Union; Ho, Alexandre.)

"FRANKS". *Fuk-lan-ki* was a term originally used by Chinese to refer to Europeans in general. The word was later corrupted to "Franks."

-G-

GAMA, VASCO DA (1460–1524). Gama was an experienced navigator and explorer, who, at the end of the 15th century, was commissioned by King Manoel of Portugal to find a viable and lucrative sea route to the East. Between 1497 and 1498, Gama succeeded in discovering this route, first round the Cape of Good Hope and then through the Indian Ocean to Goa, Cochin, and Calicut on the west Indian coast. This route was later to open up trading opportunities for ships leaving Lisbon for Goa, Macau, China, and even Japan. In 1522, Gama was appointed as the Viceroy of India. He died in 1524. (See Goa; Malacca; Portuguese Trade Routes.)

GOA. Goa, on the western coast of India, was originally a Hindu city which later came under Muslim control. In the early 16th century it became a Portuguese colony, and quickly developed forts, churches, and seminaries. Goa effectively became the capital of the Portuguese mercantile empire in the Far East. A Viceroy, appointed by the Portugal monarch, commanded the city and exercised overall control of the colonization and administration of surrounding regions including Macau. Apart from being an administrative center, Goa was also strategically located along the Lisbon-Goa-Malacca-Macau trade route in which textiles from Goa were exchanged for spices in Malacca. (See Malacca; Portuguese Trade Routes; Gama, Vasco da.)

GOVERNADOR (Governor). Before 1623 the emphasis on seasonal trading made it more appropriate for the functions of governor to be handled by the relevant Captain-Major of the Voyages to Japan. These were appointed by the Portuguese Crown or by the Portuguese authorities in India. In 1623 the Portuguese recognized the increasing importance of Macau by appointing the first full-time Captain-Major or governor, Dom Francisco de Mascarenhas, who was appointed in 1623. For China the presence of a Portuguese governor constituted a symbolic threat until the signing of the Luso-Chinese Treaties of Friendship and Trade in 1888.

Between 1623 and 1991 there have been 126 changes in the individual or group occupying the role of *governador* (see Appendix 1). According to the Organization Statute of 1976, the *Governador* is appointed by the President of the Portuguese Republic. This usually follows consultation with the local population through the *Assembleia Legislativa* and representatives of some social organizations.

The *Governador* serves a five-year term, and has both executive and legislative powers. As the head of the executive, he formulates general policy, executes laws and coordinates the civil service. These executive powers are exercised with the support of an executive structure—the *secretarios* (secretaries) and the *Conselho Consultivo* (Consultative Council). (See Captain-General; Captain-Major.)

-H-

HO (HE), ALEXANDRE. Alexandre He belongs to a liberal-oriented political group called Flower of Friendship and Development of Macao. In 1984 he became the first liberal to be directly elected to the *Assembleia Legislativa.* In 1988, He, together with other liberals, won three seats in the Assembly. Despite their success in 1988, He and his allies remained a small minority within a pro-Peking (Beijing) coalition.

Because of a lack of institutionalized channels for communication between the government and the people in Macau, many Macau Chinese have frequently used He as channel to articulate their interests and grievances. (See Flower of Friendship and Development of Macau).

HO, YIN (HE, XIAN). Ho Yin (He Xian) was a Chinese businessman in Macau who died in 1983. His business empire included the Tai Fung Bank, hotels, restaurants, and bus and taxi companies. He was accepted both by the Chinese community and by the Portuguese administration as a prominent member of society between the 1960s and the 1980s. He chaired several public utility companies and was the president of the Chinese General Chamber of Commerce, vice-president of the *Assembleia Legislativa*, and a member of the Standing Committee of the Chinese National People's Congress. His son, Edmund Ho (He), emerged as a prominent political figure in the 1980s. At present, he is the executive director and general manager of the Tai Fung Bank. He has been regarded as the most probable person to be the first ethnic Chinese governor of Macau. (See Macau Chamber of Commerce.)

-I-

ILLEGAL IMMIGRANTS. The influx of illegal immigrants has been a problem since the late 1970s. In March 1982, the Macau Government requested the members of five major chambers of commerce to register with the government all illegal immigrants employed in their factories and companies, together with their families and any family members without identity cards. As a result, a total of 29,000 people were registered. In May of the same year, the government also issued more temporary abode permits to workers who were eventually issued with identity cards in June 1985.

In January 1989, the Macau Government carried out another registration of youngsters and students under 18 who were not identity cardholders, and more than 4,500 were issued with identity cards. In the following year, the government sought to register the parents of these youngsters. As soon as this announcement was made, another 50,000 illegal immigrants came forward.

INDUSTRY. In the early years, Macau functioned almost solely as a trading port and there was little industrial development. The first industrial plant, a cannon foundry, was set up by a Portuguese by the name of Manuel Tavares Bocarro. This cannon casting industry served an important need of Portuguese trading routes between Lisbon and the East. However, in the 18th century, the industry began to decline and the foundries were closed down.

Until after the Second World War, the main industries in Macau were confined to the making of joss sticks, firecrackers, and matches for export to Southeast Asia, Europe, and America. However, from the 1930s, small-scale textile industries, shoe factories, and furniture factories also began to appear. But it was not until the 1970s and the 1980s that large-scale modern industries such as garment manufacturing, plastics, toys, and electronics began to emerge. These were largely stimulated by the attempts of Hong Kong businesses to circumvent the wave of protectionism in the West against exports from Hong Kong. These circumstances lay behind the development in the 1970s of Hong Kong-based investment in the clothing sector. Similarly in the 1980s, when the U.S. decided to withdraw the Generalized System of Preferential Treatment (GSP) scheme from Hong Kong on products such as toys and artificial flowers, this triggered a second wave of Hong Kong-based investment. Toys now account for 10% of Macau's exports.

In the future, Macau's industry is likely to be faced with strong competition from other low-cost producers, such as the Philippines and Thailand, as well as more sophisticated measures in trade protectionism.

INSTITUTO EMISSAR DE MACAU (IEM). In 1980, the government attempted to encourage the development of the financial sector by establishing the state-owned *Instituto Emissar de Macau* (IEM), which issues the currency and advises on banking regulations. From this time the number of banks increased rapidly. Apart from foreign banks, such as Citibank and Banque Nationale de Paris, there are six Chinese banks in Macau with two being affiliates of Bank of China. These Chinese banks in particular have good connections with investors in the Zhuhai Special Economic Zone.

In the same period, the *Sociedade Financeira,* was also established as a clearinghouse. However, Macau's role as a financial center is overshadowed by that of Hong Kong.

-J-

JESUITS. From the early 16th century, missionaries accompanied the traders to the East. Religious orders, such as the Jesuits, founded branches in Macau. They built churches, hospitals, and orphanages to help those in need. The Jesuits also opened and ran the Seminary of Sao Paulo, otherwise known as Madre de Deus. This was made into a university college in 1594 and began to offer the first degree courses in theology and arts in 1597. Notable Jesuits, such as Father Matteo Ricci, were regarded as the pioneers in introducing science into China.

The order suffered a setback in 1773 when the King of

Portugal demanded the dissolution of the Order because of an alleged assassination attempt. The Jesuits were expelled from Macau and the Seminaries of Sao Paulo and Sao Jose were closed. (See Catholic church; Madre de Deus School; Ricci, Matteo; Rites Controversy; Sao Paulo Church; Seminary of Sao Paulo.)

JUDICIARY. Macau has a district court (*Tribunal da Comarca de Macau*) and an Administrative Tribunal (*Tribunal Administrative de Macau*).

The district court is a local court affiliated to the higher court in Lisbon. Judges are directly appointed by the Ministry of Justice of the Portuguese Republic. There are two benches with jurisdiction in civil and criminal matters.

The Administrative Tribunal is responsible for adjudicating decisions emanating from the municipal councils and assessment and collection of taxes.

Decisions of the Macau courts are appealable to the superior Portuguese courts unless otherwise limited.

JUNE 4TH INCIDENT IN CHINA. Macau was largely untouched by the events of June 4, 1989 at T'ien-an-man (Tiananman) Square in Peking (Beijing). A demonstration involving between 50,000 to 100,000 people took place, but no organized movement with prominent leaders emerged from the protest. The Macau Government, keen to show its stable relationship with China, announced during the upheaval that there would be no change in its plan to build an international airport on Taipa Island. By contrast with Hong Kong, there was no postponement of the first meeting of the Basic Law Consultative Council and there were less demands for political reform.

JURUBACAS. The early local interpreters in Macau who were baptized and given Christian names and family names of their godparents, and finally integrated into Portuguese society.

-L-

LEAL SENADO (Loyal Senate). The *Leal Senado* was established in 1583, and is Macau's oldest local political institution. Originally it was a senatorial organization in accordance with the medieval Portuguese tradition of municipal government. After the Portuguese revolution of 1820 and its subsequent constitutional reforms, the colonial empire was reorganized and in 1834 the *Leal Senado* was converted into a municipal council. As a municipal council, it manages the urban area of the Macau Peninsula.

Before July 1988, the *Leal Senado* had eight members of whom four were appointed by the Governor. The new Electoral Law in July 1988 expanded the *Leal Senado* into a 15-member council with only three members being appointed. Its decisions on budgets and loans are subject to the Governor's approval. (See *Camara Municipal das Ilhas*.)

LIAMPO. Liampo is currently known as Ningpo (Ningbo), and is situated on the Chekiang (Zhejiang) coast. Following the ban on seatrade imposed by the Kwangtung (Guangdong) authorities in the 1520s, the Portuguese concentrated on trade in Fukien (Fujian) and Chekiang (Zhejiang) provinces. In 1540, the Portuguese began wintering regularly in Liampo. However, the Chinese authorities became increasingly irritated by the aggressive behavior of some Portuguese traders, and in 1548, the newly appointed Governor of Chekiang (Zhejiang) and Fukien (Fujian), Ch'u Yuan (Chu Yuan), moved to end the illicit trade and Liampo was destroyed. The Portuguese trading operations moved southward to Lampacao and later to Macau. By 1557 Macau had become established as the major Portuguese trading center in 1557. (See Chu Yuan.)

LICENSED GAMBLING. Gambling is a significant facet of Macau's economy, with extensive involvement of both the government and the local community. Income from gambling operations constitutes about 60% of the government's total income and 20% of the total Gross Domestic Product (GDP.)

The first step taken by the government to grant licenses for gambling was under the governorship of Captain Isidoro Francisco Guimaraes (1851–1863). In 1934 the government granted monopoly rights to all casino-style gambling. The first franchise contract was granted to Tai Xing Company whose first casinos were in the Central Hotel.

On 1 January 1962, the *Sociedade de Turismo e Diversoes de Macau* (STDM) took over as the licensed holder, and has coordinated the development of gambling into a major enterprise. By 1985, the STDM owned five casinos in Macau and a ferry service between Hong Kong and Macau. It has also been instrumental in attempts to revive horse racing and associated gambling activities. (See *Sociedade de Turismo e Diversoes de Macau*.)

LOCALIZATION OF THE CIVIL SERVICE. For most of the 1970s and 1980s the pace of localization in the Macau civil service was slow. Up to 1987, approximately 50% of the 700 professional-grade civil servants were expatriates from Lisbon. The Macanese, who constitute 3% of the population, occupied most of the middle-ranking grades, and the Chinese have normally worked at the lowest levels.

However, in May 1988, Governor Melancia, after his visit to Peking (Beijing), declared that localization of the civil service would become an official policy. In August

1988, the Macau Government drafted a bill to recognize non-Portuguese degrees or certificates, and from February 1989, Chinese (Cantonese) became an official language alongside Portuguese. By the end of 1989, all official documents were to be bilingual.

Although the Macanese have expressed reservations about localization and bilingualism, both policies are fully supported by local Chinese and by the Chinese Government.

LUSO-CHINESE TREATY OF FRIENDSHIP AND TRADE (1888). This agreement, also known as the Treaty of Peking (Beijing), was based on the protocol usually referred to as the Lisbon Agreement. This had been drafted in 1887 by the Portuguese Minister of Foreign Affairs and a delegate of the Chinese Imperial Maritime Customs. On December 1, 1888, the Governor of Macau, Tomas de Sousa Rosa, signed the Treaty. It was ratified on August 28, 1889. *Inter alia* this confirmed the "perpetual occupation and government of Macau and its dependencies by Portugal as any other Portuguese possession." However, Portugal was obliged not to "alienate Macau and its dependencies without agreement with China." In this way, China has retained a very limited sense of symbolic sovereignty over Macau. However, the question of border delineation was postponed, and this created constant frictions between the Portuguese claim that four islands comprise Macau's territory and the Chinese consent of only Taipa and Coloane. In 1928, when the treaty was renewed, the sensitive issue of border delineation was again evaded.

-M-

MA, MAN-KEE (MA, WANQI). Dr. Ma Man-kee (Ma Wanqi) is a local Chinese businessman in Macau who succeeded Ho Yin (He Xian) as the Chairman of the Macau Chinese Chamber of Commerce. He is a prominent supporter of Peking (Beijing). Up to 1990, he was a member of the Macau *Assembleia Legislativa.* He also served on the Standing Committee of the Chinese National People's Congress and the Chinese People's Political Consultative Conference of the PRC. (See Macau Chamber of Commerce.)

MACANESE (*Macaense*). The term *Macanese* is difficult to define. Many see the Macanese as a racial mixture of Portuguese and Chinese. But many of those who refer to themselves as "pure Macanese" claim to be the descendants of the original Portuguese-Malaccan combinations, and deny biological links with the Chinese population.

In Macau's early years, when the Portuguese upper class looked down on the Chinese as second-class citizens, the Macanese identified with the Portuguese. In modern times they have filled the middle-ranking positions within the civil service. However, they also resent the way in which Portuguese nationals have filled the most senior positions in the past, and the way in which the policy of localization will discriminate in favor of local Chinese in the future. (See Chinese and Macanese Dialects; Macanese Culture.)

MACANESE CULTURE. Macau has been under Portuguese influence for about 400 years, but the cultural fusion between the Portuguese and Chinese has been uneven. In the field of arts, medicine, and religion, for example, both cultures have maintained their separate identities. Overlaps have arisen, however, in areas such as Macanese dialect, architecture, and cuisine. (See Macanese.)

MACAO. Macao is rendered as "Macau" in Portuguese. Before 1955, the term Macao was used in all official documents.

MACAU CHINESE CHAMBER OF COMMERCE. The Macau Chinese Chamber of Commerce, established in 1911, is a bastion of pro-China influence. Its Chairman, Dr. Ma Man-kee (Ma Wanqi), is the most powerful locally-born entrepreneur in Macau. The Chamber consists of 2,700 members most of which are private firms. Other members include trade associations, state-owned companies, and guilds. (See Ma Man-kee (Ma, Wanqi).)

"MACAU PEOPLE RULING MACAU". Throughout Macau's history, top- and middle-ranking positions within the government have been filled by the Portuguese and the Macanese. The Chinese population has been confirmed to low-level duties.

However, the Sino-Portuguese Joint Declaration of 1987 stipulated that localization of top-level officials would be the priority and that Macau would move towards "Macau People Ruling Macau" by 1999. (See Basic Law of Macau; Macau Special Administrative Region; Sino-Portuguese Joint Declaration.)

MACAU SPECIAL ADMINISTRATIVE REGION (SAR). During the negotiations leading to the Sino-British Joint Declaration on the future of Hong Kong in 1984, the Chinese Government suggested that the question of Macau would be settled only after the Hong Kong issue has been decided. In 1987, the Sino-Portuguese Joint Declaration on Macau's future was signed and Macau is to become a Special Administrative Region of the People's Republic of China on December 20, 1999. (See Basic Law of Macau; "Macau People Ruling Macau"; Sino-Portuguese Joint Declaration; Sino-Portuguese Negotiations.)

MADRE DE DEUS SCHOOL (SEMINARY OF SAO PAULO). The Madre de Deus School was founded by the Jesuits on 1 December 1594. In 1597, it was made into a university college and the first degree courses were organized in theology and arts subjects—humanities, Greek and Latin, rhetoric, and philosophy. In 1601, 59 Jesuits, of whom 26 were priests, lived at Sao Paulo. There were also a school of Oriental languages, a school of music and one of painting. After the expulsion of the Jesuits, the college was used as an army barracks, until, in 1835, it was destroyed by fire. (See Catholic Church; Jesuits; Ricci, Matteo.)

MALACCA. In the context of early trading routes for spices, Malacca was strategically situated between the Spice Islands and Baghdad. Its status in the years prior to the Portuguese arrival was that of a protected nation under Imperial China. In 1511, Alfonso de Albuquerque, a Portuguese captain, took Malacca by force, and a Captain-General, responsible to the Viceroy at Goa, was appointed to administer the city. Malacca then became a key Portuguese trading post until 1641, when it was captured by the Dutch. (See Goa; Portuguese Trade Routes.)

MASCARENHAS, DOM FRANCISCO DE. Dom Francisco de Mascarenhas arrived in Macau in 1623 to become the first full-time *Governador*. His prime aim was to build forts to protect Macau from a potential Dutch invasion. Under his administration, the fortresses of Sao Paulo do Monet, Barra, Sao Francisco, Penha and Sao Januario were finished and the Fort of Guia was planned. Mascarenhas also established a cannon foundry.

MESQUITA, VICENTE NICOLAU DE. Mesquita was referred to by the Portuguese as "the hero of Passaleao" after his success in leading the Portuguese retaliation to the Chinese following the assassination of Amaral in 1849.

In 1849, Mesquita was a young Macanese sub-lieutenant. In the tense period following the assassination of Amaral, the Chinese stationed a strong armed force at Pakshanlan (Passaleao), about a mile beyond the Barrier Gate. The Portuguese, in retaliation, decided to counterattack, and on August 25, 1849, Mesquita led two sneak attacks to destroy the center of the Chinese fort and expel the garrison.

However, Mesquita's later career was less distinguished. In one of his periods of insanity he killed his wife and her daughter and wounded another son and daughter. He eventually committed suicide.

A monument to him was erected in 1940 opposite the *Leal Senado*. However, it was eventually destroyed in a demonstration in 1966.

-N-

NAN GUANG TRADING COMPANY. The Nan Guang Trading Company was China's sole political and commercial representative in Macau from 1949 to 1984. It was then split into the Nan Guang Company, which is the political arm, and the Nan Guang Trading Company, which is the commercial arm. The latter is under the control of the Ministry of Foreign Economic Relations and Trade of China. It runs a number of factories and retail outlets. It also acts as an agent in appointing distributors for Chinese products in Macau.

-O-

"OPEN-DOOR" POLICY OF CHINA. Since Portugal established formal diplomatic relations with China in 1979, the Portuguese administration has seen an opportunity for Macau to profit from China's "open-door" policy.

As part of this policy the nearby Chuhai (Zhuhai) area has been designated a Special Economic Zone, and Macau is able to use its China connections by exporting and re-exporting goods to and from China. As part of its plans to develop this trade further the Macau Government has approved proposals to construct a deep-water harbor in Coloane by 1991 and an international airport by 2010.

ORGANIZATION STATUTE (ORGANIC STATUTE). Following the *coup d'etat* that toppled the regime of Marcello Caetano in 1974, the Portuguese Constitution of 1976 stated that Macau is not part of Portuguese territory. Instead Macau was to be governed by a statute which would be appropriate to Macau's special situation. The *Assembleia de Republica* (the Portuguese Parliament) eventually drew up the Organization Statute as the Constitution of Macau.

This statute lays down the fundamental organization of the government system. It specifies the scope of Macau's legislative, administrative, economic, and financial autonomy. In terms of its autonomy, Macau's *Assembleia Legislativa* can initiate amendments to, or total repeal of, the Organization Statute. There is no requirement for a qualified majority in the Portuguese Parliament. Although the President of the Republic has the power to appoint and dismiss the Governor, who is politically responsible to him, the appointment is compulsorily subject to previous consultation with the local population through the *Assembleia Legislativa.* The responsibility for external representation rests with the President who may delegate such powers to the Governor. Thus when such delegation occurs, Macau may conduct her own external relations.

Macau's affiliation with Portugal has three main dimensions. Firstly, on a proposal by the Governor to the President, the *Assembleia Legislativa* can be dissolved in the public interest. Secondly, the Court of Audit can adjudicate disagreements between the government and the Administrative Court. Thirdly, the Supreme Administrative Court can hear appeals against decisions by the Governor and the Secretaries.

Following the signing of the Sino-Portuguese Joint Declaration in 1987, the promise of a "high degree of autonomy" stimulated considerable discussion on the amendment of the Organization Statute in areas such as the powers of the Governor and the possible enlarging of the membership of the *Assembleia Legislativa*. In June 1987, reform-minded liberals, such as Alexandre Ho (He), suggested a committee should be set up to amend the Organization Statute. This was met with indifference from a majority of the deputies in the *Assembleia Legislativa* who believed that China would not endorse further democratization in Macau.

-P-

PADROADO SYSTEM. The term *"Padroado Real"* referred to the royal patronage of the Catholic Church. The Portuguese Crown inherited certain rights and duties as the patron of the Roman Catholic Missions and ecclesiastical establishments in its colonial possessions in Africa, Asia, and Brazil. Initially this was mutually beneficial to both the Crown and the Church in their attempts to expand their influence. One major advantage for the Portuguese was the Papal ban on missionaries sailing to the region vaguely known as "India" except on board Portuguese ships. A second was the right to nominate or to confirm all appointments to vacant Bishoprics or other high ecclesiastical offices in Asia.

On the Church's side the chief beneficiary was the Society of Jesus, which had energetic and capable members, coupled with the support given by the Crown of Portugal.

In the mid-17th century, the Papacy began to see the arrangement as against their interests, and irrelevant to the changing political and economic situation where Portuguese power was being replaced by the British and the Dutch. Accordingly, the privileges of the Crown under the *Padroado Real* were gradually removed throughout the 17th to 18th century. (See Catholic Church; Jesuits.)

PATACA. Macau's unit of currency is the pataca (MPtc). The pataca is tied to the Hong Kong dollar at MPtc 103 = HK$100. As the Hong Kong dollar is linked to the US dollar, the value of Macau's imports and exports are affected by the changes in the value of the US dollar.

PIRES, TOME. Pires was the first Portuguese envoy to China. After Alvares' early voyages to China, the Portuguese recognized the need to establish an official relationship with China and to gain the right to settle in Chinese territory. In 1518, the Viceroy of Goa, Lopo Soares de Albergaria, sent Pires as an ambassador to China.

After waiting in Canton (Guangzhou) for two years Pires was given permission to travel northward. He was cordially received by the Emperor Chang Te (1506–1521) in Nanking (Nanjing) and was told to go to Peking (Beijing) for an official audience. However, the Emperor died soon afterwards, and Pires lost his mentor.

Around the same period another Portuguese mission, headed by Simao Peres de Andrade, was causing more antagonism with the Chinese authorities. As a result, the new Emperor, Chia Ching, together with his conservative civil service, reversed their attitude toward the Portuguese diplomats. Pires was sent to prison in Canton (Guangzhou) where he eventually died.

POPULATION. The early settlers in Macau were seafarers, many of whom brought slaves and mistresses from Goa and Malacca. By 1555, the population was estimated to be about 400 rising to about 20,000 by 1750. In the early 1900s, Macau's population stood at 75,000, a figure which was to double by the 1930s. The influx of Chinese, particularly following the war with the Japanese, increased the population to around 150,000 by the end of the Second World War. The 1981 census figure of 268,300 probably seriously underestimated the true total by failing to include large numbers of illegal immigrants.

Within the population the ratio of Chinese over Portuguese has increased over time. By 1800, there were approximately as many Chinese as Portuguese. In the subsequent period up to the early 20th century, the ratio of Chinese population continued to grow because of the unstable political conditions in China. While the numbers of Portuguese remained the same in absolute terms, their percentage of the total had by 1926 declined to its present level of around 2 to 3 percent. (See Illegal Immigrants.)

PORTUGUESE CIVIL CODE. The current legal system in Macau originates from Portugal and is based on metropolitan law. As with Portugal's other colonies, Macau's legal system became subject to the Portuguese Civil Code on 18 November 1867. Subsequently, in 1909 and 1911, Chinese customs were codified to become part of the laws of Macau. With rapid social and economic change in recent years, a range of new laws have been approved by the *Assembleia Legislativa* and the Governor under the Organization Statute of 1976.

The resumption of Chinese sovereignty in 1999 has been associated with moves towards bilingualism in law. The main laws are to be translated into Chinese and new

314 / **Portuguese Nationality Status**

laws to be drafted in both languages. By 1999, the Basic Law instead of the Portuguese Civil Code will be used in Macau. (See Basic Law of Macau; Organization Statute.)

PORTUGUESE NATIONALITY STATUS. To pave the way for a smooth transition of power in 1999, the Portuguese Government has assured full nationality status to the Macanese, and some Macau Chinese who were born in Macau before 1979, and to their children. This group of Portuguese passport-holders are entitled to right of abode in Portugal, to find employment in countries of the European Community, and to transfer their nationality to their children. It was estimated by the government in 1990 that this group amounts to 150,000, rising to a possible 200,000 by 1999. This arrangement, which was written into the Sino-Portuguese Joint Declaration as a memorandum, has largely stemmed the tide of emigration in Macau. (See Dual Nationality; Sino-Portuguese Joint Declaration; Sino-Portuguese Negotiations.)

PORTUGUESE TRADE ROUTES. Between 1560 and 1640, Macau was at the center of three trade routes between the Far East and the West. In the Macau-Malacca-Goa-Lisbon route, ships left Lisbon with metalware in March in order to arrive at Goa in September. They left Goa with cotton textiles which were, in turn, exchanged for spices in Malacca. These were shipped from Malacca to Macau for their final destinations in China and Japan. The Canton (Guangzhou)-Macau-Nagasaki route was based on the exchange of Chinese silk for Japanese silver. This route was the most profitable and was a privilege of the Portuguese Crown. Usually it was under the direction of a Captain-Major appointed by the Crown. Finally, the Macau-Manila-Mexico route involved silver coins shipped from Manila in settlement for goods imported from Macau and China. (See Gama, Vasco da; Goa; Malacca.)

-R-

RICCI, MATTEO (FATHER). The Jesuit Father Matteo Ricci arrived in Macau in 1584. He prepared for his China missions by learning to speak Chinese in the Seminary of Sao Paulo in Macau. His training as a mathematician and an astronomer allowed him to introduce much of European science to China. He arrived in Peking (Beijing) in 1600 and was allowed to set up a Christian mission by the Emperor. He died in Peking (Beijing) on 11 May 1610. (See Catholic Church; Jesuits; Sao Paulo, Church; Madre de Deus School; Seminary of Sao Paulo.)

RITES CONTROVERSY. In the 17th century, the so-called "rites controversy" arose between the various Catholic religious orders in their approach to Chinese society. The Jesuits permitted Chinese converts to continue practices such as ancestor worship, but the Dominicans and Franciscans held the opposite view.

In the face of this controversy, Pope Clement XI attempted unsuccessfully to involve the Ch'ing (Qing) Emperor K'ang-hsi (Kangxi) (1662–1723). This incident fueled the Rites Controversy and led to the persecution of Chinese Christians in Macau. At the climax of this controversy, the Augustinian fathers were expelled from Macau in 1712, and this was followed by the expulsion of the Jesuits in 1767. (See Catholic Church; Jesuits.)

-S-

SAO PAULO, CHURCH. The greatest of Macau's churches was built in 1602 adjoining the Jesuit College of Sao Paulo, the first Western college in the Far East. According to early travellers, the Church, made of clay and wood, was richly decorated and furnished. The facade of carved stone was built by Japanese Christian exiles and local craftsmen under the direction of Italian Jesuit Carlo Spinola between 1620 and 1627. After the expulsion of the Jesuits, the college was used as an army barracks, and in 1835 a fire destroyed the college and the body of the church. The surviving facade rises in four colonnaded tiers and is covered with carvings and statues which illustrate the early days of the Church in Asia. (See Catholic Church; Jesuits; Seminary of Sao Paulo.)

SEMINARY OF SAO PAULO. The Seminary of Sao Paulo was founded by the Jesuits on December 1, 1594. In 1597, it was made into a university college and offered its first degree courses. In 1601, 59 Jesuits, of whom 26 were priests, lived at Sao Paulo. There were schools of Oriental languages, of music, and of painting. After the expulsion of the Jesuits in 1767, the college was used as an army barracks until in 1835 it was destroyed by fire (See Catholic Church; Jesuits; Sao Paulo, Church; University of East Asia.)

SENADO DA CAMERA. See *Leal Senado;* Senate.

SENATE. The Senate has been Macau's major political institution since 1583 when Bishop Dom Leonardo de Sa and Bishop Carneiro took the initiative to call together Portuguese citizens in Macau to form the Senate (or *Senado da Camera*). The Viceroy of Portuguese India issued a decree in 1586 which empowered the Senate to elect its members triennially and to make judicial appointments. The Senate was composed of citizen-elected representatives, three aldermen, three legal officials, and a Secretary. It was responsible for the civil and financial matters of the settlement. The governmental power of Macau was shared between the Senate, the Magistrate (or *Ouvidor*), and the Captain-Major whose power was limited to administering the garrison. In fact, the Senate in

Macau served as an effective check on any despotic tendency of the local governor.

In appreciation of Macau's continued allegiance to Portugal even when she was controlled by the Spanish under the Union of Crowns, the Prince Regent, later King John VI, conferred in 1810 the title of *Leal Senado* (or "Loyal Senate").

In 1834, political reforms in Portugal led to a reorganization of the Portuguese empire. The *Ouvidor* and the Senate of Macau were dissolved in 1835 by the Governor, who was then vested with full powers as a civil governor, and a municipal council, still called *Leal Senado,* was set up to replace the old Senate. (See *Leal Senado* (Loyal Senate); Union of Crowns.)

SINO-PORTUGUESE JOINT DECLARATION. Between June 1986 and March 1987 four rounds of negotiations on Macau's future were held in Peking (Beijing) between a Chinese team led by Deputy Foreign Minister Chou Nan (Zhou Nan), and a Portuguese team led by the Ambassador to the United Nations, Dr. Rui Medina. On March 26, the delegates initialled a Sino-Portuguese Joint Declaration on Macau, and on April 13, premier Chao Tzu-yang (Zhao Ziyang) and Portuguese Prime Minister, Anibal Cavaco Silva, officially signed the Declaration in Peking (Beijing).

To a large extent, the Joint Declaration mirrors that of Hong Kong. The concept of "One Country, Two Systems" will apply. Essentially this means that Macau's current social and economic systems and lifestyle will remain unchanged for 50 years, even after Macau becomes a "Special Administrative Region" of China in 1999. Under the accord, Macau can participate in international bodies as an independent entity; the flow of capital will be unhindered and the Macau pataca will remain freely convertible.

However, there are differences between the two Joint

Declarations. The political arrangements for the selection of legislators and the chief executive included in the Macau pact are less "democratic" than those in the Hong Kong agreements. For instance, Annex I of the Macau pact states: "The legislature shall be composed of local inhabitants, and the majority of its members shall be elected . . . and its chief executive shall be appointed by the Central Government on the basis of the results of elections or consultations held in Macau." In contrast the Hong Kong pact states: "The legislature of the Hong Kong Special Administrative Region shall be constituted by elections."

Thus, the possibility of members being appointed to Macau's future legislature has not been ruled out. These vague but potentially crucial terms in the accord may arouse much controversy when the Macau Basic Law is finally drafted.

Similarly, a crucial point in the Hong Kong agreements gives assurances that the Chinese garrison will not interfere in the internal defence of the territory, while the Macau accord only states briefly that "the Central Government shall be responsible for the defence of the Macau SAR."

The issue of Macau nationality is also slightly different from that of Hong Kong because of the prominence of the Macanese who have already taken Macau as their permanent residence. Macanese interests have been given special consideration under the nationality arrangement in the memorandum.

Important questions facing the Sino-Portuguese Joint Liaison Group will be the dual nationality issue and the localization of the civil service and laws. Land leases will be handled by a specially appointed Land Group. Under the existing agreement, up to 20 hectares a year may be made available for leasing until 1999. (See Basic Law of Macau; Dual Nationality; "Macau People Ruling Macau"; Macau Special Administrative Region; Portuguese Nationality Status; Sino-Portuguese Joint Declaration; Sino-Portuguese Negotiations.)

SINO-PORTUGUESE NEGOTIATIONS. Although the post-revolutionary government of Portugal offered to return Macau to China three times between 1974 and 1977, China rejected each offer—largely because the change in Macau's status might shock Hong Kong. In return for Portuguese willingness to postpone returning Macau to China, China permitted Macau to democratize the legislature but would not permit any demand for independence. The terms of a secret agreement concluded between China and Portugal in 1979 stated that Portugal was to continue administering Macau, but sovereignty belonged to China. The date of returning Macau to China was to be settled through negotiations when the time was thought to be appropriate by both sides.

In subsequent negotiations, Portuguese diplomats proposed that Macau should be returned to Chinese rule in the year 2004. China rejected this proposal and insisted on the reunification of Macau before 2000. In 1987, the Sino-Portuguese Joint Declaration on Macau's future was signed specifying that Macau would become a Special Administrative Region of the PRC on 20 December 1999. (See Basic Law of Macau; Dual Nationality; "Macau People Ruling Macau"; Macau Special Administrative Region; Organization Statute; Portuguese Nationality Status; Sino-Portuguese Joint Declaration.)

SOCIEDADE DE TURISMO E DIVERSOES DE MACAU (STDM). See Macau Tourism and Entertainment Company.

SOUSA, LEONEL DE. Sousa was a sixteenth-century native of the Algarve region of Portugal who married and settled in Chaul on the west coast of India before he sailed eastward as the commodore of a fleet bound for Japan. While in Canton (Guangzhou) in 1553–54, he signed an agreement with a provincial Chinese Admiral in charge of the Kwangtung (Guangdong) coastal regions of Sheung Chuen and Lampacao. As a result of this agreement, Sino-Portuguese trade gained official status and the Portuguese were allowed to trade in Canton (Guangzhou) and other Kwangtung (Guangdong) ports. In exchange for this official recognition, the Portuguese agreed to place themselves under the surveillance of the Chinese authorities and to pay tax.

SUMMERS INCIDENT. James Summers was a Protestant teacher of St. Paul's College in Hong Kong in the late 1840s who was at the center of a minor diplomatic storm between Portugal and Britain. In June 1849, British and American warships took part in a regatta in Macau. Before the contest, there was a Corpus Christi procession, and when the host came by Summers was reluctant to doff his hat even when ordered by a priest and, later, by the Governor, Amaral. As a result, he was jailed.

A senior British officer, Captain Henry Keppel, demanded Summers be released arguing that he was subject to British extraterritorial rights. This was rejected by the Macau authorities. Keppel and a party of men then freed Summers by force, shooting one jailer and hurting some others. Diplomatic protests led to the British government making a formal apology, censuring Keppel, and granting a pension to the family of the dead jailer.

SUN, YAT-SEN (SUN, YIXIAN). Dr. Sun Yat-sen (Sun Yixian), the founder of the Chinese Republic, had many connections with Macau in his early years. Dr. Sun was born in 1866 in Xiangshan county, which comprised Macau and other nearby areas. In 1892, he graduated from the Hong Kong College of Medicine for Chinese. Soon he went to Macau to work as a volunteer medical officer in the

Kiang Wu Hospital. He was the first Chinese to practice Western medicine in Macau. His expertise made him well-known among citizens and he built up good connections with many important people in Macau. He also founded a newspaper to advocate revolutionary ideas. He was a key figure in the successful attempt to overthrow the Ch'ing (Qing) dynasty and became the first President of the Chinese Republic. Dr. Sun died on March 12, 1925. (See also Hong Kong entry.)

-T-

TOURISM. Tourism and gambling are important elements in the Macau economy, probably accounting for about 25% of the total Gross Domestic Product (GDP) in the 1980s. Their importance was formally recognized as early as 1960 with government legislation to promote tourism in Macau, including the establishment of a Tourism and Information Center as an independent authority within the Government of Macau. (See Licensed Gambling; Macau Tourism and Entertainment Company.)

TREATY OF TIENTSIN (TIANJIN) 1862. After the Opium War, China signed a number of treaties with foreign powers recognizing their rights of trade and administration in Chinese territories. The Portuguese saw these as a chance to obtain Macau formally and permanently. In 1862, Macau's Governor, Isidoro de Guimaraes, was appointed as the ambassador to China to negotiate a treaty. With the mediation of the French ambassador, Guimaraes succeeded in lifting Macau's Ground Rent payment and terminating the presence of the customs officers who symbolized Chinese claims to sovereignty over Macau. The Treaty of Tientsin (Tianjin) was therefore initialled on August 13, 1862 giving full recognition of Macau as a Portuguese colony. However, two years later, when the Treaty was due for ratification, the Chinese discovered that the French translation of the Treaty had stipulated to Portugal the severance of Macau. China therefore refused to ratify the Treaty, and further negotiations failed to conclude any formal agreement.

TREATY OF WANG-HSIA (WANGXIA). (Sino-American Treaty of Friendship and Trade) 1844. The signing of the Treaty of Nanking (Nanjing) in 1842 ceding Hong Kong to Great Britain signalled China's weakness to the outside world. In February, 1844, the U.S. Ambassador, Caleb Cushing, was instructed by President Taylor to establish trading relations with China which would enable the Americans to enjoy similar rights as the British. In June, 1844, Kiying, the top-ranking Chinese official who ratified the Treaty of Nanking (Nanjing), came south to Wangxia to negotiate with the Americans. Under the threat to use force, Kiying hastily compromised. The Treaty of Wangxia, which declared "perfect, permanent, universal peace" between the two countries, was signed on July 3. It provided the Americans with the right to reside, to trade, and to set up consulates in the trading ports. In addition, it secured extraterritorial rights for American citizens in China.

-U-

UNION OF CROWNS. Between 1580 and 1640, Portugal was, in essence, occupied by Spain.

Following the deaths of the young King of Portugal and his aged uncle, Philip II of Spain came forward to claim the Crown and successfully invade Portugal in December, 1580. The so-called Union of the Crowns meant Portugal ceased to be an independent state, but was subjected to Spanish rule. All Portuguese territories, including Macau, came under Spanish influence. However, in 1640, a revolution led by the Duke of Braganca, a descendant of the Portuguese royal family and later King Joao IV of Portugal, drove the Spanish out and ended the Union of Crowns.

Throughout the period of Spanish rule, Macau still pledged allegiance to the old Royal Portuguese Crown, and as a reward, King Joao IV bestowed on the city the title: "City of the Name of God, None Other More Loyal." (See City of the Name of God).

UNIVERSITY OF EAST ASIA. The University of East Asia was established largely in 1981 by a Hong Kong business, the Ricci Island West Company, as the only university in Macau.

In the face of the rapid socioeconomic development the University was established to meet the needs for higher education in Macau and the wider region of East Asia. It is a full member of the International Association of Universities. The three founding colleges were the University College, the Junior College, and the Graduate College.

The University was taken over by the Macau Government in February 1988 and a process of restructuring began. The Junior College merged with the Polytechnic Institute in early 1990 to become the Macau Polytechnic.

BIBLIOGRAPHY

INTRODUCTORY ESSAY

There is relatively little literature on Macau, especially in English. However, many early documents written in Portuguese by missionaries and early explorers have been incorporated into a few serious historical accounts. Boxer, C. R. *The Great Ship from Amacon, Fidalgos in the Far East,* and *Seventeenth Century Macau,* are outstanding pioneering works in the area. More recent publications are Coates, A. *A Macau Narrative, Macau and the British,* and *City of Broken Promises.*

More recently the opening up of China trade, has led to a greater interest in Macau's links with the Pearl River Delta. This development coincides with the founding of the East Asia University and the Center of Macau Studies. An important interdisciplinary study is Cremer, R. D. *Macau: City of Commerce and Culture.* Hong Kong: UEA Press, 1987. It provides extensive treatment of historical, cultural, and commercial features of the territory. Another useful volume of similar scope is the collection of papers presented at the Conference on *Industrial Economy of Macau in the 1990s.* Hong Kong: UEA Press, China Economic Research Center, 1990 (papers edited by Cremer, R. D.)

1. HISTORY

1.1. General History

Clemens, J., *Discovering Macau,* Hong Kong: Macmillan, 1977.

Coates, Austin, *A Macau narrative,* Hong Kong: Heinemann, 1978.

326 / Bibliography, Macau

Cremer, R.D., *Macau: city of commerce and culture,* Hong Kong: UEA Press, 1987.

—., *Macau: city of commerce and culture. Second edition: continuity and change,* Hong Kong: API Press, 1991.

Jones, P.H.M., *Golden guides to Hong Kong and Macau,* Hong Kong: Far East Economic Review, 1969.

Silva, F.A., *The sons of Macao: their history and heritage,* San Francisco, California: UMA, 1979.

Wang Hung-cao, *History of Macau,* Hong Kong: Commercial Business, 1987. (In Chinese)

Yuan Bong-jian and Yuan Gui-shau, *Brief history of Macau,* Hong Kong: Middle Current, 1988. (In Chinese)

1.2. Early Period

Boxer, C.R., *Four centuries of Portuguese expansion: 1415–1825 a Succinct Survey,* Berkeley, CA.: University of California Press, 1961.

Braga, J.M., *The Western pioneers and their discovery of Macau,* Macau: Imprensa Nacional, 1949.

Luis, Keil, *Jorge Alvares: the first Portuguese to go to China.* Macau: Instituto Cultural de Macau, 1990.

Usellis, William R., *The origin of Macau,* Chicago, IL: University of Chicago, 1958.

1.3. Colonial Period

Ball, James Dyer, *Macao: the Holy City; the gem of the orient earth,* Canton: China Baptist Publication Society, 1905.

Boxer, Charles Ralph, *Fidalgos in the Far East: 1550–1770,* Hong Kong: Oxford University Press, 1968.

————., *The great ship from Amacon: annals of Macau and the Old Japan trade: 1555–1640,* Lisbon: Centro De Estudos Historicos Ultramarinos, 1959.

————., *Seventeenth century Macau in contemporary documents and illustrations,* Hong Kong: Heinemann, 1984.

Braga, J.M., *Hong Kong and Macau: a record of good fellowship,* Hong Kong: Graphic Press, 1951.

Coates, Austin, *Macau and the British 1637–1842,* Hong Kong: Oxford University Press, 1988.

Guillen-Nunez, Cesar, *Macau,* Hong Kong: Oxford University Press, 1984.

Hanna, Willard Anderson, *A trial of two colonies,* New York: American Universities Field Staff Inc, 1969.

Ljungstedt, Anders, *An historical sketch of the Portuguese settlement in China,* Boston: Munroe, 1836.

Montalto de Jesus, C.A., *Historic Macau,* Oxford: Oxford University Press, 1984.

Souza, George Bryan, *The survival of empire: Portuguese trade and society in China: the South China Sea 1630–1754,* Cambridge: Cambridge University Press, 1986.

Yen, Ching-hwang, *Coolies and mandarins,* Singapore: Singapore University Press, 1985.

1.4. Decolonization Period

Chang, Joane, "Macau waiting in the wings as Peking (Beijing) sets the political stage for 1997" in *South China Morning Post,* January 14, 1988.

The Chinese, "Macau's registration for illegal immigrants", No. 106, May, 1990 (In Chinese).

Economist Intelligence Unit, *Country report: Hong Kong and Macau;* London. The Economist. Various issues.

Economist Intelligence Unit, Regional Reference Series, *China, Japan and Asian NICs: economic structure and analysis,* 1988, pp. 111–112.

Far East Economic Review, *Asian Yearbook 1990,* Hong Kong: Far East Economic Review, 1989.

Kan Tang, *Hong Kong and Macau: history in search of a future,* Taipei: WACL/APACL ROC Chapter, 1989.

Lo, Shui-hing, "Aspects of political development in Macao" in *China Quarterly.* 120. Dec., 1989, pp.837–851.

Macau Handbook Publication Committee, *Macau handbook,* Macau: Ao Men Ryh Bao, 1978; 1983; 1988.

Moshey, Sachs, ed., *World mark encyclopedia of the nations: Volume IV,* New York: John Wiley & Sons, 1976.

Pai Shing Semi-Monthly, "Drafting of the Macau Basic Law: Nationality Bill and Protection of Human Rights", No.213, April 1, 1990 (In Chinese).

————., "Macau's illegal immigrants as a Time Bomb", No. 214, April 16, 1990. (In Chinese)

2. POLITICS AND GOVERNMENT

Afonso, R., and Pereira, F.G., "The constitution and legal system" in *Macau: city of commerce and culture.* Edited by Cremer, R. D. Hong Kong: UEA Press, 1987.

————., "The political status and government institutions of Macau" in *Hong Kong Law Journal.* Vol.16, Jan. 1986, pp.28–57.

Caracterizacao dos recursos humanos da administracao publica de Macau, Macau: Governo de Macau, 1986.

Constituicao da Republica Portuguesa, (CRP), April 2, 1976.

Economist Intelligence Unit, *Country report: Hong Kong and Macau;* London: The Economist. Various issues.

Mendes, C., *Direito comparado,* Lisbon: AAFDL, 1982/83.

Wesley-Smith, P., "Macau" in *Constitutions of Dependancies and Special Sovereignties.* Edited by A. P. Blaustein and P. M. Blaustein. New York: Oceana, 1985.

3. Society

3.1. Architecture

Graca, J., *Fortificacoes de Macau, concepcao e historia,* 1st Portuguese edition, Instituto Cultural de Macau, 1985.

Hugo-Brunt, Michael, *An architectural survey of the Jesuit seminary church of St. Paul's, Macau,* Hong Kong: Hong Kong University Press, 1954.

————. *The convent and church of St. Dominic at Macao,* Hong Kong: Hong Kong University Press, 1961.

Liang, S. C., *A pictorial history of Chinese architecture: a study of the development of its structural system and the evolution of its types,* Cambridge, MA: Massachusetts Institute of Technology, 1984.

Simpson, Colin, *Asia's bright balconies: Hong Kong, Macao, Philippines,* Sydney: Angus and Robertson, 1962.

Teixeira, Manuel, *The Church of St. Paul in Macau.* Lisbon: Centro de Estudos Historicos Ultramaninos da Junta de Investigacoes Cientificas deo Ultrammar, 1979.

Wong, S. K., *Macau architecture, an integrate of Chinese and Portuguese Influences,* Macau: Imprensa Nacional, 1970.

3.2. Arts, Literature, and Culture

Azeved. R. A., de, *A influencia da cultura Porttuguesa em Macau, Bibliography Breve,* Lisbon: ICALP, 1984.

Borget, A., *La Chine et les Chinois,* Paris: Goupil et Vibert, 1842.

Boxer, C. R., "A note on the Interaction of Portuguese and Chinese Medicine at Macao and Peking," *Boletim od Instituto Luis de Camoes.* Vol.8, 1974, pp.33–54.

Clunas, C., *Chinese export watercolours,* London: Victoria and Albert Museum, 1984.

Cotton, J. J., "George Chinnery, artist, (1774–1852)," *Bengal: Past and Present.* Vol. 27, 1924.

Hillard, H., *My Mother's Journal: A Young Lady's Diary of Five Years Spent in Manila, Macao and the Cape of Good Hope,* Edited by K. Hillard. Boston: George H. Ellis, 1900.

Hong Kong Museum of Art, *George Chinnery: his pupils and influence,* Hong Kong: Urban Council, 1985.

Hunter, W. C., *Bits of old China,* Shanghai: Kelly & Walsh, 1911.

Hutcheon, R. *Chinnery:the man and the legend.* (Second edition) Hong Kong: Formasia, 1989

———., *Souvenirs of Auguste Borge,* Hong Kong: South China Morning Post, 1979.

Luis de Camoes Museum, *George Chinnery: Macau*, Macau: Leal Senado, 1986.

Martyn, Gregory, *Dr. Thomas Boswall Matson (1815–1860): physician and amateur artist in China*, London: Martyn Gregory, 1985.

Odell, Kathleen, *Chinnery in China: a novel*, London: Murray, 1971.

Scholberg, Henry, *Bibliography of Goa and the Portuguese in India*, New Delhi: Promilla, 1982.

3.3. Society

Boxer, C. R., *Portuguese society in the tropics*, Madison, WI: University of Wisconsin Press, 1965.

Skinner, George W., *Modern Chinese society: an analytical bibliography*, Stanford, CA: Stanford University Press, 1973.

————., "Marketing and social structure in rural China" in *Journal of Asian Studies*. Vol.24, pp.3–34, 195–228, 363–399, 1964–65.

4. THE ECONOMY

American Chamber of Commerce (AMCHAM), "Doing business in Macau surveyed," in March 1985, pp.14–17.

Ao Men Ryh Bao, "Guangdong-Macau economic and trade relations have developed quickly in recent years," January 13, 1986.

Asian Pacific Center, *The markets of Asia/Pacific: Hong Kong and Macau*, Aldershot, England: Gower Publishing Co., 1982.

Bank of China, "Nan Guang trading company of Macau" *Hong Kong-Macau Economic Quarterly*. Issue 11, 1982, pp.63–64.

China economic news, Economic Information & Consultancy Company, Hong Kong, 1980–1985.

The Commercial and Credit Bureau, *The Comacrib industrial and commercial Manual: China and Hong Kong,* Shanghai: 1936.

Cremer, R.D., *Industrial economy of Macau in the 1990s,* Hong Kong: UEA Press, China Economic Research Center, 1990.

Far Eastern Economic Review, *Asia Yearbook,* various issues.

Feitor, R., "Macau's modern economy" in Cremer, R.D., *Macau: City of Commerce and Culture,* Hong-kong: UEA Press, 1987.

Hong-kong and Shanghai Banking Corporation, *Macau,* Hong Kong: 1989.

Kamm, J. T., "Guangdong's SEZs" in *The China Business Review,* March-April, 1980, pp.28–31.

Kamm, J. T., "Pearl River Delta Review" in *Journal of the American Chamber of Commerce in Hong Kong,* October 1983, pp.14.

———., "Trading and investing in Zhuhai" in *Canton Companion.* Issue II, 1979, Hong Kong: Far East Publications.

Macau Government Printing Press, *Sectoral policies investment Plan, 1984: analysis of the economic and financial situation of the territory,* Macau: 1984.

Peng Chi-jui, *Hong Kong and Macau,* Hong Kong: Business Commercial, 1986.

Sit, V., Cremer, R.D., and Wong, S.L. *Entrepreneurs and Enterprises in Macau,* Hong Kong: Hong Kong University Press, 1991.

Ting, Tien-fook, *PRC business firms in Hong Kong and Macau,* Hong Kong: American Chamber of Commerce (AMCHAM), 1988.

Wong, Hon-keung, *Economy of Macau,* Macau: Journal "Va Kio,"
1988. (In Chinese)

——— (ed.), *Almanaque of Macau's economy,* Macau: Journal of "Va
Kio," 1983, 1984/1986. (In Chinese)

APPENDICES

APPENDIX 1: LIST OF GOVERNORS

1623	Dom Francisco Mascarenhas
1626	Dom Filipe Lobo
1630	Dom Jeronimo da Silveira
1631	Manuel da Camara de Noronha
1636	Domingos da Camara de Noronha
1638	Dom Sebastiao Lobo da Silveira
1645	Luis de Carvalho e Sousa
1646	Dom Diogo Coutinho Docem
1647	Dom Joao Pereira
1650	Joao de Sousa Pereira
1654	Manuel Tavares Bocarro
1664	Manuel Coelho da Silva
1667	Dom Alvaro da Silva
1670	Manuel Borges da Silva
1672	Antonio Barbosa Lobo

1678	Antonio de Castro Sande
1679	Luis de Melo Sampaio
1682	Belchior do Amaral de Meneses
1685	Antonio da Mesquita Pimentel
1688	Andre Coelho Vieira
1691	Dom Francisco da Costa
1693	Antonio da Silva e Melo
1694	Gil Vaz Lobo Freire
1697	Cosme Rodrigues de Carvalho e Sousa
1697	The Municipal Senate (Leal Senado da Camara)
1698	Pedro Vaz de Siqueira
1700	Diogo de Melo Sampaio
1702	Pedro Vaz de Siqueira (2d time)
1703	Jose da Gama Machado
1706	Diogo do Pinho Teixeira
1710	Francisco de Melo e Castro
1711	Antonio de Siqueira de Noronha
1714	Dom Francisco de Alarcao Sotto Maior
1718	Antonio de Albuquerque Coelho
1719	Antonio da Silva Telo e Meneses

1722	Dom Cristovao de Severim Manuel
1724	Antonio Carneiro de Alcacova
1727	Antonio Monis Barreto
1732	Antonio de Amaral Meneses
1735	Dom Joao do Casal
1735	Cosme Damiao Pinto Pereira
1738	Manuel Pereira Coutinho
1743	Cosme Damiao Pinto Pereira (2d time)
1747	Antonio Jose Teles de Meneses
1749	Joao Manuel de Melo
1752	Dom Rodrigo de Castro
1755	Francisco Antonio Pereira Coutinho
1758	Dom Diogo Pereira
1761	Antonio de Mendonca Corte-Real
1764	Jose Placido de Matos Saraiva
1767	Diogo Fernandes Salema e Saldanha
1770	Dom Rodrigo de Castro (2d. time)
1771	Diogo Fernandes Salema e Saldanha (2d. time)
1777	Dom Alexandre da Silva Pedrosa Guimaraes
1778	Joas Vicente da Silveira Meneses

1780   Antonio Jose da Costa

1781   Dom Francisco de Castro

1783   Bernardo Aleixo de Lemos e Faria

1788   Francisco Xavier de Mendonca Corte Real

1789   A Commission (Lazaro da Silva Ferreira, the Chief Justice, and Manuel Antonio da Costa Ferreira, Commandant of the Forces)

1790   Dom Vasco Luis Carneiro de Sousa e Faro

1793   Jose Manuel Pinto

1797   Dom Cristovao Pereira de Castro

1800   Jose Manuel Pinto (2d. time)

1803   Caetano de Sousaa Pereira

1806   Bernardo Aleix de Lemos e Faria (2d. time)

1808   Lucas Jose de Alvarenga

1814   Lucas Jose de Alvarenga (2d. time, but did not take office)

1817   Jose Osorio de Castro de Albuquerque

1822   Committee, under Major Paulino da Silva Barbosa, set up the Absolutist Regime

1823   Government Council restored the Conservative regime

1825   Joaquim Mourao Garces Palha

1827   Government Council

1830	Joao Cabral de Estefique
1833	Bernardo Jose de Sousa Soares Andrea
1837	Adriao Acacio da Silveira Pinto
1843	Jose Gregorio Pegado
1846	Joao Ferreira do Amaral
1849	Government Council
1850	Pedro Alexandrino da Cunha
1850	Government Council
1851	Francisco Antonio Goncalves Cardoso
1851	Isidoro Francisco Guimaraes
1863	Jose Rodrigues Coelho do Amaral
1866	Jose Maria da Ponte e Horta
1868	Antonio Sergio de Sousa
1872	Januario Correia de Almeida
1874	Jose Maria Lobo de Avila
1876	Carlos Eugenio Correia da Silva
1879	Joaquim Jose da Graca
1883	Tomas de Sousa Rosa
1886	Firmino Jose da Costa
1889	Francisco Teixeira da Silva

1890	Custodio Miguel de Borja
1894	Jose Maria de Sousa Horta e Costa
1897	Eduardo Augusto Rodrigues Galhardo
1900	Jose Maria de Sousa Horta e Costa (2d. time)
1904	Martinho Pinto de Queiros Montenegro
1907	Pedro de Azevedo Coutinho
1908	Jose Augusto Alves Rocadas
1909	Eduardo Augusto Marques
1910	Alvaro de Melo Machado
1912	Anibal Augusto Sanches de Miranda
1914	Jose Carlos da Maia
1918	Artur Tamagnini de Sousa Barbosa
1919	Henrique Monteiro Correia da Silva
1923	Rodrigo Jose Rodriques
1925	Manuel Firmino de Almeida Maia Magalhaes
1926	Artur Tamagnini de Sousa Barbosa (2d. time)
1931	Joaquim Anselmo de Mata Oliveira
1932	Antonio Jose Bernardes de Miranda
1935	Joao Pereira Barbosa
1937	Artur Tamagnini de Sousa Barbosa (3d. time)

1940   Gabriel Mauricio Teixeira

1947   Albano Rodrigues de Oliveira

1951   Joaquim Marques Esparteiro

1957   Pedro Correia de Barros

1959   Jaime Silverio Marques

1962   Antonio Adriano Faria Lopes dos Santos

1966   Jose Manuel de Sousa e Faro Nobre de Carvalho

1974   Jose Eduardo Martinho Garcia Leandro

1981   Vasco de Almeida e Costa

1986   Joaquim Germano Pinto Machado Correia da Silva

1987   Carlos Mantey Melancia

Appendix 2: A Brief Outline History of Macau

1152	Establishment of Xiangshan County and Macau under its administration.
1277	Duan Zong, the young emperor of the South Sung (Song) Dynasty together with 50,000 followers, reached Macau to avoid attack by Mongolians; the beginning of inhabitation in Macau.
1488	Temple Ama was built.
1498	Vasco da Gama reached Goa of India.
1510	Alfonso de Albuquerque of Portugal occupied Goa.
1511	Portuguese occupied Malacca.
1513	Jorge Alvares reached Tuen Mun and started to trade with China.
1517	Fernao Peres de Andrade and Tome Pires, envoy of Portugal, were admitted to Kwangtung (Guangdong) to negotiate for trading relations with China.
1519	An expedition, led by Samao Pires d' Andrade, built fortification on Neilingding Island.
1535	Foreign trade office of China relocated in Macau; Portuguese ships were allowed to moor in Macau.
1553	Portuguese landed on Macau.
1556	Portuguese poets exiled to Macau, writing the famous nationalistic poem *Os Lusiadas*.

1557	Portuguese obtained the leasehold of Macau by paying tribute.
1564	Jesuits reached Macau.
1569	Nagasaki in Japan became the trading post of Portugal.
1573	Portuguese in Macau began to pay ground rent to Chinese government. A barrier gate, or "border" gate was built.
1575	Pope of Rome decreed the establishment of the Macau diocese.
1580	Union of the Portuguese and Spanish Crowns.
1581	Leonardo de Sa became first Bishop of the diocese of Macau.
1582	Portuguese signed a land lease with China, agreed to pay an annual rent of 500 taels of silver to the Xiangshan County.
1584	Establishment of the Senate.
1586	Viceroy of Goa approved of Macau's status as a self-governing city.
1601	Dutch ships first appeared in Macau to request for lease and trade.
1604	First Dutch invasion failed.
1605	Portuguese built city wall without Chinese permission.
1607	Second Dutch Invasion failed.
1622	Portuguese won brilliantly in the third Dutch invasion.

1623   Dom Francisco Mascarenhas, the first formal Captain-General assumed office.

1627   Fourth serious Dutch invasion failed.

1631   Holland seized Malacca, thus severing the trade route between Goa and Macau; Portuguese trade suffered setback.

1635   First British ship reached Macau.

1642   Macau pleaded loyalty to the new king of Portugal; Macau was bestowed the name: "City Of The Name Of God. There Is None More Loyal."

1644   Ch'ing (Qing) policy toward Macau unchanged.

1685   China opened four ports with Macau being one of them for foreign trade; establishment of customs offices in Macau.

1701   Portugal and Holland joined the Grand Alliance against France.

1703   Portugal and Britain signed a friendship treaty.

1709   King of Portugal announced Macau's Senate should be filled by "old Christian, pure Portuguese."

1717   Imperial decree forbade Chinese ship to trade in the "Southern Sea," Macau was exempted; British and French ships were not allowed to trade in Kwangtung (Guangdong), but could only anchor in Taipa.

1746   Preaching to Chinese in Macau forbidden.

1762   Expulsion of the Jesuits; three years after suppression of the Society in Portugal.

1773	Britain sold opium into Kwangtung (Guangdong).
1784	First American trading ship in Macau.
1796	China banned opium for the first time.
1802	Portugal gave monopoly right to Macau for opium trade; Britain failed in an attempt to invade Macau.
1808	Britain occupied Macau, but left under the pressure of Chinese threat.
1822	Internal revolt of the Portuguese in Macau was held down by the Kwangtung (Guangdong) authority.
1839	Lin Tse-hsu checked and forbade opium trade in Macau.
1842	Hong Kong ceded to Britain in the Convention of Nanking (Nanjing); five ports in China opened for foreign trade.
1843	Portugal sent envoys to Peking (Beijing) to negotiate for Macau's status.
1844	China and United States signed the Treaty of Wanghsia (Wangxia) in Macau.
1845	King of Portugal announced Macau as a free port unilaterally; appointed Ferreira do Amaral as governor.
1846	Amaral practiced expansionist policies, taxing Chinese.
1849	Subjects in Macau taxed incoming ships, expanded the territory beyond its "border," demolished the

Chinese Customs office, expelling its officers, and devastated Chinese graveyards.

1849   Assassination of Amaral; revenge led by Vicente Nicolau de Mesquita.

1851   Portuguese seized Taipa.

1852   Portuguese and British engaged in the coolies trade.

1862   Treaty of Tientsin (Tianjin) negotiated between China and France in representation of Portugal; France signed the treaty.

1863   Portuguese demolished the city wall.

1864   China refused to ratify the Treaty of Tientsin (Tianjin).

1873   Portuguese banned coolie trade in Macau; Kiang Wu Hospital was established.

1874   Portuguese demolished old barrier gate and built a new one.

1883   Macau and Timor were combined as an overseas province of Portugal under the control of Goa.

1887   Conclusion of the Treaty of Friendship and Trade between China and Portugal, confirmed the perpetuate occupation of Macau by Portuguese, but the question of border delimitation was evaded.

1890   Portuguese integrated Green Island into Macau's territory.

1892   Dr. Sun Yat-sen (Sun Yixian) graduated from Hong Kong College of Medicine for Chinese and worked as a doctor in Kiang Wu Hospital of Macau.

1902	Establishment of the first bank in Macau.
1909	China and Portugal negotiated in Hong Kong about the delimitation of border, meeting unconcluded.
1928	Expiration of the 1887 Luso-Chinese Treaty; negotiated and signed a new Treaty of Friendship and Trade, but avoided the issue of Macau's border delimitation.
1937	Japan invaded China, Chinese refugees fled to Macau.
1945	Refugees returned to China.
1948	Beginning of air traffic between Macau and Hong Kong, but ended with the crash of a plane.
1949	Founding of the People's Republic of China.
1951	Korean War, Macau joined the United Nations embargo; Macau termed as a province officially.
1955	Portugal announced Macau as an overseas province.
1957	Portugal decreed exports from Macau be duty-free to Portuguese territories.
1961	Portugal confirmed Macau as a tourist center with the power to establish gambling businesses.
1966	Conflict between Macau police and local leftist.
1967	Spill-over from the Cultural Revolution in PRC.

1972	China claimed Macau's sovereignty in the United Nations.
1974	Military revolution in Portugal.
1976	Enactment of the Organic Statute, formation of the Legislative Assembly.
1977	Macau currency linked with Hong Kong Dollar.
1979	Establishment of Sino-Portuguese diplomatic relationship; Macau becomes "Chinese Territory under Portuguese Administration."
1981	The University of East Asia was established.
1984	Dissolution of the Legislative Assembly by Governor Costa.
1986	Sino-Portuguese negotiations in the future of Macau.
1987	Signing of the Sino-Portuguese Joint Declaration.
1988	Formation of the Basic Law Drafting Committee; Alexandre Ho (He) and two other liberals won three seats in the Legislative Assembly; Electoral Union won the majority of seats in the Legislative Assembly.
1989	Formation of the Basic Law Consultative Committee.
1990	Governor Melancia resigned from office.
1991	Canvassing of public opinion on the Basic Law.
1992	Submission of the revised draft Basic Law to the Standing Committee of the National People's Congress.

1993   Final draft of the Basic Law for approval.

1999   Macau as a Special Administrative Region of the
             People's Republic of China.

APPENDIX 3: TABLES

3.1. Table 1: Population of Macau

Year	Total	Chinese(%)	Portuguese	Others
1555	400	n.a		n.a
1563	>5,000	n.a		n.a
1578*	10,000	n.a		n.a
1621*	≈20,000	n.a		n.a
1640*	40,000	n.a		n.a
1743	5,500	2,000(37.0)	3,400	100
1750*	20,000	n.a		n.a
1839	≈13,000	7,033(54.1)	5,601	350
1910	74,866	71,021(94.8)	3,601	244
1920	83,984	79,807(95.0)	3,816	361
1927	157,175	152,738(96.8)	3,846	591
1937*	164,528	n.a		n.a
1939	245,194	239,803(97.8)	4,624	767
1941*	>50,000	n.a		n.a
1945*	150,000			
1950	187,772	183,105(97.5)	4,066	601
1960	169,299	160,764(94.9)	7,974	561
1970	248,636	240,008(96.5)	7,467	1,161
1980	268,300	n.a.		n.a
1981	295,300	n.a.		n.a
1982	321,500	n.a.		n.a
1983	342,700	n.a.		n.a
1984	375,500	n.a.		2,911
1985	408,500	n.a.		2,769
1986	423,200	n.a.		3,243
1987	443,300	n.a.		3,923
1988	443,500	n.a.		3,546

Key: *   Figures not so frequently quoted
     n.a. not applicable

Major Sources: 1. Wong, Hon-keung, *Macau Economy*, 1988.
              2. Macau Government, *Yearbook of Statistics*, various issues:
                 1981–88.
              3. Wong, Hon-keung, *Almanaque of Macau's Economy*, 1984/1986.

Points to be noted:

1. Government statistics are available from 1910 onward. A census is taken every ten years approximately. The interim figures in the 1980s are deduced mainly by accounting for the births and deaths, immigrations, and emigrations.

2. At the end of the 1970s, there was a surge of illegal immigrants entering Macau. The numbers are not included in the official figures, but most have been granted Portuguese citizenship under the prevailing government policy.

3.2. Table 2: Age Distribution (Census, 1981)

	1981	1982	1983	1984	1985
			(in percentage)		
Under 15	22.5	21.9	21.4	21.2	21.2
15–59	70.8	71.6	72.1	72.6	72.6
60 and over	8.3	7.9	7.7	7.4	7.2

Source: Macau Government, *Yearbook of Statistics,* 1985.

3.3. Table 3: Population Distribution by Area (Census, 1981)

Macau Peninsula	238,562	91.12%
Taipa	5,568	2.13%
Coloane	4,231	1.62%
Marine	13,445	5.13%

3.4. Table 4: Macau's Export and Import Growth, 1979–1989

Year	Export	Import
	(in Ptc. million)	
1979	3,821	3,832
1982	4,449	4,441
1983	5,653	5,402
1984	7,305	6,385
1985	7,181	6,179
1986	8,630	7,318
1987	11,234	9,017

352 / Appendix, Macau

| 1988 | 12,003 | 10,376 |
| 1989* | 5,824 | 5,876 |

*First half of 1989

Source: Cremer, R. D., ed., *Industrial Economy of Macau in the 1990s,* Hong Kong: UEA Press, 1990.

3.5. Table 5: Macau's Value of Industrial Production for Export

	1976	1983	1987
		(in Ptc. million)	
Garments	864	1814	4009
Toys	4	422	1100
Electrical & Electronics	N.A.	211	400

Source: Wong Hon-keung, *Almanaque of Macau's Economy,* various issues.
Cremer, R. D., Ibid.

WADE-GILES AND PINYIN SYSTEMS

Chinese dynasties, personal names, places and terms in this book are identified using both the Wade-Giles and Pinyin systems.

WADE-GILES	PINYIN
Canton (Kwangtung)	Guangzhou
Chang Ch'un Ch'iao	Zhang Chun Qiao
Chao Tsu-yang	Zhao Ziyang
Chiang Ch'ing	Jiang Qing
Chiang Kai-shek	Jiang Jieshi
Ch'in	Qin
Ch'ing	Qing
Ch'uanpi	Chuanbi
Chou En-lai	Zhou Enlai
Chou Nan	Zhou Nan
Fukien	Fujien

WADE-GILES	PINYIN
Fung Shui	Feng Shui
Han	Han
Hua Kuo-feng	Hua Guofeng
Hsu Chia-t'un	Xu Jiatun
Kwangsi	Guangxi
Kwangtung	Guangdong
Kuomingtang	Guomingdang
Lin Tse-hsu	Lin Zexu
Ma Man-kee	Ma Wanqi
Mao Tse-tung	Mao Zedong
Ming	Ming
Nanking	Nanjing
Peking	Beijing
San-on	Xin-an
Sham Chun	Shenzhen

WADE-GILES	PINYIN
Sham Chun	Shenzhen
Shantau	Swatow
Shen-yang	Shenyang
Sui	Sui
Sun Yat-sen	Sun Yixian
Sung	Song
Szechwan	Sichuan
T'ang	Tang
Teng Hsiao-p'ing	Deng Xiaoping
T'ien-an-man	Tiananman
Tientsin	Tianjin
Tungkuan	Dongguan
Wang Hung Wen	Wang Hong Wen
Wei Hai Wei	Weihaiwei
Yao Wen Yuan	Yao Wen Yuan
Yeh Ming-ch'en	Yeh Mingchen

ABOUT THE AUTHORS

ELFED VAUGHAN ROBERTS was educated at the University of Wales and taught in higher education in the United Kingdom for a number of years. In 1978 he was appointed to lecture in Political Science at the University of Hong Kong. He has a wide number of publications relating to Hong Kong's political developments and possible scenarios for the future. His most recent works are *Political Dictionary for Hong Kong* by Stephen Davies and Elfed Roberts (Macmillan, 1990) and *Social Sciences: A Foundation Course: Politics* (Open Learning Institute of Hong Kong, 1991).

PETER BRADSHAW is employed by the Open University in the United Kingdom. In that capacity he has a wide range of experience in preparing advanced learning material for students as well as teaching responsibilities. His experience in this field led him to be seconded to Hong Kong University where he oversaw the preparation of the Social Sciences Foundation Course materials, all of which are now completed and available in the territory in published form.

SUM NGAI LING was educated at the University of Hong Kong, where she obtained a number of advanced degrees. She was, until recently, a senior teacher at one of the most prestigious schools in the territory and was instrumental in writing and publishing highly regarded texts in the field of social studies and political science.